MERCEDES-BENZ

SLK R171 series

2004-2011

Brian Long

Essential Buyer's Guide Series
Alfa Romeo Giulia GT Coupé (Booker)
Alfa Romeo Giulia Spider (Booker)
Audi TT (Davies)
Austin Seven (Barker)
Big Healeys (Trummel)
BMW E21 3 Series (1975-1983) (Reverente)
BMW E30 3 Series 1981 to 1994 (Hosier)
BMW GS (Henshaw)
BMW X5 (Saunders)
BSA 350 & 500 Unit Construction Singles (Henshaw)
BSA 500 & 650 Twins (Henshaw)
BSA Bantam (Henshaw)
Citroën 2CV (Paxton)
Citroën ID & DS (Heilig)
Cobra Replicas (Ayre)
Corvette C2 Sting Ray 1963-1967 (Falconer)
Ducati Bevel Twins (Falloon)
Ducati Desmodue Twins (Falloon)
Ducati Desmoquattro Twins – 851, 888, 916, 996, 998, ST4 1988 to 2004 (Falloon)
Ducati Overhead Camshaft Singles, "The Book of the (Falloon)
Fiat 500 & 600 (Bobbitt)
Ford Capri (Paxton)
Ford Escort Mk1 & Mk2 (Williamson)
Ford Mustang – First Generation 1964 to 1973 (Cook)
Ford Mustang – Fifth generation/S197 (Cook)
Ford RS Cosworth Sierra & Escort (Williamson)
Harley-Davidson Big Twins (Henshaw)
Hinckley Triumph triples & fours 750, 900, 955, 1000, 1050, 1200 – 1991-2009 (Henshaw)
Honda CBR FireBlade (Henshaw)
Honda CBR600 Hurricane (Henshaw)
Honda SOHC Fours 1969-1984 (Henshaw)
Jaguar E-Type 3.8 & 4.2-litre (Crespin)
Jaguar E-type V12 5.3-litre (Crespin)
Jaguar Mark 1 & 2 (All models including Daimler 2.5-litre V8) 1955 to 1969 (Thorley)
Jaguar S-Type – 1999 to 2007 (Thorley)
Jaguar X-Type – 2001 to 2009 (Thorley)
Jaguar XJ-S (Crespin)
Jaguar XJ6, XJ8 & XJR (Thorley)
Jaguar XK 120, 140 & 150 (Thorley)
Jaguar XK8 & XKR (1996-2005) (Thorley)
Jaguar/Daimler XJ 1994-2003 (Crespin)
Jaguar/Daimler XJ40 (Crespin)
Jaguar/Daimler XJ6, XJ12 & Sovereign (Crespin)
Kawasaki Z1 & Z900 (Orritt)
Land Rover Series I, II & IIA (Thurman)
Land Rover Series III (Thurman)
Lotus Seven replicas & Caterham 7: 1973-2013 (Hawkins)
Mazda MX-5 Miata (Mk1 1989-97 & Mk2 98-2001) (Crook)
Mercedes Benz Pagoda 230SL, 250SL & 280SL roadsters & coupés (Bass)
Mercedes-Benz 280-560SL & SLC (Bass)
MG Midget & A-H Sprite (Horler)
MG TD, TF & TF1500 (Jones)
MGA 1955-1962 (Crosier)
MGB & MGB GT (Williams)
MGF & MG TF (Hawkins)
Mini (Paxton)
Morris Minor & 1000 (Newell)
Moto Guzzi 2-valve big twins (Falloon)
New Mini (Collins)
Norton Commando (Henshaw)
Peugeot 205 GTI (Blackburn)
Porsche 911 (964) (Streather)
Porsche 911 (993) (Streather)
Porsche 911 (996) (Streather)
Porsche 911 Carrera 3.2 (Streather)
Porsche 911SC (Streather)
Porsche 924 – All models 1976 to 1988 (Hodgkins)
Porsche 928 (Hemmings)
Porsche 930 Turbo & 911 (930) Turbo (Streather)
Porsche 944 (Higgins)
Porsche 986 Boxster (Streather)
Porsche 987 Boxster & Cayman (Streather)
Rolls-Royce Silver Shadow & Bentley T-Series (Bobbitt)
Subaru Impreza (Hobbs)
Triumph 350 & 500 Twins (Henshaw)
Triumph Bonneville (Henshaw)
Triumph Herald & Vitesse (Davies)
Triumph Spitfire & GT6 (Baugues)
Triumph Stag (Mort)
Triumph Thunderbird, Trophy & Tiger (Henshaw)
Triumph TR6 (Williams)
Triumph TR7 & TR8 (Williams)
Vespa Scooters – Classic 2-stroke models 1960-2008 (Paxton)
Volvo 700/900 Series (Beavis)
VW Beetle (Cservenka & Copping)
VW Bus (Cservenka & Copping)
VW Golf GTI (Cservenka & Copping)

Those Were The Days ... Series
Alpine Trials & Rallies 1910-1973 (Pfundner)
American 'Independent' Automakers – AMC to Willys 1945 to 1960 (Mort)
American Station Wagons – The Golden Era 1950-1975 (Mort)
American Trucks of the 1950s (Mort)
American Trucks of the 1960s (Mort)
American Woodies 1928-1953 (Mort)
Anglo-American Cars from the 1930s to the 1970s (Mort)
Austerity Motoring (Bobbitt)
Austins, The last real (Peck)
Brighton National Speed Trials (Gardiner)
British and European Trucks of the 1970s (Peck)
British Drag Racing – The early years (Pettitt)
British Lorries of the 1950s (Bobbitt)
British Lorries of the 1960s (Bobbitt)
British Touring Car Racing (Collins)
British Police Cars (Walker)
British Woodies (Peck)
Café Racer Phenomenon, The (Walker)
Don Hayter's MGB Story – The birth of the MGB in MG's Abingdon Design & Development Office (Hayter)
Drag Bike Racing in Britain – From the mid '60s to the mid '80s (Lee)
Dune Buggy Phenomenon, The (Hale)
Dune Buggy Phenomenon Volume 2, The (Hale)
Endurance Racing at Silverstone in the 1970s & 1980s (Parker)
Hot Rod & Stock Car Racing in Britain in the 1980s (Neil)
Last Real Austins 1946-1959, The (Peck)
Mercedes-Benz Trucks (Peck)
MG's Abingdon Factory (Moylan)
Motor Racing at Brands Hatch in the Seventies (Parker)
Motor Racing at Brands Hatch in the Eighties (Parker)
Motor Racing at Crystal Palace (Collins)
Motor Racing at Goodwood in the Sixties (Gardiner)
Motor Racing at Nassau in the 1950s & 1960s (O'Neil)
Motor Racing at Oulton Park in the 1960s (McFadyen)
Motor Racing at Oulton Park in the 1970s (McFadyen)
Motor Racing at Thruxton in the 1970s (Grant-Braham)
Motor Racing at Thruxton in the 1980s (Grant-Braham)
Superprix – The Story of Birmingham Motor Race (Page & Collins)
Three Wheelers (Bobbitt)

Rally Giants Series
Audi Quattro (Robson)
Austin Healey 100-6 & 3000 (Robson)
Fiat 131 Abarth (Robson)
Ford Escort MkI (Robson)
Ford Escort RS Cosworth & World Rally Car (Robson)
Ford Escort RS1800 (Robson)
Lancia Delta 4WD/Integrale (Robson)
Lancia Stratos (Robson)
Mini Cooper/Mini Cooper S (Robson)
Peugeot 205 T16 (Robson)
Saab 96 & V4 (Robson)
Subaru Impreza (Robson)
Toyota Celica GT4 (Robson)

WSC Giants
Audi R8 (Wagstaff)
Ferrari 312P & 312PB (Collins & McDonough)
Gulf-Mirage 1967 to 1982 (McDonough)
Matra Sports Cars – MS620, 630, 650, 660 & 670 – 1966 to 1974 (McDonough)

Biographies
A Chequered Life – Graham Warner and the Chequered Flag (Hesletine)
Amédée Gordini ... a true racing legend (Smith)
André Lefebvre, and the cars he created at Voisin and Citroën (Beck)
Chris Carter at Large – Stories from a lifetime in motorcycle racing (Carter & Skelton)
Cliff Allison, The Official Biography of – From the Fells to Ferrari (Gauld)
Edward Turner – The Man Behind the Motorcycles (Clew)
Driven by Desire – The Desiré Wilson Story
First Principles – The Official Biography of Keith Duckworth (Burr)
Inspired to Design – F1 cars, Indycars & racing tyres: the autobiography of Nigel Bennett (Bennett)
Jack Sears, The Official Biography of – Gentleman Jack (Gauld)
Jim Redman – 6 Times World Motorcycle Champion: The Autobiography (Redman)
John Chatham – 'Mr Big Healey' – The Official Biography (Burr)
The Lee Noble Story (Wilkins)
Mason's Motoring Mayhem – Tony Mason's hectic life in motorsport and television (Mason)
Raymond Mays' Magnificent Obsession (Apps)
Pat Moss Carlsson Story, The – Harnessing Horsepower (Turner)
Tony Robinson – The biography of a race mechanic (Wagstaff)
Virgil Exner – Visioneer: The Official Biography of Virgil M Exner Designer Extraordinaire (Grist)

General
11/2-litre GP Racing 1961-1965 (Whitelock)
AC Two-litre Saloons & Buckland Sportscars (Archibald)
Alfa Romeo 155/156/147 Competition Touring Cars (Collins)
Alfa Romeo Giulia Coupé GT & GTA (Tipler)
Alfa Romeo Montreal – The dream car that came true (Taylor)
Alfa Romeo Montreal – The Essential Companion (Classic Reprint of 500 copies) (Taylor)
Alfa Tipo 33 (McDonough & Collins)
Alpine & Renault – The Development of the Revolutionary Turbo F1 Car 1968 to 1979 (Smith)
Alpine & Renault – The Sports Prototypes 1963 to 1969 (Smith)
Alpine & Renault – The Sports Prototypes 1973 to 1978 (Smith)
Anatomy of the Works Minis (Moylan)
Armstrong-Siddeley (Smith)
Art Deco and British Car Design (Down)
Autodrome (Collins & Ireland)
Autodrome 2 (Collins & Ireland)
Automotive A-Z, Lane's Dictionary of Automotive Terms (Lane)
Automotive Mascots (Kay & Springate)
Bahamas Speed Weeks, The (O'Neil)
Bentley Continental, Corniche and Azure (Bennett)
Bentley MkVI, Rolls-Royce Silver Wraith, Dawn & Cloud/Bentley R & S-Series (Nutland)
Bluebird CN7 (Stevens)
BMC Competitions Department Secrets (Turner, Chambers & Browning)
BMW 5-Series (Cranswick)
BMW Z-Cars (Taylor)
BMW Boxer Twins 1970-1995 Bible, The (Falloon)
BMW Cafe Racers (Cloesen)
BMW Custom Motorcycles – Choppers, Cruisers, Bobbers, Trikes & Quads (Cloesen)
BMW – The Power of M (Vivian)
Bonjour – Is this Italy? (Turner)
British 250cc Racing Motorcycles (Pereira)
British at Indianapolis, The (Wagstaff)
British Cars, The Complete Catalogue of, 1895-1975 (Culshaw & Horrobin)
British Custom Motorcycles – The Brit Chop – choppers, cruisers, bobbers & trikes (Cloesen)
BRM – A Mechanic's Tale (Salmon)
BRM V16 (Ludvigsen)
BSA Bantam Bible, The (Henshaw)
BSA Motorcycles – the final evolution (Jones)
Bugatti Type 40 (Price)
Bugatti 46/50 Updated Edition (Price & Arbey)
Bugatti T44 & T49 (Price & Arbey)
Bugatti 57 2nd Edition (Price)
Bugatti Type 57 Grand Prix – A Celebration (Tomlinson)
Caravan, Improve & Modify Your (Porter)
Caravans, The Illustrated History 1919-1959 (Jenkinson)
Caravans, The Illustrated History From 1960 (Jenkinson)
Carrera Panamericana, La (Tipler)
Chrysler 300 – America's Most Powerful Car 2nd Edition (Ackerson)
Chrysler PT Cruiser (Ackerson)
Citroën DS (Bobbitt)
Classic British Car Electrical Systems (Astley)
Cobra – The Real Thing! (Legate)
Competition Car Aerodynamics 3rd Edition (McBeath)
Concept Cars, How to illustrate and design (Dewey)
Cortina – Ford's Bestseller (Robson)
Coventry Climax Racing Engines (Hammill)
Daily Mirror 1970 World Cup Rally 40, The (Robson)
Daimler SP250 New Edition (Long)
Datsun Fairlady Roadster to 280ZX – The Z-Car Story (Long)
Dino – The V6 Ferrari (Long)
Dodge Challenger & Plymouth Barracuda (Grist)
Dodge Charger – Enduring Thunder (Ackerson)
Dodge Dynamite! (Grist)
Dorset from the Sea – The Jurassic Coast from Lyme Regis to Old Harry Rocks photographed from its best viewpoint (Belasco)
Dorset from the Sea – The Jurassic Coast from Lyme Regis to Old Harry Rocks photographed from its best viewpoint (souvenir edition) (Belasco)
Draw & Paint Cars – How to (Gardiner)
Drive on the Wild Side, A – 20 Extreme Driving Adventures From Around the World (Weaver)
Ducati 750 Bible, The (Falloon)
Ducati 750 SS 'round-case' 1974, The Book of the (Falloon)
Ducati 860, 900 and Mille Bible, The (Falloon)
Ducati Monster Bible (New Updated & Revised Edition), The (Falloon)
Dune Buggy, Building A – The Essential Manual (Shakespeare)
Dune Buggy Files (Hale)
Dune Buggy Handbook (Hale)
East German Motor Vehicles in Pictures (Suhr/Weinreich)
Fast Ladies – Female Racing Drivers 1888 to 1970 (Bouzanquet)
Fate of the Sleeping Beauties, The (op de Weegh/Hottendorff/op de Weegh)
Ferrari 288 GTO, The Book of the (Sackey)
Ferrari 333 SP (O'Neil)
Fiat & Abarth 124 Spider & Coupé (Tipler)
Fiat & Abarth 500 & 600 – 2nd Edition (Bobbitt)
Fiats, Great Small (Ward)
Fine Art of the Motorcycle Engine, The (Peirce)
Ford Cleveland 335-Series V8 engine 1970 to 1982 – The Essential Source Book (Hammill)
Ford F100/F150 Pick-up 1948-1996 (Ackerson)
Ford F150 Pick-up 1997-2005 (Ackerson)
Ford GT – Then, and Now (Streather)
Ford GT40 (Legate)
Ford Model Y (Roberts)
Ford Small Block V8 Racing Engines 1962-1970 – The Essential Source Book (Hammill)
Ford Thunderbird From 1954, The Book of the (Long)
Formula 5000 Motor Racing, Back then ... and back now (Lawson)
Forza Minardi! (Vigar)
France: the essential guide for car enthusiasts – 200 things for the car enthusiast to see and do (Parish)
From Crystal Palace to Red Square – A Hapless Biker's Road to Russia (Turner)
Funky Mopeds (Skelton)
Grand Prix Ferrari – The Years of Enzo Ferrari's Power, 1948-1980 (Pritchard)
Grand Prix Ford – DFV-powered Formula 1 Cars (Pritchard)
GT – The World's Best GT Cars 1953-73 (Dawson)
Hillclimbing & Sprinting – The Essential Manual (Short & Wilkinson)
Honda NSX (Long)
Inside the Rolls-Royce & Bentley Styling Department – 1971 to 2001 (Hull)
Intermeccanica – The Story of the Prancing Bull (McCredie & Reisner)
Italian Cafe Racers (Cloesen)
Italian Custom Motorcycles (Cloesen)
Jaguar, The Rise of (Price)
Jaguar XJ 220 – The Inside Story (Moreton)
Jaguar XJ-S, The Book of the (Long)
Jeep CJ (Ackerson)
Jeep Wrangler (Ackerson)
Karmann-Ghia Coupé & Convertible (Bobbitt)
Kawasaki Triples Bible, The (Walker)
Kawasaki Z1 Story, The (Sheehan)
Kris Meeke – Intercontinental Rally Challenge Champion (McBride)
Lamborghini Miura Bible, The (Sackey)
Lamborghini Urraco, The Book of the (Landsem)
Lambretta Bible, The (Davies)
Lancia 037 (Collins)
Lancia Delta HF Integrale (Blaettel & Wagner)
Land Rover Series III Reborn (Porter)
Land Rover, The Half-ton Military (Cook)
Laverda Twins & Triples Bible 1968-1986 (Falloon)
Lea-Francis Story, The (Price)
Le Mans Panoramic (Ireland)
Lexus Story, The (Long)
Little book of microcars, the (Quellin)
Little book of smart, the – New Edition (Jackson)
Little book of trikes, the (Quellin)
Lola – The Illustrated History (1957-1977) (Starkey)
Lola – All the Sports Racing & Single-seater Racing Cars 1978-1997 (Starkey)
Lola T70 – The Racing History & Individual Chassis Record – 4th Edition (Starkey)
Lotus 49 (Oliver)
Marketingmobiles, The Wonderful Wacky World of (Hale)
Maserati 250F In Focus (Pritchard)
Mazda MX-5/Miata 1.6 Enthusiast's Workshop Manual (Grainger & Shoemark)
Mazda MX-5/Miata 1.8 Enthusiast's Workshop Manual (Grainger & Shoemark)
The book of the Mazda MX-5 Miata – The 'Mk1' NA-series 1988 to 1997 (Long)
Mazda MX-5 Miata Roadster (Long)
Maximum Mini (Booij)
Meet the English (Bowie)
Mercedes-Benz SL – R230 series 2001 to 2011 (Long)
Mercedes-Benz SL – W113-series 1963-1971 (Long)
Mercedes-Benz SL & SLC – 107-series 1971-1989 (Long)
Mercedes-Benz SLK – R170 series 1996-2004 (Long)
Mercedes-Benz SLK – R171 series 2004-2011 (Long)
Mercedes-Benz W123-series – All models 1976 to 1986 (Long)
MGA (Price Williams)
MGB & MGB GT– Expert Guide (Auto-doc Series) (Williams)
MGB Electrical Systems Updated & Revised Edition (Astley)
Micro Caravans (Jenkinson)
Micro Trucks (Mort)
Microcars at Large! (Quellin)
Mini Cooper – The Real Thing! (Tipler)
Mini Minor to Asia Minor (West)
Mitsubishi Lancer Evo, The Road Car & WRC Story (Long)
Montlhéry, The Story of the Paris Autodrome (Boddy)
Morgan Maverick (Lawrence)
Morgan 3 Wheeler – back to the future!, The (Dron)
Morris Minor, 60 Years on the Road (Newell)
Moto Guzzi Sport & Le Mans Bible, The (Falloon)
Motor Movies – The Posters! (Veysey)
Motor Racing – Reflections of a Lost Era (Carter)
Motor Racing – The Pursuit of Victory 1930-1962 (Carter)
Motor Racing – The Pursuit of Victory 1963-1972 (Wyatt/Sears)
Motor Racing Heroes – The Stories of 100 Greats (Newman)
Motorcycle Apprentice (Cakebread)
Motorcycle GP Racing in the 1960s (Pereira)
Motorcycle Road & Racing Chassis Designs (Noakes)
Motorhomes, The Illustrated History (Jenkinson)
Motorsport In colour, 1950s (Wainwright)
MV Agusta Fours, The book of the classic (Falloon)
N.A.R.T. – A concise history of the North American Racing Team 1957 to 1983 (O'Neil)
Nissan 300ZX & 350Z – The Z-Car Story (Long)
Nissan GT-R Supercar: Born to race (Gorodji)
Northeast American Sports Car Races 1950-1959 (O'Neil)
Nothing Runs – Misadventures in the Classic, Collectable & Exotic Car Biz (Slutsky)
Off-Road Giants! (Volume 1) – Heroes of 1960s Motorcycle Sport (Westlake)
Off-Road Giants! (Volume 2) – Heroes of 1960s Motorcycle Sport (Westlake)
Off-Road Giants! (volume 3) – Heroes of 1960s Motorcycle Sport (Westlake)
Pass the Theory and Practical Driving Tests (Gibson & Hoole)
Peking to Paris 2007 (Young)
Pontiac Firebird (Cranswick)
Porsche Boxster (Long)
Porsche 356 (2nd Edition) (Long)
Porsche 908 (Födisch, Neßhöver, Roßbach, Schwarz & Roßbach)
Porsche 911 Carrera – The Last of the Evolution (Corlett)
Porsche 911R, RS & RSR, 4th Edition (Starkey)
Porsche 911, The Book of the (Long)
Porsche 911SC 'Super Carrera' – The Essential Companion (Streather)
Porsche 914 & 914-6: The Definitive History of the Road & Competition Cars (Long)
Porsche 924 (Long)
The Porsche 924 Carreras – evolution to excellence (Smith)
Porsche 928 (Long)
Porsche 944 (Long)
Porsche 964, 993 & 996 Data Plate Code Breaker (Streather)
Porsche 993 'King Of Porsche' – The Essential Companion (Streather)
Porsche 996 'Supreme Porsche' – The Essential Companion (Streather)
Porsche Racing Cars – 1953 to 1975 (Long)
Porsche Racing Cars – 1976 to 2005 (Long)
Porsche – The Rally Story (Meredith)
Porsche: Three Generations of Genius (Meredith)
Preston Tucker & Others (Linde)
RAC Rally Action! (Gardiner)
RACING COLOURS – MOTOR RACING COMPOSITIONS 1908-2009 (Newman)
Racing Line – British motorcycle racing in the golden age of the big single (Guntrip)
Rallye Sport Fords: The Inside Story (Moreton)
Renewable Energy Home Handbook, The (Porter)
Roads with a View – England's greatest views and how to find them by road (Corfield)
Rolls-Royce Silver Shadow/Bentley T Series Corniche & Camargue – Revised & Enlarged Edition (Bobbitt)
Rolls-Royce Silver Spirit, Silver Spur & Bentley Mulsanne 2nd Edition (Bobbitt)
Runways & Racers (O'Neil)
Russian Motor Vehicles – Soviet Limousines 1930-2003 (Kelly)
Russian Motor Vehicles – The Czarist Period 1784 to 1917 (Kelly)
RX-7 – Mazda's Rotary Engine Sportscar (Updated & Revised New Edition) (Long)
Scooters & Microcars, The A-Z of Popular (Dan)
Scooter Lifestyle (Grainger)
SCOOTER MANIA! – Recollections of the Isle of Man International Scooter Rally (Jackson)
Singer Story: Cars, Commercial Vehicles, Bicycles & Motorcycle (Atkinson)
Sleeping Beauties USA – abandoned classic cars & trucks (Marek)
SM – Citroën's Maserati-engined Supercar (Long & Claverol)
Speedway – Auto racing's ghost tracks (Collins & Ireland)
Sprite Caravans, The Story of (Jenkinson)
Standard Motor Company, The Book of the
Subaru Impreza: The Road Car And WRC Story (Long)
Supercar, How to Build your own (Thompson)
Tales from the Toolbox (Oliver)
Tatra – The Legacy of Hans Ledwinka, Updated & Enlarged Collector's Edition of 1500 copies (Margolius & Henry)
Taxi! The Story of the 'London' Taxicab (Bobbitt)
Toleman Story, The (Hilton)
Toyota Celica & Supra, The Book of Toyota's Sports Coupés (Long)
Toyota MR2 Coupés & Spyders (Long)
Triumph Bonneville Bible (59-83) (Henshaw)
Triumph Bonneville!, Save the – The inside story of the Meriden Workers' Co-op (Rosamond)
Triumph Motorcycles & the Meriden Factory (Hancox)
Triumph Speed Twin & Thunderbird Bible (Woolridge)
Triumph Tiger Cub Bible (Estall)
Triumph Trophy Bible (Woolridge)
Triumph TR6 (Kimberley)
TT Talking – The TT's most exciting era – As seen by Manx Radio TT's lead commentator 2004-2012 (Lambert)
Two Summers – The Mercedes-Benz W196R Racing Car (Ackerson)
TWR Story, The – Group A (Hughes & Scott)
Unraced (Collins)
Velocette Motorcycles – MSS to Thruxton – New Third Edition (Burris)
Vespa – The Story of a Cult Classic in Pictures (Uhlig)
Volkswagen Bus Book, The (Bobbitt)
Volkswagen Bus or Van to Camper, How to Convert (Porter)
Volkswagens of the World (Glen)
VW Beetle Cabriolet – The full story of the convertible Beetle (Bobbitt)
VW Beetle – The Car of the 20th Century (Copping)
VW Bus – 40 Years of Splitties, Bays & Wedges (Copping)
VW Bus Book, The (Bobbitt)
VW Golf: Five Generations of Fun (Copping & Cservenka)
VW – The Air-cooled Era (Copping)
VW T5 Camper Conversion Manual (Porter)
VW Campers (Copping)
You & Your Jaguar XK8/XKR – Buying, Enjoying, Maintaining, Modifying – New Edition (Thorley)
Which Oil? – Choosing the right oils & greases for your antique, vintage, veteran, classic or collector car (Michell)
Works Minis, The Last (Purves & Brenchley)
Works Rally Mechanic (Moylan)

For post publication news, updates and amendments relating to this book please visit www.veloce.co.uk/books/V4653

www.veloce.co.uk

First published in October 2015 by Veloce Publishing Limited, Veloce House, Parkway Farm Business Park, Middle Farm Way, Poundbury, Dorchester DT1 3AR, England. Fax 01305 268864 / e-mail info@veloce.co.uk / web www.veloce.co.uk or www.velocebooks.com. ISBN: 978-1-845846-53-4 UPC: 6-36847-04653-8 Readers with ideas for automotive books, or books on other transport or related hobby subjects, are invited to write to the editorial director of Veloce Publishing at the above address. British Library Cataloguing in Publication Data – A catalogue record for this book is available from the British Library. Typesetting, design and page make-up all by Veloce Publishing Ltd on Apple Mac. Printed in India by Replika Press.

MERCEDES-BENZ

SLK R171 series

2004-2011

Brian Long

VELOCE PUBLISHING
THE PUBLISHER OF FINE AUTOMOTIVE BOOKS

Contents

Introduction & Acknowledgements

The original SLK had been introduced in 1996, allowing buyers to enjoy the special experience of open-top Mercedes-Benz motoring without the expense attached to the SL models. The innovation, safety and quality one expects from a Stuttgart thoroughbred was there, with greater emphasis on the fun-to-drive element, and the R170 model duly picked up over 40 international awards. Demand outstripped supply, with many moving to the marque for the first time, and requests for a more sporting character were acknowledged in a 2000 face-lift.

When the second generation SLK (the R171) was introduced in 2004, it followed the concept of the original car, carrying over an improved version of the innovative folding metal roof, for instance, but also fell into line with trends one could see in other Mercedes model lines, becoming overtly sporty to match the revival of the company's glory days in the motorsport arena. Naturally, in this 'green' era in which we live, the engineers had to back up advances in performance and chassis technology with cleaner emissions and enhanced safety, and, in each respect, they succeeded. This book traces the R171 SLK's history, from initial development through to the last one built in the spring of 2011, taking in all the variations in each of the main markets along the way ...

As always, because of the use of contemporary photography as a matter of policy, these books cannot possibly be done

without a great deal of help from the factory. As with the author's earlier SL and SLK books, I would particularly like to record my sincere appreciation for the services of Gerhard Heidbrink at Daimler AG in Stuttgart – a more helpful chap would be hard to find, and this book simply wouldn't have been possible without his kind co-operation.

I should also like to thank Nils Beckmann and Joerg Rupp in Stuttgart for managing to drag me into the 21st century on the parts book front, Silvie Kiefer for patiently looking after me on the digital archive side, Kenichi Kobayashi at Miki Press, the extensive research facilities at the Japan Motor Industry Federation (JMIF) in Tokyo, Rob Halloway at Mercedes-Benz UK, and Robert Moran and Christian Bokich of Mercedes-Benz USA. There have been many, many others, but to list them all would take another book!

Like the R170 sister title, also published by Veloce, I hope this book will appeal to past owners, present owners, those thinking of ownership, and followers of Mercedes-Benz lore alike. Incidentally, I've had several people mention the inclusion of a buying section, but please forgive me for not writing one – a worthwhile, in-depth guide would call for a lot of space, and I believe the limited number of pages we have to play with are better assigned to the history of the car. I hope you understand this, and, assuming I'm still alive and kicking, start looking out for an R172 edition about ten years from now!

Brian Long
Chiba City, Japan

S NY 2626

1

History of the Brand

The name of Mercedes-Benz, along with the three-pointed star trademark that goes with it, is recognised the world over as a symbol of prestige, exemplifying the highest levels of German engineering and quality. Before moving onto the book's main subject, it's worthwhile reflecting on the history of the brand, and what made it so renowned, to help put things into perspective ...

The Mercedes-Benz story begins with two pioneers of the motor industry – Gottlieb Daimler and Carl Benz. Somewhat surprisingly, despite the fact that both were German-born, with both of them recognised as leading lights in the fledgling automotive trade, based less than 60 miles (100km) away from each other, they never actually met. Nonetheless, the coming together of the two companies they founded is what concerns us here, with the Daimler-Benz business using the Mercedes-Benz badge on the majority of its road vehicles from the late-1920s onwards.

Gottlieb Daimler (1834-1900).

Birth of the Daimler marque

Gottlieb Daimler was born in Schorndorf, a stone's throw to the east of Stuttgart, on 17 March 1834. Daimler didn't come from an engineering background (in fact, his father was a baker), but it was obvious from an early age that this was to be Daimler's destiny, for, as well as learning Latin, he attended technical drawing school as a young boy.

Although he began his apprenticeship with a local gunsmith, as soon as his four years were up, he began studying engineering in greater depth, augmenting his academic work with practical experience gained in the field in France and Britain.

On settling back in Germany, Daimler moved around for a while, although his appointment as Technical Director of the Gasmotoren-Fabrik Deutz AG (founded by Nikolaus August Otto

Wilhelm Maybach at the controls of a belt-driven Daimler from 1895, with Gottlieb Daimler to his right.

– the father of the four-stroke, 'Otto-cycle' engine) in 1872 was an important step in his career, with Wilhelm Maybach (1846-1929), whom he'd first met as a colleague in 1864, already present as his right-hand man.

However, in time a rift grew between Daimler and the Cologne-based manufacturer, with Daimler and Maybach wanting to develop faster-running petrol engines that could release more power. Ultimately, in 1882, Gottlieb Daimler decided to go it alone and opened a small workshop at the back of his villa in Cannstatt, on the outskirts of Stuttgart, with Maybach working alongside him to help nurture this new technology.

A number of single-cylinder, air-cooled petrol engines were duly designed and built, one being used to power the world's first motorcycle in 1885. There was also a four-wheeled horseless carriage, actually produced for Daimler's wife as a birthday present, which made its initial runs during the autumn of 1886. Within a short space of time, the engines were finding various applications on land, rails, water, and even in the air. After building a second car in 1889, this time powered by a water-cooled V-twin, it was obvious that Daimler and Maybach were moving in the right direction, and investors soon began knocking on the door of the large new factory in Cannstatt.

The Daimler Motoren Gesellschaft (DMG) was registered on 28 November 1890, its purpose being to manufacture and market Daimler engines and related products. In addition, there was a great deal of licensing activity in this new and exciting field of engineering, with Panhard & Levassor of France being one of the first to sign up. There was also a company founded in America bearing Daimler's name (with William Steinway of Steinway piano fame behind it), and another in England thanks to the business dealings of Frederick Simms and Harry Lawson.

As so often happens once investors get involved, though, profits start to dominate decisions, and the desire to experiment usually has to be tempered with the sale of products to satisfy short-term requirements. Maybach was forced to leave the Cannstatt company due to a clash of policy, and Daimler's health was failing – a situation not helped by the internal conflict with members of the DMG Board. Perhaps unsurprisingly, Daimler ultimately resigned from the company he'd founded in October 1894.

Daimler and Maybach duly joined forces again (they'd remained close friends even after the latter left the DMG), this time bringing Daimler's son, Paul, into the fold, and between them they designed a 2.1-litre four-cylinder engine equipped with Maybach's innovative spray-nozzle carburettor. Known as the Phönix, it was a landmark unit, and, following some political manoeuvring from Frederick Simms, the pair was asked to return to the Daimler Motoren Gesellschaft on new, more favourable terms.

Gottlieb Daimler died on 6 March 1900, although Wilhelm Maybach continued his work before becoming heavily involved with aero-engine production for the famous Zeppelin airship concern. After the Great War, Maybach marketed a short-lived series of luxury cars under his own name, with the brand being revived recently for a Mercedes-Benz flagship saloon.

Genesis of the Benz brand

Carl Benz was born in Mühlberg on 25 November 1844. The son of a train driver, after leaving school, he went to the Karlsruhe Polytechnic to study mechanical engineering, and duly moved around a number of firms following his graduation, gaining practical experience in a wide range of fields, from building locomotives, to designing machinery and even iron bridges.

Carl Benz (1844-1929).

Joining forces with August Ritter, Benz established his own engineering shop in Mannheim, about 55 miles (90km) north of Stuttgart, in August 1871, but the partnership was short-lived, with Benz ultimately buying out Ritter. The small workshop was not a success, though, and Benz turned his attention to developing two-stroke engines (there were too many patents already registered against four-stroke powerplants) in the second half of 1877, with the first unit running successfully two years later.

By late 1882, the Benz engine had attracted investors, and Gasmotorenfabrik Mannheim was established, although Benz left the company within a few months of starting it as the shareholders tried to influence things too much. For instance, Benz wanted to produce a motor vehicle, but a quick financial return on supplying engines was favoured by the majority of people. Having put up production facilities as his stake in the business, Carl Benz was left with no option but to start from scratch.

Luckily, on 1 October 1883, Max Rose and Friedrich Esslinger came to Benz's aid in helping to form a new company, Benz & Co Rheinische Gasmotorenfabrik, Mannheim. Not long after, many of the patents applying to the four-stroke engine were declared null and void, allowing Benz to begin developing a new, fast-running powerplant based on the Otto-cycle. By 29 January 1886, a patent had been filed on the world's first, purpose-built vehicle to be powered by a petrol engine – the three-wheeled Benz Patent Motorwagon. Refinements were made, and the car was duly put into series production, the 'Model 3' version thereby providing the foundation stone for the automotive industry.

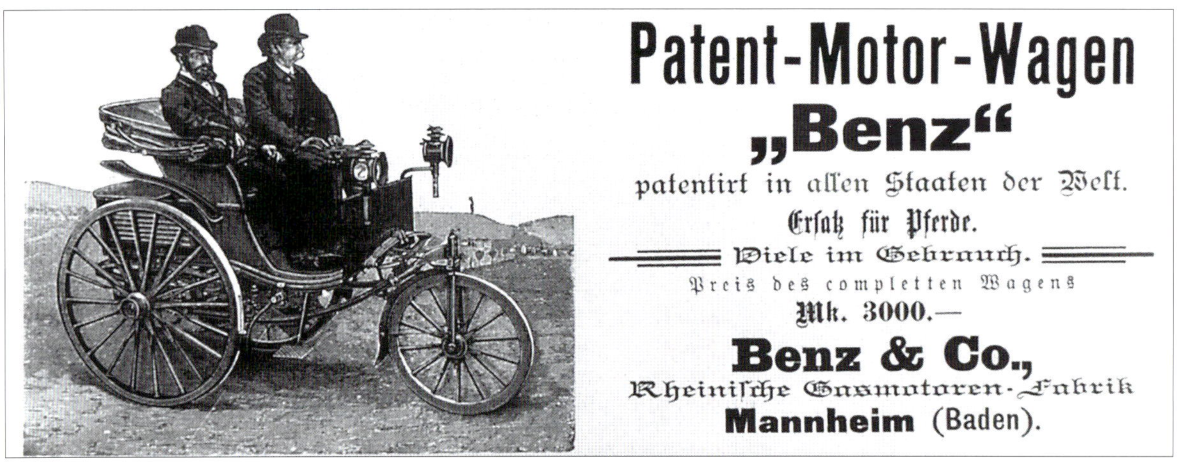

An advert for the Benz Patent Model 3, with Carl Benz driving, and Josef Brecht beside him – a close friend and business associate, who was later a director of the Benz & Cie concern.

Ironically, in the spring of 1890, despite Benz & Co being Germany's second largest engine manufacturer, Carl Benz once again found himself alone in business. But new partners were promptly found, and Benz continued to innovate, with four-wheeled cars being produced, new steering systems designed, and the horizontally-opposed (boxer) engine being developed, amongst other things.

The four-wheeled Velo, introduced in April 1894, was a huge commercial success by the standards of the day (around 1200 were built), allowing a new company, Benz & Cie. AG, to be registered in May 1899. However, blinded by their bid to compete with a flood of cheaper machines built in France, Benz had become disillusioned with the people running the firm, and resigned in January 1903.

Inside the Daimler Motoren Gesellschaft (DMG) works at Untertürkheim, the moment being captured in 1905. By this time, Daimler in Coventry, England, had long since found its own direction in terms of design and manufacturing, but William Steinway would soon start building Mercédès cars under licence in the States.

A new century, a new age

Daimler and Benz were still rivals at the turn of the century. The companies bearing their names fought in the showrooms graced by the rich and famous, and in the long-distance races and hillclimbs of Europe.

As it happens, the competition link provided the birth of the Mercedes brand. Shortly after Gottlieb Daimler passed away,

A 40hp Mercédès-Simplex from 1901 – a development of the 35hp model the gave birth to the Mercédès brand.

Mercédès advertising from 1910.

Emil Jellinek (an Austrian businessman who, among other things, sold Daimlers to wealthy clients in the south of France) entered a couple of Daimlers in the Nice-La Turbie hillclimb using his pseudonym 'Mercédès' – the name of his daughter.

Following the fatal accident of one of the drivers, Jellinek proposed a number of changes that would not only improve safety, but also enhance the sporting nature of the vehicles to satisfy the needs of his customers. He requested a reduction in weight, a lower body, and a longer wheelbase in order to cope with the

A magnificent Mercédès showroom in Berlin pictured just before the Great War. Note the racer in the foreground – Mercédès was highly-successful in top class competition at this time, both in Europe and America.

greater power outputs he outlined. Jellinek promised to purchase a large number of these vehicles in return for distribution rights in France, Belgium, the Austro-Hungarian Empire and America, but also requested that they carry the 'Mercédès' badge.

A deal was struck on 2 April 1900, and Wilhelm Maybach set about designing the first Mercédès in conjunction with Paul Daimler without delay. By the end of the year, Jellinek had taken delivery of the first of the line – a racing car that ultimately provided the foundation stone for the modern automobile, with a low-slung, pressed steel chassis frame playing host to a 5.9-litre, 35hp engine cooled by a honeycomb radiator, and a gate for the gearchange.

The Mercédès was raced with a great deal of success, and many variations were produced for regular road use, from an 8/11hp version all the way up to a 9.2-litre 60hp model. The Mercédès (the name being registered as a trademark by the DMG in 1902), set the standard for the day in the high-class car market, and was built under licence by numerous manufacturers.

Luckily, the DMG Board had made preparations for expansion in advance of its commercial success, buying a large piece of land in Untertürkheim on the eastern edge of Stuttgart in August 1900. This would duly become the spiritual home of Mercedes-Benz, operational at the end of 1903.

Six-cylinder engines followed in 1906, and there was a limited run of Knight sleeve-valve models just before the First World War. Meanwhile, the famous three-pointed star had been registered as a trademark, with approval eventually coming in February 1911. The three arms within the star represent the land, sea and air, and indeed, each has been conquered in the Stuttgart company's own inimitable way over the years: the outer ring was first added in 1921.

Shortly after the Great War, when the conflict had, if nothing else, allowed technology, metallurgy and production techniques to make great advances, the first supercharged Mercédès made its debut, and on 30 April 1923, Ferdinand Porsche was draughted in from Austro-Daimler to replace Paul Daimler as Chief

Benz advertising from 1913, the 82/200hp car referring to a racing model. The Benz marque was also very active in competition on both sides of the Atlantic.

The Benz works in Mannheim, just before the turn of the century.

A four-cylinder 10/30hp Benz saloon from 1923.

Engineer, bringing overhead camshafts and front-wheel brakes to the marque in a series of exceptionally elegant supercharged models.

In the meantime, Benz & Cie AG came to the fore, modernizing its range via conventional two- and four-cylinder cars designed by Marius Barbarou. The move towards reasonably-priced machines allowed the Benz business to clock up world-leading sales of around 600 units a year at the turn of the century, but the policy was out of step with that of Carl Benz himself. As mentioned earlier, he gave up his post as Chief Engineer, although he did remain on the Supervisory Board until his death on 4 April 1929.

While all this political manoeuvering was going on, Carl Benz had formed a new company with his son Eugen on 9 June 1906, called C Benz Söhne. By 1908, it had turned to car production after demand for the gas engines it was building fell off. This particular business, based in Ladenburg, to the east of Mannheim, was duly handed over to Eugen and his younger brother, Richard, in 1912. However, with the problems associated with the German economy following the First World War, the firm officially stopped building cars in 1923.

Benz & Cie AG continued down its safe path with its vehicle line-up, with a racing programme, and diesel engine and aero-engine development going on in the background. The Benz badge gained its laurel wreath in the summer of 1909, and a take-over of Süddeutsche Automobilfabrik Gaggenau GmbH not long after provided Benz with a ready-made line of commercial vehicles.

Meanwhile, Hans Nibel had been put in charge of car design from 1910. Interestingly, Nibel's own love of racing (he'd been involved with the machine that formed the basis for the 'Blitzen Benz' record breaker) spawned a number of competition cars, and the Benz marque duly found favour with a wealthy clientele. One of the most ardent supporters of the brand was Prince Henry of Prussia – the brother of Kaiser Wilhelm II.

Benz introduced its first six-cylinder powerplant in 1914. This was actually an aero-engine, but the company stuck almost exclusively to straight-sixes for its road cars following the First World War. During the war years, Benz had produced some magnificent aero-engines, including four-valve per cylinder units and a V12 prototype. It also emerged from the conflict as a leading light in the field of diesel technology.

The merger of two great houses

Following the end of the First World War, Germany suffered greatly at the hands of hyperinflation. Such conditions are naturally far from ideal for manufacturers of expensive goods, and with Deutsche Bank holding a huge amount of shares in both the Daimler Motoren Gesellschaft and Benz & Cie AG, it was decided that a syndicate be formed in order to save production costs. An agreement of mutual interest was duly signed on 1 May 1924, with a full merger and the birth of Daimler-Benz AG taking place on 28 June 1926.

A domestic advert proclaiming the merger of two of the greatest names in the German car industry, if not the world.

A 500K Special Roadster on display at the 1936 Berlin Motor Show.

Although the company was known as Daimler-Benz, the cars were marketed using the Mercedes-Benz name, with Mercedes officially losing the accents along the way. Only two Benz models made it into the Mercedes-Benz passenger car programme, and both were gone by 1927. A new badge, combining the Mercedes-Benz name, Benz laurels, and the familiar three-pointed star had been registered soon after the merger.

There were straight-eights from October 1928, and following the departure of Ferdinand Porsche at the end of the year, Hans Nibel took over sole responsibility as the company's Chief Engineer: the pair had been sharing the post since the merger.

Despite the difficult financial climate in the wake of the Wall Street Crash, the marque entered the mid-1930s with some magnificent creations, with the SS and SSK giving way to the 500K and 540K. By this time, the company was producing a range of vehicles that went from the modest 1.3-litre saloon, with its NA

Racing hero Rudolf Caracciola in action with the SSK in 1930. Caracciola duly went on to win the European Hillclimb Championship.

Poster celebrating Hermann Lang's victory in the Tripoli Grand Prix with the W125 – one of the cars that helped create the 'Silver Arrows' legend.

four at the rear, all the way up to the 7.7-litre supercharged eight with its glamorous coachbuilt bodies.

Meanwhile, 1934 had witnessed the debut of the first of the Silver Arrows – the ultra-modern W25 Grand Prix car. This was followed by a string of successful models that, combined with the might of the Auto Union team, put Germany at the forefront of the motorsport scene until the outbreak of the Second World War. Record breakers were also built, based on the GP cars, and brought the new Autobahn network into use in a rather unexpected fashion – the straight, level roads being perfect for the challenge to find the fastest man on Earth.

Following Hans Nibel's death in 1934, Max Sailer took over as the head of design and R&D. Sailer had been associated with the Stuttgart marque for decades, most visibly as a racing driver of note in the vintage era. During Sailer's watch, products as diverse as the 540K, the 170V and 170H, and the 260D (the world's first diesel series-built passenger car) were released. The factory also built the first batch of VW30 test vehicles during the spring of 1937 – the ancestors of the Volkswagen Beetle.

Then, of course, 1939 brought with it conflict, first in Europe, and then on a global scale. Virtually all the historic Untertürkheim factory had been destroyed during successive Allied bombing runs in November 1943 and September 1944. Other plants were either destroyed or badly damaged, too, making it difficult for Daimler-Benz to bounce back once the hostilities came to an end in 1945.

The immediate postwar years

Fritz Nallinger had been appointed Chief Engineer in 1940, taking over from Max Sailor. Having been in charge of commercial vehicle development since May 1935, he was already a trusted and highly-experienced member of the Daimler-Benz team, and therefore an ideal candidate for the job.

Like so many manufacturers, Daimler-Benz warmed over some of its prewar designs as part of the rebuilding process, releasing its first postwar car (ignoring utilitarian versions and commercial vehicles) in July 1947 – the bread-and-butter 1.7-litre 170V four-door sedan. By October that year, 1000 had been built, but commercials and repair work dominated the scene in Stuttgart as the transition from military to civilian production took place.

Research and development work recommenced in the middle of 1948. Soon after, the Unimog was unveiled, and car production reached 1000 units a month. Granted, it was still less than half the figure posted in the years leading up to the war, but for Dr Wilhelm Haspel, the company's Chairman, it must have seemed like a definite and most welcome sign of imminent recovery.

Two new 170-series variants (the 170S and 170D) joined the line-up in May 1949, and production continued until 1955, by which time the 180 had been introduced as a stablemate. The 170V and 170D were revised in June 1950, receiving, among other things, more powerful engines. Their popularity helped Daimler-Benz breeze towards a landmark figure of 50,000 postwar passenger cars built in October that same year.

Safety considerations were already starting to play an important role in vehicle development at Daimler-Benz. Karl Wilfert (in charge of body development at the Sindelfingen plant) filed a patent for a safety door lock in 1949, and Bela Barenyi came up with the passenger safety cell in 1951. In principle, both of these inventions are still in use to this day.

1951 witnessed the revival of six-cylinder engines with the launch of the 2.2-litre 220 series (W187) and the three-litre 300 (W186 II) models unveiled in Frankfurt in the latter half of April. The 300 quickly picked up the 'Adenauer' nickname, as the German Chancellor, Konrad Adenauer, was a staunch supporter of the model, and was rarely seen in public without one. The sporting two-door 300S (W188) made its debut later in the year at the Paris Salon.

The 170-series was updated again in 1952, with new models augmenting revised ones, but the debut of the 300SL sports-racer was perhaps the most telling sign that Daimler-Benz was back, its reputation being restored in the showrooms and on the track. A convincing win at Le Mans was followed by a deal with Max Hoffman, which secured a good sales outlet for Mercedes-Benz cars in America. Hoffman also handled Porsche, VW, Alfa Romeo and Jaguar imports for the US, incidentally.

September 1953 marked the arrival of the slab-sided 'Ponton' series, giving the styling cue for a whole new generation of Mercedes-Benz models. It was launched in 1.8-litre four-cylinder guise (W120), but a 2.2-litre six-cylinder version (W180) had joined the line-up by the following spring as a replacement for the W187 model.

The Mercedes-Benz line-up in 1951, which was still very much a range of warmed-over prewar machines to get production rolling again after the conflict. However, the six-cylinder 300 in the foreground was a new model.

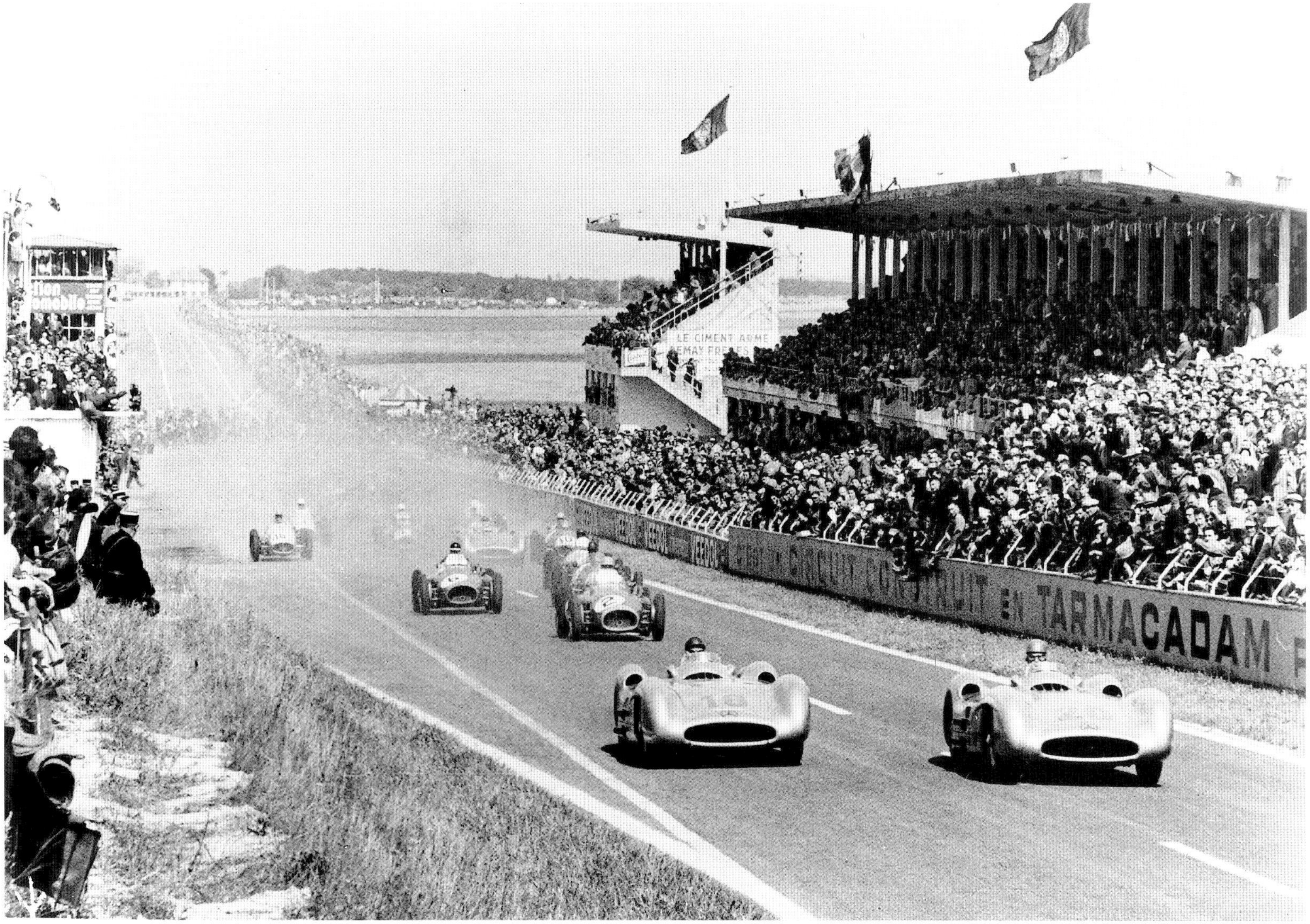

Mercedes-Benz made its long-awaited return to Grand Prix racing in 1954 with the 2.5-litre, normally-aspirated W196 model, fielded with both streamlined and open-wheeled bodies. Making their debut at Rheims in July (the race seen here), the straight-eight machines went on to dominate the GP scene in 1954 and 1955 in much the same way as the prewar Silver Arrows had.

On the sporting front, 300SL and 190SL prototypes made their debut at a show in New York in early 1954, in the same year as the W196 Grand Prix car hit the tracks. As expected, it was a winner straight out of the box, and continued to dominate wherever it went in the following season, too. Supremacy with the 300SLR in the 1955 Mille Miglia was sadly overshadowed by the Le Mans disaster, where many spectators died following a freak accident, and Mercedes withdrew from racing soon after. A second magnificent era in motorsport had come to an end.

In the meantime, Daimler-Benz of North America Inc was founded in Delaware on 7 April 1955 to handle US imports. With so many new models coming in 1956, such as the 190, 219 and 220S, the timing couldn't have been better. Interestingly, though, in April 1957 (the month after the 300SL Roadster made

The 190SL (foreground) and second generation 300SL on the production line at the tail-end of the fifties.

its debut), a deal was struck with the Curtiss-Wright concern, and the Studebaker-Packard Corporation took on responsibility for the sales of Mercedes-Benz cars and diesel engines in the States. A subsidiary of Studebaker-Packard called Mercedes-Benz Sales Inc (MBS) was duly formed in August 1958, although this fell by the wayside at the start of 1965, when Mercedes-Benz of North America Inc (MBNA) took over US operations.

Back in Germany, the passenger car range was overhauled in time for the 1958 Model Year, and during that sales season, power-assisted steering and seatbelts became an option long before the latter became a legal requirement. Other safety-minded introductions included a new wedge-pin door lock, and a proper crash test programme, which began in earnest at the tail-end of 1959.

Ironically, considering they were bitter rivals in prewar racing, Daimler-Benz acquired a majority interest in Auto Union during 1958. In the following year, plans to take a stake in BMW were thwarted, although the remaining shares in Auto Union were secured at the end of 1959. The company was eventually sold to Volkswagen in 1964, signalling a revival of the Audi name (one of the four firms brought together under the Auto Union marque), later merging it with NSU. Today, Auto Union is ably represented by Audi AG: its cars carrying the same four rings on their noses as the prewar racers designed by Professor Ferdinand Porsche after he moved from the Mercedes camp. Audi is still owned by the VW group, which has since merged with Porsche. It's a small world in the German car industry!

Meanwhile, September 1958 brought with it a new fuel-injected 220SE (W128) model. Success in the field of long-distance rallying took the place of victories on the track, and success in the showrooms is easy to quantify with annual production averaging around 100,000 units a year by this time, plus around 55,000 commercial vehicles to add to this total.

The modern era

The 1959 Frankfurt Show heralded a new era for Daimler-Benz, with the first of the 'Fintail' series models lining up alongside a revised four-cylinder 'Ponton' line. These original 'Fintail' cars (W111) were six-cylinder saloons, replacing the 'Ponton' sixes, although by 1961, two-door fixed head and drophead models had been launched (with disc brakes and an automatic transmission adding technical appeal), as well as a new W110 four-cylinder range, bringing the 'Ponton' era to an end, and a flagship W112 three-litre model. The 'Fintail' variants were a perfect blend of modernity and tradition, and allowed Mercedes to make huge steps forward in the field of safety – the introduction of crumple zones being a case in point.

The SL range was also brought up-to-date during 1963, when the 230SL (W113) replaced the 190SL and 300SL, bridging the gap between the two in many ways, but the modern styling was another sign that the Mercedes-Benz brand had moved on a generation. Similar lines were chosen for the upmarket 1964

A batch of 'Fintail' saloons (in four- and six-cylinder guise) about to be delivered to a dealer, circa 1962. The 'Fintail' models, originally introduced in late 1959, replaced the 'Ponton' series.

Advertising for the 230SL, released soon after its success on the 1963 Spa-Sofia-Liège Rally.

The Mercedes-Benz 250/8 (W114) of 1968 vintage. Note the four-cylinder 'Fintail' also on the line, along with the W108 bodyshell in the background.

V8-engined 600 – a stately vehicle available as a 5/6-seater or 7/8-seater on an extended wheelbase.

Things moved forward again in September 1965, when the W108 and W109 models replaced the 'Fintail' six-cylinder saloons, although the two-door models and four-cylinder W110 line continued for a while longer, duly joined by the 250SL before augmenting the 280SL and a new range of '/8' machines that took the place of the 'Fintail' fours at the start of 1968. These W114 and W115 cars were a thoroughly modern interpretation of traditional Mercedes thinking, overseen by Dr Hans Scherenberg, who took over the responsibility for product development following the retirement of Professor Fritz Nallinger at the end of 1965. As 1968 continued, the 300SEL 6.3 broke cover, along with an attractive W114 coupé body, which eventually went into production during the following year.

The 3.5-litre V8 engine made its debut at the 1969 Frankfurt Show, powering 300SEL 3.5 (W109) and two-door W111 variants, although the event was probably best remembered for the world premiere of the Wankel-engined C111. This magnificent creation was perhaps too far ahead of its time, although it's a shame that more wasn't done with the rotary engine – after a few more C111 prototypes, as with so many companies that had paid NSU for patent rights, the RE adventure came to an end.

In 1970, Hermann J. Abs resigned as Chairman of the Daimler-Benz AG Supervisory Board, handing the reins to Franz Heinrich Ulrich. A few months later, Dr Joachim Zahn was made Chairman of the Board of Management, while the Hanomag truck concern became a wholly-owned subsidiary of the Stuttgart giant (the tractor side of the business was separated and sold to Massey Ferguson).

The 280SE 3.5 and 280SEL 3.5 saloons were added to the W108 series in early 1971, although it was the R107 SL that stole the limelight. Introduced in April, the two-seater V8 roadster was

An English language advert from the early part of the 1970s, featuring the 280SE 3.5 (W108), powered by a V8 engine.

joined by a slightly longer tin-top version (the C107, or SLC) at the end of the year. Not long after, a new batch of W114 models joined the range, giving Mercedes-Benz a particularly sporting ambience in time to compliment the luxury W116 S-Class, announced at the 1972 Paris Salon. Eventually, 4.5-litre V8 engines were added to the S-Class and SL line-up, as well as long-wheelbase variants on the big saloons.

Mercedes-Benz UK Ltd was formed as 1974 dawned, the same year in which the SL line gained a six-cylinder engine option, while 1975 saw the launch of the 450SEL 6.9 – a true wolf in sheep's clothing. With a workforce of roughly 150,000 at this time, annual production during 1975 stood at 350,098 cars and 229,302 trucks.

Tranquility

After years of running countless model variations alongside each other – some, like the W111 two-door models, lasting six years beyond their four-door counterparts – the introduction of the W123-series saloons in January 1976 brought with them a sense of calm. Although a few of their '/8' predecessors were allowed to continue for a little while longer, compared with other model changeovers, it was a clean progression this time around. From now on, the W123s would take up the mid-range (as what would became known as the E-Class), the saloon, coupé and estate models augmenting the S-Class saloons at the top of the line, and the SL/SLC sports cars.

Dr Wilfried Guth was at the helm of the Supervisory Board by now, and one of his first decisions to make the new estate version of the W123 at the Bremen plant – first established by Borgward in 1938, but inherited by Daimler-Benz after the Hanomag takeover. This gradual move from commercial vehicle to passenger car production would duly become significant for fans of Mercedes sports cars at the end of the 1980s.

At the end of 1977, an all-alloy V8 was introduced on the 450SLC 5.0, while at the other end of the scale, a turbo-diesel engine was launched for the 300SD saloon. On 14 October that year, the 5,000,000th postwar passenger car left the line at Sindelfingen. Interestingly, the first million cars built after the conflict had taken 16 years to complete, whilst this last batch of a million had taken just two years. A few weeks later, Hans Scherenberg retired, leaving Werner Breitschwerdt in charge of product development.

Daimler-Benz had first toyed with ABS brake systems in 1970, but they ultimately became available in December 1978. Two months later, the long-running G-Wagen off-roader (Mercedes' answer to the Range Rover) was introduced, originally developed as a joint-project with Steyr-Daimler-Puch.

The supremely elegant W126 S-Class series was introduced at the 1979 Frankfurt Show, powered by 2.8-litre straight-sixes, or all-alloy 3.8- and 5.0-litre V8s. Production began on the state-of-the-art lines at Sindelfingen in December, which is when Joachim Zahn retired, allowing Dr Gerhard Prinz to become the new Chairman of the Board of Management of Daimler-Benz AG.

The W123 and SL/SLC models inherited new engines in 1980, and the availability of ABS brakes became more widespread. Airbags and seatbelt pretension systems became listed in the following year, keeping Daimler-Benz very much at the forefront of safety innovation and technology. 1981 also saw the last of the 600s built, as well as the first of the W126 coupés – the 380SEC and 500SEC ranking as one of the author's all-time favourites from the postwar era, even though they brought about the end of the SLC series.

The W116 S-Class model taking part in a 1978 press event promoting ABS braking technology.

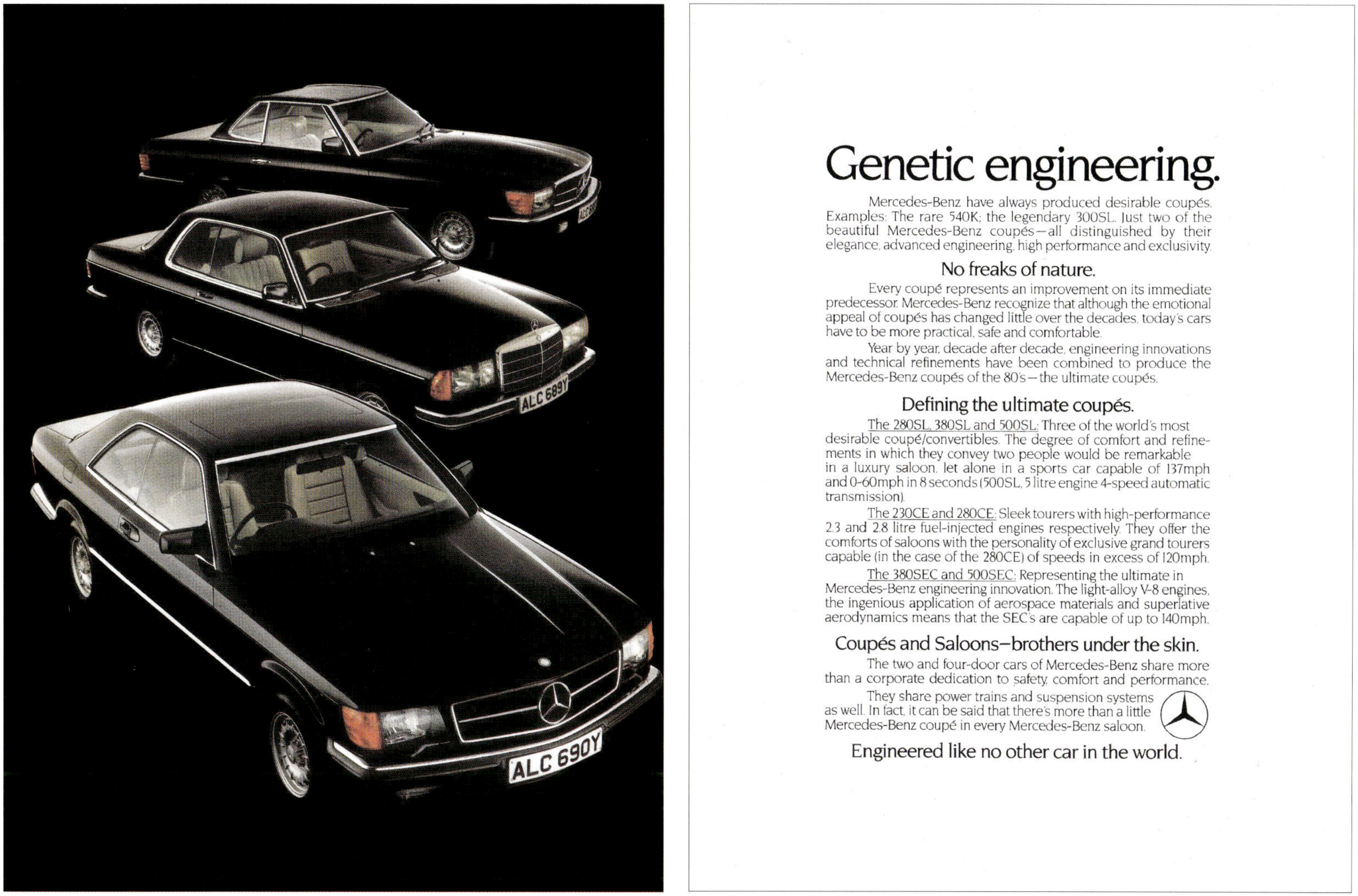

A British advert from 1983 featuring the supremely elegant W126-based SEC coupé, the W123-based CE coupé, and the R107 SL model. The contemporary S-Class was available in saloon (SE), lwb saloon (SEL) and coupé (SEC) guise, while the W123 was sold in saloon, lwb saloon, estate (T) and coupé (C/CE) form.

An all-new compact car, the 190/190E (W201), was announced in November 1982, bringing forth a predecessor to today's C-Class. A diesel-powered 190D was added in 1983, along with a high-performance 16v model, which managed to claim a number of world speed records a few weeks before it was launched.

With the death of Gerhard Prinz, Professor Werner Breitschwerdt stepped up to take on the Chairman's role, while Dr Rudolf Hörnig took over as head of R&D in May 1984. Catalytic converters became an option in Germany soon after, while particulate filters were employed on diesel cars, pointing the way for others to follow in a world that suddenly became aware of the 'Green' side of automotive engineering.

The respected W123-series was replaced by a new line of W124 models at the end of 1984, with styling closely resembling that of the W201. When the 1985 Frankfurt Show opened its doors for business, all three lines – the C-Class, E-Class and S-Class

The Sauber-Mercedes C9 Group C car of 1988. The following race season marked the true return of the 'Silver Arrows' in more ways than one.

(including the SL) – had been face-lifted, and new technologies, such as ASD (an automatic locking differential), ASR (an early form of traction control) and 4MATIC (an automatic four-wheel drive system) had been presented to the public. Rightfully proud of its traditional engineering, Daimler-Benz had shown it was capable of moving with the times, taking advantage of the latest electronics wizardry.

W124-based coupés were introduced at the 1987 Geneva Show, and Edzard Reuter replaced Werner Breitschwerdt in the Chairman's office a few months later. At the same time, at the 1987 Frankfurt Show, new diesel engines were announced for W201 and W124 series cars, and the W126 series was given uprated V8 engines.

1988 brought with it news of Mercedes-Benz officially returning to motorsport, with a Group A programme, and a prestigious Group C one, building on the success of the Swiss Sauber team. Swapping black paint for silver, the Group C cars were in form from the off in the following season, taking the WSPC title with ease in 1989, and then again in 1990.

Enhancing the marque's new-found sporting image, the technologically-advanced R129 SL was launched at the 1989 Geneva Show, fielded with a pair of three-litre straight-sixes and a five-litre V8. There was also a 190E 2.5-16 Evolution announced at the event, produced as a 500-off homologation special to further the chances of the top Group A racing teams (an Evo II was built in 1990).

The R129-type SL pictured at the time of its launch.

With so many different interests in a wide range of companies, Daimler-Benz AG was restructured in mid-1989, with Professor Werner Niefer named as Chairman of the Board of Management for the Mercedes-Benz AG wing. A face-lifted W124-series was announced soon after, and by the spring of 1990, all Mercedes passenger cars were powered by fuel-injected engines to give cleaner emissions.

Professor Hartmut Weule took over as the R&D boss in September 1990, and in the following month, closer ties were forged with AMG (the famous tuning company), and the 500E was introduced as the flagship of the W124 range, duly built at the Porsche factory in the Zuffenhausen district of Stuttgart.

The W140 S-Class made its debut at the 1991 Geneva Show, with three-, four-, five- and six-litre powerplants, the latter being an exotic V12. By the autumn, a large range of AMG models had joined the fray, as well as a four-seater convertible based on the W124 series (officially going on sale in the summer of 1992), and a C112 experimental sports car with a gullwing body configuration.

Mercedes officially withdrew from racing at the end of 1991, but new S-Class coupés were announced at the 1992 Detroit Show in January, and work continued on alternative fuel units in the background. The 600SL kept up the momentum, followed by a revised engine line-up for the W124 and W140 models later in the year.

A replacement for the 190 – the W202 C-Class – was launched in mid-1993, bringing with it a new form of model designation. The recently-released 600SL became the SL600 overnight as a result, but it was timely for the new engines adopted on the six-cylinder SLs, and the face-lifted W124s, which were correctly termed as E-Class models. It was all change in the administration offices, too, with Helmut Werner named as the new Chairman of the Board of Management at Mercedes-Benz AG.

September 1993 brought with it a concept that duly became the A-Class, new AMG models, and a revised G-Wagen, keeping the off-roader alive and well. Then, in November, the company announced it was taking a stake in Britain's Ilmor Engineering, which signalled a wish to enter the Formula One and Indycar arena.

More S-Class and E-Class variants put in an appearance at the 1994 Geneva Show in March, but it was the Turin Show, which opened a month later, that held the most interest for sports car fans, as that was where the SLK prototype made its debut.

Many companies talk of having pedigree. However, with so many landmark machines to its name and a rich history created by some of the biggest names in the industry, it's fair to say that few can match the bloodlines behind the Mercedes-Benz brand ...

The AMG Story

The Mercedes brand has always managed to attract the attentions of tuning companies, but few are as synonymous with the Stuttgart maker as AMG of Burgstall, Baden-Württemberg, and later Affalterbach, a few miles to the north-east of Stuttgart.

AMG was officially founded in June 1967 by Hans-Werner Aufrecht (who'd worked for Daimler-Benz, and had been in the competition department building engines in the glory days of the 1950s) and Erhard Melcher. For the first ten years of its history, AMG concentrated on engine and suspension development to further its highly-successful racing programme, but body kits and wheels were added to the firm's catalogue, and ultimately complete cars were built and offered for sale, either in turnkey guise or to the specific requests of customers.

In 1983, AMG developed a four-valve per cylinder head for the V8, leading to signature vehicles like the Hammer, but it also provided the foundation stone for further expansion; not just in Germany, but in places as far afield as America and Japan. The bored-out, six-litre 32v conversion on the five-litre V8, around since 1987, would duly provide enthusiasts with the 500SL 6.0 AMG.

The real breakthrough, however, came in October 1990, when AMG secured a deal in which its tuning parts could be sold and fitted via Mercedes-Benz dealerships, and complete cars started filtering through into domestic showrooms by May 1991. In addition, the racing programme was treated as a partnership, with the works DTM cars being prepared by Aufrecht's company. On 1 January 1999, DaimlerChrysler bought a 51 per cent stake in AMG, sealing the relationship once and for all with the foundation of Mercedes-AMG GmbH.

AMG racers from the past and present ...

2

The Earlier SLK Models

The idea of selling a smaller, lighter and less expensive open sports car alongside the flagship SL was nothing new at Daimler-Benz, as the 190SL had been marketed as a stablemate for the 300SL in the late-fifties and early-sixties. With Mercedes model lines expanding at a good rate of knots, and the contemporary SL becoming more and more exclusive in a market suddenly awash with cheaper convertibles, the time was right to revive the concept ...

The first SLK prototype – the so-called 'Studie SLK' – was displayed at the 1994 Turin Show, which opened in late-April. In many ways, it was riding on the wave of enthusiasm created by the Mazda MX-5 – a vehicle introduced in February 1989 that single-handedly revived the market for small, lightweight and affordable convertibles.

It was indeed a strange twist of fate when makers all over Europe were trying to recapture a sector of the market that had once been almost exclusively theirs, but had been abandoned in the face of US proposals to ban open cars. Thankfully, the idea was never implemented, but the threat was serious enough to dissuade further development on convertibles. One only needs to think of the Jaguar XJ-S and Triumph TR7 to see what the outcome was, while Porsche went the Targa route, and Daimler-Benz designed the SLC as a back-up plan in case the R107 SL found a frosty reception in the States.

Anyway, sales of the MX-5 were brisk to say the least, and new lightweight sports (LWS) models were being launched left, right and centre. By the time the SLK concept model had made an appearance, it was already finding itself in fierce competition with open cars from the likes of Lotus, Alfa Romeo, Fiat, BMW, MG, AC and Porsche. Not all of them were available in showrooms in 1994, but they were known quantities, and the Mercedes marketing men were doing their best to get people to

The 'Studie SLK' rightfully generated a lot of excitement when it was first displayed at the 1994 Turin Show. A lot of details would be changed, but at least Mercedes stayed true to the basic concept for the production car, already in the process of being signed off in the background.

delay their final decisions on purchasing by tempting them with the SLK show car.

As it happens, the SLK was very much a hint of Helmut Werner's vision for the future of the Mercedes brand, with its sporting image enhanced by the company's first involvement in

F1 racing for four decades (as an engine supplier to the Sauber team) a month before the Turin Show, and Al Unser Jr winning the Indianapolis 500 with a Penske-Mercedes PC23 a month after the Italian event. The timing was certainly good!

The marketing campaign stepped up another gear in October 1994, when a second prototype was displayed at the Paris Salon. This was more luxurious than sporting, and was fitted with a power-operated folding metal roof – a feature that was duly carried over to production models, and gave the SLK a huge advantage in the practicality stakes. The idea wasn't particularly new, but this was the first time that a roof like this had been made available in such a compact form, allowing the boot to still act as a luggage compartment, and just as importantly, at reasonable cost, with only a small price premium over a traditional ragtop configuration. Ultimately, in January 1996, Daimler-Benz got together with its Stuttgart neighbour Porsche to form Car Top Systems Fahrzeugdachsysteme GmbH in Hamburg. The CTS concern would serve both companies well in the development and manufacture of roof systems for their respective sports car models.

The timing was once more well-planned, for at the end of October, less than two weeks after the Paris Salon closed its doors for another couple of years, Mercedes-Benz presented its new Formula One car, launched in partnership with the British McLaren team. The partnership had to wait until March 1997 for its first win, but after that, it was easy to recall the domination of the 'Silver Arrows' of yore, not only in F1, but in the American CART (Indycar) series as well.

Birth of the R170 SLK

There were a number of important factors governing the R170 SLK package. The car had to be significantly smaller and lighter than the profitable SL (the R129 series at the time) to justify its place in the showroom, and also significantly cheaper. This doesn't sound too difficult, but keeping a level of safety and body rigidity that is expected of a Mercedes open car isn't so easy, especially when running on a tight budget. There was also an enviable reliability record to uphold, quality feel to be retained, and the inclusion of the 'Variodach' power roof seen on the Paris Salon show car – something that allowed the SLK to hold a niche position in the market, but also added expensive and weight, as well as a headache for the engineering team from a number of angles.

With the thoroughly-modern W202 C-Class (finished on paper, but yet to find its way into the showrooms) chosen to provide a lot of the donor parts, including a shortened version

This is the vehicle shown at the 1994 Paris Salon, complete with its 'Variodach' folding metal roof, which dropped underneath the double-hinged bootlid to give the car a remarkably clean look from a styling point of view, as well as a number of practical advantages.

The R170 SLK taking shape in the styling studio at Sindelfingen.

of the floorpan, the design slowly but surely took shape as the concept was refined. A total of 15 scale models were whittled down to just one by March 1993.

Michael Mauer, a key design team member whose presentation model was the one chosen for further development, stated in the 1990s: "There was more variation than normal in the early sketches. We tried a number of different themes, from rounded, retro-SL designs through to modern, hard-edged ones. Simply doing a retro design didn't link up with our determination that the SLK should be a market leader for six or seven years. We wanted to combine a future-orientated shape with support design that reminded people of our history, such as the power bulges on the bonnet, and the SL-inspired face. We wanted more sporting proportions than the SL, so reduced the overhangs. The SL is our idea of an elegant sporting car. The SLK should look more youthful and dynamic."

As one can see from the accompanying table, the downsizing of the body was achieved readily enough, although the target weight of 1200kg (2640lb) set in 1993 was never going to be realised. Ultimately, however, a saving of around half-a-ton was made compared to the contemporary SL by the time everything was finished – a massive and admirable reduction that would allow ample performance from a smaller power-unit, along with enhanced handling and fuel economy.

The styling was authentic Mercedes, with certain features borrowing from the past, others keeping the car in line with its contemporary stablemates, and a few pointing towards the future. The front mask looked like a scaled-down version of the R129 in many respects, with shades of the face-lifted version (introduced in September 1995) showing through. The grille and lighting units were less aggressive, though, and the pair of power bulges in the bonnet was a reminder of the W198 300SLs of yore.

Dimensions

This table helps put the SLK's size into perspective, comparing the dimensions of the new car with the early 190SL (W121) and the R129 models, which represented the contemporary SL line at the time of the SLK's launch. The data on the Japanese interloper, credited with reviving the two-seat LWS (lightweight sports car) as a breed, provides a useful bench mark for reference, as does that for the Porsche Boxster – another open car that was making an impact, born in the same era as the SLK.

	SLK (R170)	**190SL (W121)**	**500SL (R129)**	**Mazda MX-5**	**Porsche Boxster**
Length	3995mm/157.3in	4220mm/166.1in	4470mm/176.0in	3970mm/156.3in	4315mm/169.9in
Wheelbase	2400mm/94.5in	2400mm/94.5in	2515mm/99.0in	2265mm/89.2in	2415mm/95.1in
Width	1715mm/67.5in	1740mm/68.5in	1812mm/71.3in	1675mm/65.9in	1780mm/70.1in
Front Track	1488mm/58.6in	1430mm/56.3in	1535mm/60.4in	1405mm/55.3in	1455mm/57.3in
Rear Track	1485mm/58.5in	1475mm/58.1in	1523mm/60.0in	1420mm/55.9in	1508mm/59.4in
Height	1289mm/50.7in	1320mm/52.0in	1293mm/50.9in	1235mm/48.6in	1290mm/50.8in
Weight	1325kg/2915lb	1140kg/2508lb	1800kg/3960lb	940kg/2068lb	1250kg/2750lb

Note: The height entry is that for a hardtop or when the top is in the raised position, while the width is for the body only, and does not include mirrors – these took the overall width to 1947mm (76.6in) in the case of the SLK. The rear track for the SLK is that with 16- or 17-inch wheels, which decreased by 15mm (0.6in) if 15-inch wheels were fitted. The weight is for the supercharged SLKs.

From the side, short overhangs, a low roofline and the strong double wedge styling formed by the rise of the front wing towards the bulkhead, and then a second rise from the B-post back (the join being disguised by the large door mirror) helped give the SLK a compact profile, its height being reduced visually by the use of black paint below the sill from one end of the car to the other. The smooth nose, steeply-raked windscreen and high tail helped keep the Cd down to a very reasonable 0.33, or 0.35 for the grades with wider wheel and tyre combinations. In keeping with the overall design, the alloy wheels were kept simple, free of styling gimmicks.

Around the back, the taillights followed W202 practice rather than SL lines, being triangular in shape, with the bootlid sitting almost the full width of the car to allow the roof to drop underneath it out of sight. When the roof was down, the twin roll-over bars behind the seats were revealed, enhancing safety and giving the SLK a distinctive styling feature at the same time.

Inside, the excesses of the 1994 show cars were left behind, but by Mercedes-Benz standards, the well-equipped interior was very youthful, as the target audience for the SLK was far younger than the average client that favoured the Stuttgart marque. It was also more sporting than the norm, with bucket seats and the availability of colourful two-tone upholstery, although things like the fake carbon on the centre console drew a mixed reaction from the motoring press. Interestingly, due to its thinner seat pads and a series of rapid advances in the various safety systems employed in modern cars, the SLK felt just as roomy as the much larger SL, and a wide selection of oddment storage boxes made it almost as practical, too.

Once the styling had been finalised, prototype testing began in earnest – a process aided by so many drivetrain and chassis components having been sourced from the compact C-Class saloon series that had been launched in mid-1993.

Three power-unit options were listed initially – all fuel-injected straight-fours, and two of them supercharged, although one of the latter was restricted to a very limited number of EU markets where taxes were extremely high on cars with engine capacities above a 2-litre threshold. These M111 lumps, with an alloy head and cast iron block, can be traced back to the W124 saloons, although numerous improvements had been adopted by the time they found their way into the SLK, not least the addition of variable intake camshaft timing, introduced in 1996.

One of the many SLK prototypes on test. The SLK went through an exhaustive testing programme, both in the hallowed halls of Stuttgart, and in tens of thousands of road miles in extremes of heat, cold, humidity, and dust.

The base model was a normally-aspirated 1998cc unit with an 89.9mm bore and a 78.7mm stroke. With a 10.4:1 compression ratio, it developed 136bhp and 140lbft of torque, and could be linked to a Getrag five-speed manual gearbox, or one of the new electronically-controlled 5G-Tronic five-speed automatics, first presented to the press in February 1995 alongside the ESP safety system.

The Italian, Greek and Portuguese markets were treated to a supercharged version of the same engine, and with a lower 8.5:1 c/r and different engine management system (Bosch as opposed to VDO on the NA unit), it delivered a healthy 192bhp and 199lbft of torque. This engine option could be bought with a manual transmission only.

Finally, there was the supercharged 2295cc unit used in the SLK230 Kompressor model, which was often the only vehicle available in many of the major export markets. With a 90.9mm bore and 88.4mm stroke, a Bosch black box, and an 8.8:1 c/r, it developed 193bhp at 5300rpm, along with 207lbft of torque. There was a 5MT gearbox for most of the big Mercedes outlets, although some markets were restricted to the 5AT unit that was an option in Europe, and the US at the time of the car's launch.

The chassis setup was based on contemporary C-Class practice, but with spring and damper rates, as well as the wheel travel, suitably tuned and adjusted to be more in keeping with a sports car.

Safety was also of paramount importance. Although the weight crept above target during development, the SLK was ultimately as strong and safe as the vast majority of saloons on the road.

At the front, the suspension was made up of a broad-based lower wishbone carrying the inboard coil spring, and also providing a connection for the gas-filled telescopic shock absorber close to the wheel. A trackrod end then attached the lengthy steering knuckle and hub carrier, which was located at the top by a very narrow control arm, or a second wishbone, if you want to call it that. The anti-roll bar ran in front of the suspension, with the steering mechanism aft of it.

The multi-link rear suspension was based on a hefty cradle that connected to the body with rubber bushes at four points. A short control arm carried the inboard coil spring and the outboard damper, and the other four arms (giving five links in all) then secured and located the hub carrier.

The familiar recirculating ball PAS (power-assisted steering) system was employed, albeit with a quicker ratio than the saloons, and came with a damper in the linkage to take out road shocks transmitted to the steering wheel.

The servo-assisted, dual-circuit brake system came with ABS (anti-lock braking system) as standard. A 288mm (11.3in) diameter ventilated disc was used up front with a floating caliper on the leading edge, while a solid 278mm (10.9in) disc was specified for the rear, complete with a fixed caliper on the trailing edge and an integral drum so that shoes could be used for the handbrake mechanism.

Supercharged cars came with ASR (standing for Antriebsschlupfregelung), while the normally-aspirated model was available with ETS – a very basic, low-speed electronic traction control system that wasn't able to govern engine power. ASR, on the other hand, was a state-of-the-art traction control system, managing the rear brake activation and power sent to the rear wheels as soon as slippage was detected, in order to give the best possible traction in all conditions.

The normally-aspirated model came with 7J x 15 seven-spoke alloy rims shod with 205/60 HR-rated rubber at both ends, although the sculptured cut-outs made it look like a traditional steel disc wheel. Supercharged cars had regular seven-spoke alloys, but with 16-inch diameter rims, and different widths front to rear – 7J with 205/55 VR-rated tyres up front, and 8J combined with 225/50s at the back.

Mercedes-Benz designations

For many years, Mercedes-Benz models have been identified by a vehicle class letter (or series of letters) and a number, which usually relates to an engine size. It's a system that has continued to this day, with C 350 being a C-Class saloon with a 3.5-litre power-unit, although the engine displacements don't always tie-up precisely in the way they used to.

The designation that interests us the most at this stage in the story, however, is SL, as in 190SL and so on. The '190' denotes a 1.9-litre powerplant, while 'SL' is short for Sport and Licht – in English, this would translate into a description of a lightweight sports (LWS) model.

For reference, the addition of an 'R' suffix (to make SLR) distinguished the 300SLR sports-racer from the 3-litre 300SL production road cars, while a 'C' (to make SLC) denotes a coupé version of the SL, introduced in the 1970s.

One will also come across a 'K' quite often in Mercedes circles, which used to refer to short chassis models in prewar days (as in Kurz), but nowadays is usually taken to mean Kompressor, the German for supercharger. Having said that, the SLK model was sold in normally-aspirated and supercharged guise using the same SLK moniker for both vehicle types. We can therefore safely say that in the case of the R170, the SLK designation stands for a shortened version of the SL.

An early SLK200 with the prime movers in the R170 project – Dieter Zetsche (centre, aka Dr Z) and Jürgen Hubbert, seen here on the left, and responsible for passenger car development. Zetsche was Hubbert's boss at the time of the SLK project, but when Hubbert was promoted to executive status in 1995, Helmut Petri (right) moved up to take his place.

While the 1996 Geneva Show was used to launch a new line of C- and E-Class estates, the 66th Turin Show, held the following month, was reserved to give the R170 SLK a full share of the limelight. The scene was set for another date in Turin ...

The early SLK production cars

Beginning officially in July 1996 (a month later than originally forecast, and quite some time after the April launch), production of the SLK took place in the Bremen plant, a factory originally established by the Borgward concern in 1938, but taken over by Daimler-Benz in 1971. Although the site was used by Mercedes for light commercial vehicles initially, as well as estate versions of the W123, the 190 had been made there, and production of the SL moved there, too, as soon as the R107 series run came to an end, giving way to the R129 model.

German buyers could choose from the DM 46,000 SLK200 or DM 53,000 SLK230 Kompressor. These models were very well equipped by lightweight sports car standards, with the power top, electric windows and mirrors, remote central locking, plus a whole host of minor items coming as part of the package. Major options included an automatic transmission, air-conditioning, leather trim, seat heaters, headlight washers, and audio equipment. There was also an AMG bodykit available, as well as larger AMG wheels.

US sales began in March 1997, with American buyers receiving a fully-loaded model based on the automatic SLK230 Kompressor. Listed at $39,700, it was priced similar to the Porsche Boxster, and around $10,000 more expensive than the BMW Z3, although the only options were metallic paint, heated seats and mobile phone/CD-changer packages

One of the first SLK230 Kompressor models, with its roof partially closed to show the innovative mechanism. The SLK went from coupé to convertible or vice versa in just 25 seconds, with no more effort required than the flick of a switch.

– everything else was standard, making the car tip the scales at 1370kg (3014lb).

UK-based enthusiasts were also restricted to an SLK230 Kompressor model. Launched at the 1996 British International Motor Show at the NEC, it was also equipped with a 5AT gearbox only, as were the Japanese and Australian versions of the car, released in February 1997. For 1998, Australia added an SLK200 model to the line-up, although it was never sold in the other major rhd markets.

The domestic 1998 Model Year cars came with the Brake Assist (BAS) safety system, first announced in late-1996. Developed by Daimler-Benz and Lucas Industries, this system measured the speed and force with which the brake pedal was applied, and if an emergency stop was detected, increased braking force up to the maximum the ABS system would allow. In addition, ASR became an option on the normally-aspirated model, taking the place of ETS, and the Assyst service reminder feature was added at the same time. By April 1998, ASR had become a standard

Engine bay of the SLK230 Kompressor model.

Right and below: One of the early German-registered press cars, and the typical interior of a domestic model. Note the trim, which was very much in keeping with the youthful image the marketing people were trying to project with the SLK.

fitment on all SLK models, and a 'Speedtronic' limiter feature was added to the 'Tempomat' cruise control system in the middle of the year.

It was the 1999 Model Year that was the important one for US buyers, with a manual gearbox becoming available (the automatic transmission was shifted to the option list as a result), BAS becoming standard, and the AMG bodykit and alloy wheels being made available via the $3990 'Sport Package.'

On the subject of individuality, the first Designo consulting centre had opened at the Sindelfingen plant in November 1995. This allowed customers to order cars with special interior and exterior finishes, adding to the enjoyment of purchasing a new car and the years of ownership ahead. Five more centres were planned for Germany, although the Designo name would eventually hold worldwide appeal. As the original model entered its final season, Americans were given the chance to buy a couple of Designo SLK models with special paint and trim, as well as a 'Limited Edition' car, the latter introduced in December 1999.

In the background

While all the activity surrounding the SLK was taking place, there were several important events happening on the corporate front in Stuttgart. Jürgen Schrempp was named as the new Chairman of the Board of Management at Daimler-Benz AG in May 1995, a month before the launch of the twin-headlight W210 E-Class saloon. The fresh front mask design had first been revealed in a concept car displayed at the 1993 Geneva Show, and it became something of a Benz signature for a little while.

A 1998 Japanese advert featuring the AMG CLK-GTR.

At the 1995 Frankfurt Show, held in September, the crowds were treated to a series of upgrades for the SL and C-Class, as well as the launch of the E50 AMG saloon. The AMG name was flying high in both the DTM and ITC touring car racing series at this time, the competition programme being treated as a partnership between the Stuttgart and Affalterbach companies. As it happens, AMG had secured a deal in which its tuning parts could be sold and fitted via Mercedes-Benz dealerships in October 1990, and complete cars began filtering through into domestic showrooms by May 1991. The two concerns would become closer still in the future, with Mercedes taking a 51 per cent stake in the firm in January 1999, but their relationship, even at this stage, brought forth a range of officially approved tuning parts to allow owners greater individuality, and the success on the tracks was a magnificent marketing tool for all concerned.

The S-Class coupés were face-lifted two months after the SLK production car was launched, giving rise to a new CL-Class designation. The sporty two-door CLK coupé (C208) was announced at the 1997 Detroit Show. Based on the C-Class, it resembled the concept car displayed at the Geneva Show way back in 1993, and would go on to be immensely popular, helping to push annual passenger car production up to 726,686 units. The tin-top version was joined by a convertible model in March 1998.

Klaus-Dieter Vöhringer took the place of Hartmut Weule as the head of the R&D section at about the same time as the CLK was unveiled, while the E280 and E320 models that made their debut in Amsterdam in February were the first vehicles to make use of the all-new M112 V6 engines featuring three valves per cylinder and twin ignition. A new generation of 4MATIC was also announced, with permanent four-wheel drive. In the following month, it was the turn of the new A-Class to take a bow in Geneva, where the SLK picked up the 'Cabrio Of The Year' award, selected by an international jury.

The business was restructured again in April 1997, with Mercedes-Benz AG merged into Daimler-Benz AG. More importantly, the new vee-engine plant in Bad Cannstatt (touted as the "factory of the future") was officially opened at the same time, allowing the production of M112 and M113 units in an efficient and eco-friendly manner. The one-millionth engine was built there just three years later.

The CLK-GTR homologation special was also presented in April, featuring a V12 engine and a lightweight carbonfibre body. Only 25 were built, but it was enough to qualify the car for the FIA GT Championships – a series that the model would quickly go on to dominate.

May 1997, and another new vehicle range was launched in the shape of the M-Class SUV, which was initially built in America. The C-Class cars were given a mild face-lift in the following month, and more models were added to the line at the Frankfurt Show in September, alongside a selection of fresh E-Class variants.

A few days later, the 1997 Tokyo Show played host to the debut of the Maybach luxury saloon concept vehicle. It would eventually go into production, thus reviving a treasured name from the past, in mid-2002.

Meanwhile, the company opened its third Advanced Design Studio outside Germany in February 1998, this time in Como, Italy. The others had been established in Irvine (CA) in the States in 1991, and in Yokohama, Japan, during the following year.

The first of the 'smart' microcars were presented shortly after in the spring of 1998, although it's probably fair to say that sports car fans were far more interested in the face-lifted SL range, announced at the Turin Show that April.

In the first week of May 1998, news broke of one of the biggest merger deals in the history of the motor industry, as America's Chrysler Corporation joined forces with Daimler-Benz AG to form a new company called DaimlerChrysler AG. The merger was approved at an EGM for shareholders in September, and completed in November. Jürgen Schrempp now shared the Chairman's post with Robert Eaton.

The W220 S-Class was launched at the 1998 Paris Salon, with the company's huge new proving grounds at Papenburg opening for business at around the same time. With the workforce now standing at over 440,000 people, passenger car production had hit a staggering 947,517 units in 1998.

The 1999 Detroit Show was selected as the venue to present the 5.4-litre supercharged Vision SLR coupé concept, suitably impressing the crowds gathered before it. A couple of months later, in Geneva, the new CL-Class (C215) was unveiled, along with the CLK 55 AMG. As it happens, a whole new range of AMG machines was launched in April 1999, with the SL 73 AMG being considered the flagship of the line.

A face-lifted E-Class (W210) was presented in July 1999, with the CLK updated in the following month. The relentless pace of development continued, with a roadster version of the V8-powered Vision SLR being displayed at the 1999 Frankfurt Show. New engines were announced for the S-Class at the same time, making the most of the latest in diesel technology, and before the year came to an end, the AMG range expanded once more, just after the celebrations surrounding Mercedes-Benz winning another F1 driver's title with Mika Hakkinen were beginning to die down.

The 190SL: the original SLK

Back in the fifties, Mercedes was selling its race-inspired 300SL to a small group of connoisseurs; its size restricted not so much by desire, but by price. The bottom line is, the majority of car enthusiasts would have liked a 'Gullwing' SL in their garage, but at almost $9000 in the States (just $2000 shy of the average house price at the time), it was simply out of reach.

The marketing chaps were well aware of this fact, and equally aware of the kudos attached to the SL badge thanks to the competition exploits of the first 300SL model, which was a pure racer that won just about everything worth winning in Europe, as well as delivering a stirring performance in the Carrera Panamericana. As such, plans were laid for a more reasonably-priced SL to be sold alongside its 3-litre stablemate from the start.

The announcement of the two new Mercedes sports cars in February 1954 at the International Motor Sports Show in New York had enthusiasts in raptures – the 3-litre, fuel-injected 300SL, with styling based on the 1953 SL prototype, and the much simpler, smaller-engined 190SL. Although it would be some time before either SL made it into the showrooms (the second Type W198 300SL, for instance, wasn't built until six weeks after the New York exhibition had ended, and even that was still a pre-production prototype), it was no coincidence that they were announced just as the latest W196 F1 car was about to hit the Grand Prix scene.

Walter Häcker (seated in the car) going over the final styling details on a pre-production prototype of the W121 190SL.

Another view of the pre-production prototype in the design studio at Stuttgart, featuring a completely different bonnet profile to the car displayed in New York at the beginning of 1954. The blister over the rear wheelarch was also added at the last minute, bringing the car into line with the 300SL.

Series production of the 190SL convertible started in May 1955, about six months behind schedule. This was rather ironic, given that the 190SL was always going to provide Daimler-Benz with better volume sales in the States than the 300SL. However, people had an image of the 'Gullwing' body whenever the SL moniker was muted, hence the model release order, and the smaller car could then waft by on the fame of its bigger brother by using the same Sport Licht badge.

While it's fair to say the 300SL was built using many production parts sourced from the regular road car line, the ratio was much higher in the 190SL. Even the chassis was based on a shortened Type 180 pressed-steel floorpan, rather than a dedicated tubular spaceframe, whilst most of the running gear and chassis components were simply lifted straight out of the Type 180 parts bins. This reduced cost and development time, with advantages far outweighing the disadvantages for the manufacturer.

Styled under the watchful gaze of Walter Häcker, the final prototype was exhibited at the Geneva Show in the spring of 1955. Compared with the 1954 show car, the bonnet, bumpers

A very early 190SL for the North American market. The US was by far the most important outlet for European sports cars, of course, with the 190SL introduced to Stateside buyers at a reasonable $3998.

Contemporary colour shot showing a 190SL in Singapore.

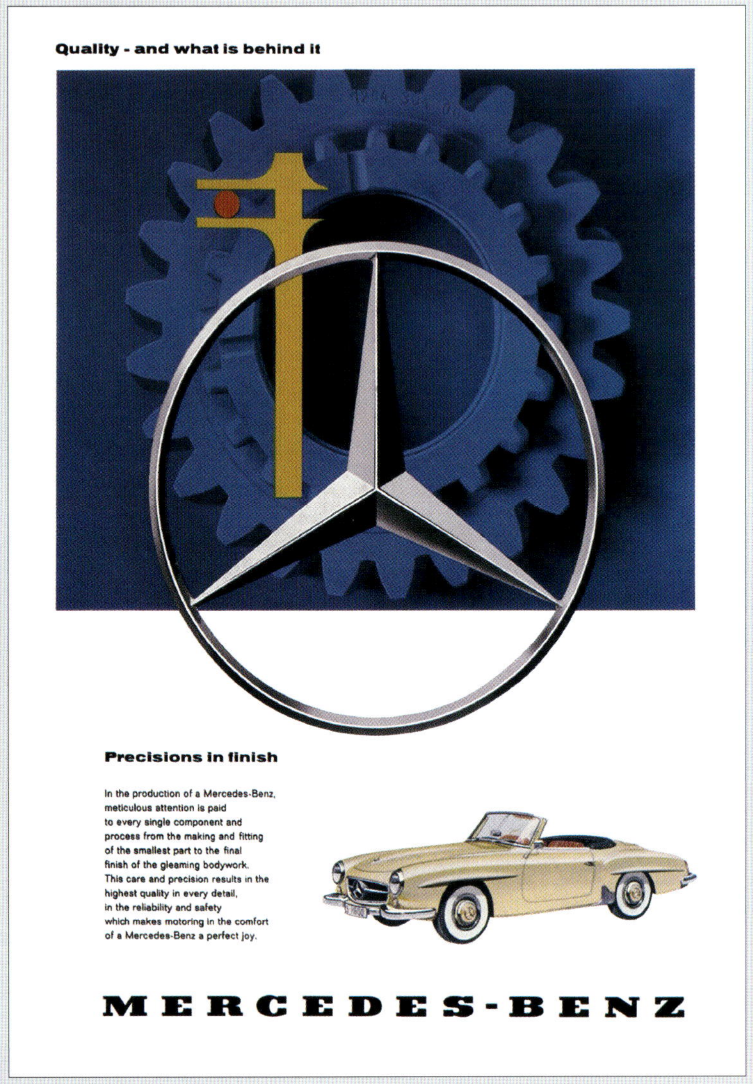

Above and right: Two pieces of advertising for the 190SL – one in German, and one in English. The 190SL may not have been quite as glamorous as the 300SL, but it was an accomplished sporting tourer that was infinitely more affordable to buy and run.

and lights were revised, and the grille and rear wings brought more into line with the 300SL, although the 'Ponton' styling influence was still very much in evidence on the latter.

A hardtop was available from the off, giving the buyer the choice of a convertible roadster (with soft top only), or a car with a hardtop, supplied with or without a hood. Interestingly, the hardtop model was called a coupé in official paperwork, and came with additional chrome trim on the sills and wheelarch blisters. Early hardtops were crafted from aluminium, but were made from pressed steel from the spring of 1956.

The body itself was largely all-steel on the 190SL, although the front and rear lids and door skins were aluminium. Even lighter doors were announced in the New York press material and appeared in several catalogues thereafter. These, along with a lightweight aero-screen and removal of the bumpers helped reduce weight for those wishing to go racing at weekends.

On a more practical note, while the 300SL had next to nothing in the way of trunk space due to its oversized fuel tank, with a parcel shelf behind the seats providing the main luggage area, the 190SL had a good-sized boot. Fitted luggage was available from the maker for both cars. In addition, a third transverse jump-seat was listed for the 190SL, fitting in behind the two front ones, or a bench-style front seat was another option.

The engine was a high output 1897cc sohc four, with the same bore as the 300SL, but a shorter 83.6mm stroke. This bore/

stroke combination was quite different to that of the original Type 180, adding 130cc to the cubic capacity, which had started out at 1767cc for the sedans, but it was duly adopted for the 1956 190 series, as well as the Type 180a of 1957 vintage. In the 190SL, a pair of twin-choke Solex carburetors and an 8.5:1 compression ratio gave 105bhp DIN at 5700rpm, with power taken to the rear wheels through a four-speed manual transmission.

Using the Type 180 floorpan allowed the Daimler-Benz engineers to employ the sedan's front subframe arrangement for the SL, with the engine, gearbox and front suspension system carried on an independent pressed-steel cradle that was then attached to the body via rubber mounts to isolate NVH – an incredibly advanced feature for the time. The concept was further refined in January 1956, thanks to an improvement in the way the engine was mounted in the subframe.

The suspension itself was quite conventional, with fabricated upper and lower arms at the front, coil springs around damper units, and an anti-roll bar. The back end featured a low-pivot swing axle with the addition of revised, fairly hefty trailing links to give superior roadholding, the handling situation being further helped by the adoption of 13-inch wheels and tyres, which, although of unusually small diameter for the day, had the effect of reducing the roll centre height.

Braking was via drums all-round, but with the drums themselves made from cast iron rather than the expensive Al-Fin bimetal (ribbed alloy sleeves over cast drums) items used on the 3-litre car. They were still finned, at least, for enhanced heat dissipation, while a servo was initially

A 190SL from 1958, seen here with its hardtop in place. The later-style hardtop, introduced in October 1959, gave far better rearward visibility.

offered as an option before becoming standard shortly after production began. Steering, meanwhile, was via the familiar recirculating-ball system for so long championed by the men in Stuttgart; lhd or rhd was available, unlike the 300SL coupé, which was officially sold with left-hand drive only.

The 190SL was subjected to a number of detail changes over the years. By far the most important were carried out in time for the 1960 Model Year, when the engine's compression ratio was upped to 8.8:1 to maintain power output at 105bhp (120bhp SAE), and a new hardtop was introduced to give better visibility. A total of 25,881 190SLs had been built by the time production ended in February 1963.

Tail of the 1960 MY 190SL. It's actually easier to date a 190SL from the rear view: the larger rear lights seen here had been introduced in June 1956, and whilst always fitted to US cars, rear bumper guards had become standard for all markets in July 1957, when they were modified to carry the number plate lights. The 1960 MY hardtop gives another clue (fitted to this car in other press pictures from the time), but about the only significant change applied after that was made to the bootlid lock, which was separated from the lift during 1960.

The R170 face-lift

The 2000 Detroit Show was used to announce the face-lifted version of the R170 SLK, although it was very low-key, with similar press material handed out at the Brussels Show in Europe. No cars were displayed, although those visiting the Stateside event were treated to an appearance from the Mercedes Vision SLA concept car – a small open two-seater based on the A-Class, but featuring a number of styling cues that pointed towards the future of the SLK.

When the face-lifted car finally went into production, in February 2000, the SLK inherited some new styling touches and a completely new engine line-up. A revised SLK200 Kompressor model provided the latest entry-level machine for the majority of markets, the SLK230 Kompressor continued in updated guise, and the normally-aspirated V6-powered SLK320 grade became the new flagship of the compact two-seater range.

On the styling side, there was a new front bumper assembly and air dam, with softer profiles and an impression of greater volume (largely thanks to the deletion of the black paint on the lower edges of the vehicle), while the grille was finished in a lighter colour to make it stand out more. Xenon headlights became an option, too.

The side repeater lamps were dropped in favour of indicators being added to the freshly-designed door mirrors, and new 16-inch alloy wheels were adopted on the SLK230 Kompressor and SLK320 models (the original 15-inch rims were carried over for the two-litre car). There were also colour-keyed door handles, along with revised side skirt styling.

Around the back, there was another new bumper assembly, the light units were subtly different, and the oval-shaped exhaust pipes matched the other styling touches applied to the face-lifted car. The lack of a boot lock (moved out of sight, underneath the boot plinth), gives another identifying feature.

As it happens, the body was strengthened (and therefore made safer when combined with other changes made under the skin) at the same time, and the fuel tank capacity was increased from 53 litres (11.6 Imperial, or 14.0 US gallons) to 60 litres (13.2 Imperial, or 15.9 US gallons), extending the car's range by a useful amount. As such, the new cars were much heavier than their predecessors, with the SLK230 Kompressor gaining 60kg (132lb) after the face-lift, for instance. Even the two-litre machine

Several views of the face-lifted SLK200 Kompressor model, highlighting the fact that the four-cylinder cars had a different lower apron at the front compared with the V6 models, along with 'Kompressor' badging on the side of the front wings.

Exterior of the SLK320, which had 16-inch five-spoke alloys, as opposed to six-spoke versions for the 2.3-litre models. Look carefully, and one can just make out the larger front brakes used on the V6 cars.

The stylish interior of an automatic SLK320 with 'Calyptus Linea' wood trim. The colour of the gauge faces was changed to a shade called 'Mussel' during the face-lift.

tipped the scales at 1365kg (3003lb), while the V6 model seen here had a 1405kg (3091lb) kerb weight.

In a bid to keep up with what the competition was doing, the interior of the SLK was given a makeover of epic proportions, with the overall impression changing from youthful and sporty to luxurious with a hint of sportiness. Material selection had a lot to do with this change in moods, with new 'Arezzo' cloth and fresh leather shades, as well as different trim that looked more inviting, with the seats moving away from the pure bucket shell concept (or at least making it less obvious), the end of the carbonfibre-style facing pieces, and a simpler approach to things like the steering wheel design.

While the two-tone theme was carried over, the quickest way to sum up the interior transformation is in the replacement of the carbon-type trim pieces for engine-turned aluminium ones on the centre console and door handle surrounds, with the lighting switch and air vent escutcheon panels now having a plain black finish. As an option, though, the aluminium sections could be replaced by one of two shades of wood trim for those looking for a more luxurious atmosphere.

Moving on to the engines - of the M111 power-units, the smaller four gained a new engine management system and supercharger, as well as a revised head that allowed a higher 9.5:1 compression ratio. That notwithstanding, in a bid to keep abreast of EU emission regulations, power dropped from 192bhp to just 163, although a choice between six-speed manual and five-speed automatic transmissions (the latter now coming with a 'Touchshift' selector) held great appeal in the showroom. A number of minor tweaks on the 2.3-litre version kept power virtually unchanged (up 4bhp, in fact), and fuel economy improved thanks to the latest 6MT and 5AT gearboxes.

The V6 was a 3199cc (89.9mm x 84.0mm) all-alloy M112 unit, which was unusual in having three valves per cylinder (one exhaust valve and two inlets) working via a single overhead camshaft on each bank. With fuel-injection, dual ignition, variable length intake manifold technology, and a 10.0:1 c/r, the engine delivered 218bhp at 5700rpm, along with 229lbft of torque at between 3000 and 4600rpm. Again, six-speed manual or five-speed automatic transmissions were available.

On the chassis front, the suspension was stiffened and lowered by 5mm (0.2in), gaining a rear anti-roll bar along the way, and the Electronic Stability Programme (ESP), first introduced in the early part of 1994, was made standard across the SLK line. This replaced the ASR traction control system used previously, although it built

Display version of an M112 V6 from the time, the cutaway sections clearly showing its internal workings, along with those of the automatic transmission tacked onto the back. The SLK's engine bay had been made to accept a V6 from the off.

on the latter's hardware, using the ABS sensors to determine the onset of oversteer or understeer, and selectively reducing engine torque or applying one of the rear brakes to bring the car back into control. Finally, to keep the additional performance in check, the V6 model was given larger front brakes. These measured 300mm across (11.8in), which is 12mm (0.5in) greater than the disc diameter found on the four-cylinder models, although all cars shared the same rear brake setup.

Final years of the R170

Without taxes (VAT was 16 per cent in Germany at the time), the face-lifted SLK200 Kompressor was priced at DM 51,800 at the start of 2000, while the SLK230 Kompressor commanded DM 56,900, and the SLK320 a cool DM 66,900 in manual guise. Standard equipment and options were pretty much carried over if we use equivalent model lines, although air-conditioning was standard on the V6 grade.

Sales of the face-lifted car began in the States just a few weeks after the Detroit Show closed its doors, with the newcomer officially classed as an early 2001 model in the US. The V6-engined SLK320 joining the line-up was naturally the biggest news for fans of the two-seater, priced at $43,900 - $5000 more than the face-lifted 2.3-litre supercharged car, which was actually cheaper than before.

Whereas leather and wood trim were classed as options in Germany, things were simplified somewhat for American buyers, with the four-cylinder machine coming with aluminium trim pieces on the centre console and door handle surrounds, while the six-cylinder car came with wood trim as standard, extending to the steering wheel and gearshift; leather upholstery was standard across the board. The 'Sport Package' was continued, bringing with it the AMG bodykit and wheels, and two 'Designo' models were available.

As in Germany and most other parts of Europe, British enthusiasts had three grades to choose from. Australians also had the full line-up, although Japanese buyers were restricted to the 2.3- and 3.2-litre models, as per the North American market.

Above and left: The SLK 32 AMG with its unique alloy wheels and interior. The gentleman in the car is Bernd Schneider, by the way – the multiple German Touring Car (DTM) champion for Mercedes and AMG.

In the background, Bob Eaton retired in March 2000, just as the new W203 C-Class was being launched. Dieter Zetsche and Wolfgang Bernhard were sent from Stuttgart to the US to hold the fort, as what amounted to a take-over rather than a merger emerged. A little while later, as the empire building continued on Schrempp's watch, DaimlerChrysler took a one-third stake in Japan's Mitsubishi Motors in July 2000.

The Frankfurt Show, usually a showcase for the German manufacturers, was a low-key affair for Mercedes in 2000, with the launch of the new C-Class Sports Coupé (C203) being the highlight. Not long after, the company withdrew from the US CART racing scene in order to concentrate its efforts on Formula One and touring cars – motorsport arenas in which the Mercedes-Benz marque was enjoying great success. Then, in January, visitors to the 2001 Detroit Show witnessed the official public launch of a couple of new C-Class models and the rapid SLK 32 AMG.

The 156mph (250kph) SLK 32 AMG was a fully-engineered model, with the folks at AMG going a lot further than adding the optional bodykit and wheels to make a new grade. For starters, the 3.2-litre V6 was supercharged and intercooled, and had virtually all its internal components modified, as well as a new exhaust system. With a Bosch ME management system and 9.0:1 compression ratio, it delivered 354bhp (over 60 per cent more power than the normally-aspirated V6) at 6100rpm, and a huge 332lbft of torque at 4400rpm. The fact that the car was 90kg (198lb) heavier than the SLK320 hardly seemed to matter, although the torque output

The SLK 'Special Edition,' launched in the spring of 2002.

Another view of the SLK 32 AMG, this particular model being fitted with the regular AMG alloys, rather than the more ornate version sold as standard. These were available as a no-cost option (NCO).

restricted transmission options to a 5AT only, albeit coming with a sporting 'Speedshift' feature to make the 'box more responsive. The suspension was duly uprated, as was the braking system, the AMG car inheriting huge 334mm (13.1in) diameter vented discs at the front, and 300mm (11.8in) ones at the rear end.

Changes were made to the interior, too, the AMG car coming with a host of special features, such as AMG sports seats with integrated headrests, leather trim (including a unique grey combination) matched with a blackened wood veneer, a different steering wheel, and a new instrument pack. With Germany gearing up for the Euro, the SLK 32 AMG was introduced at €49,000 (plus taxes), while the SLK200 Kompressor model was now valued at €26,900, the SLK230 Kompressor was listed at €29,400, and the SLK320 at €34,700.

The AMG car was added to the Stateside line-up in the spring of 2001, filtering through to UK showrooms as the 2002 season began. As something of a swansong, the SLK 'Special Edition' was launched in April 2002, followed by the 'Final Edition' ten months later. The final R170 models were ultimately built in April 2004, with production amounting to 311,222 units over the eight-year run.

Corporate news

The all-new R230 SL was announced at the end of July 2001 in readiness for the 2002 Model Year. By adopting the vario-roof design that had made its debut on the R170 SLK, this was the first of the modern SLs to move away from a traditional soft top (with separate hardtop) configuration. An R230 version of the SL 55 AMG was launched at the 2001 Frankfurt Show, along with a couple of other AMGs, with the supercharged engine duly winning several awards.

At the end of 2001, with annual car production reaching almost one-and-a-quarter million units, a small ceremony was held at the Sindelfingen plant to commemorate the production of 20,000,000 passenger cars at the plant since the cessation of hostilities in WWII. Not long after, in January 2002, the new W211 E-Class made its debut at the Brussels Show. A couple of weeks later, the company announced the new M271 four-cylinder engine incorporating a number of advanced technologies pointing the way towards the future, with supercharging, intercooling, four valves per cylinder, adjustable camshaft positioning, and Lanchester-type balance shafts being part of the specification. One of the first applications was the C209-type CLK, launched at the Geneva Show; a drophead version followed a year further down the line.

The stunning SLR McLaren (left), pictured here with a 'Gullwing' 300SL. Both cars pushed the performance envelope during their respective eras.

The Chrysler Crossfire

The Chrysler Crossfire was an interesting spin-off from the Daimler-Benz and Chrysler merger, built by Karmann in Germany between February 2003 and December 2007. Why is it included in this book? Well, the platform and many of the components are shared with those of the R170 SLK320, with the rare SRT-6 variants coming with the supercharged AMG engine. The first season was restricted to coupé bodies, although a convertible augmented the line for the 2005 season onwards. In all, 76,014 cars were produced during the Crossfire's life cycle, with just under 43,000 of them having the closed bodywork. The SRT-6, available with both body configurations, was indeed rare, with just 4071 sold in total, including 2571 coupés.

The Chrysler Crossfire in fixed-head coupé guise. (Courtesy Chrysler)

The R230 version of the legendary Mercedes-Benz SL model.

The 2002 Paris Salon witnessed the launch of face-lifted versions of the W220 S-Class and C215 CL models, as well as new C- and E-Class variants, and a fresh six-cylinder R230 SL model – the SL350. Unlike the early postwar years, when model ranges were few and stayed much the same for decades, there was seemingly no let-up in the stream of new vehicles.

Dr Thomas Weber took over responsibility for R&D on the first day of 2003, while the 2003 Detroit Show, which opened on 11 January, witnessed the launch of the twelve-cylinder SL600 model, as well as that of the E-Class estate.

September 2003 saw the announcement of the 7G-Tronic automatic gearbox, a 7AT unit developed in-house to give better performance and improved economy at the same time. It was first seen on the eight-cylinder cars, including the SL range. Hardly pausing for breath, Mercedes displayed the SLR McLaren, Vision CLS study vehicle (eventually launched as the supremely elegant CLS production car in March 2004), a four-door 'smart' model, and a bi-fuel version of the E-Class at the 2003 Frankfurt Show. The bi-fuel car was a sign of the times, although the Stuttgart maker was in fact experimenting with all sorts of 'Green' technology behind the scenes, ranging from fuel cell vehicles to conventional EVs, through to diesel-based hybrids.

Just before Christmas 2003, the company introduced a new clear coat paint using advanced nanotechnology to help prevent coachwork scratches. The E, S, CL, SL and SLK ranges were the first to employ this new paint, although it spread to the other model lines soon after. At the same time, a new 3.5-litre V6 (M272) engine was presented to the press. Using four-valve per cylinder technology, it was first seen in the new R171 SLK, launched at the 2004 Geneva Show. The next chapter takes up the story from there ...

3

Ready for the Showroom

"For all its appeal, and despite various updates, we had trouble thinking of [the original SLK] as a real sports car. Small-scale grand tourer, yes. Sports car, not quite. That changes with the arrival of the second generation. The bobtail cuteness of the original gives way to a grown-up look that echoes the theme of other SLs, including the mighty SLR McLaren. All in all, a much more serious SLK." – *Car & Driver*, January 2005.

The various elements that made up the R170 face-lift were simply cosmetic and mechanical tweaks, executed in order to keep an older model up-to-date, even if the styling side of things gave the SLK a new level of maturity. However, the change in designation to R171 was completely justified with the latest car, which was given an all-new drivetrain, a sportier chassis setup, and a slightly larger body to improve safety and comfort levels.

Indeed, the R171 came with a 2430mm (95.7in) wheelbase, which was 30mm (1.2in) longer than that specified for the outgoing model, and an overall length of 4082mm (160.7in). The width was listed at 1777mm (70.0in), or 1969mm (77.5in) including the mirrors, while the track was 1530mm (60.2in) at the front and 1541mm (60.7in) at the rear on the base cars; the overall height was 1297mm (51.1in). The six-cylinder and AMG cars were a fraction wider and had different track measurements, incidentally, but whichever way one looks at it, compared with the last of the R170s, the new car was a touch bigger all-round, with only the height remaining virtually the same as before.

The extra bulk was simply a sign of the times, for even the Mazda MX-5 Miata grew by around 40mm (1.6in) in length and width during its transformation from NB to NC series in 2005, despite huge efforts to keep the car as light and compact as possible. One thing was for sure: the R171 SLK was significantly smaller than the contemporary SL, which was by then 4535mm (178.5in) long and 1827mm (71.9in) wide without door mirrors, or 2045mm (80.5in) with them. It's fair to say the R230 SL was a huge car for a strict two-seater, but the difference in sizes and pricing would keep the SL and SLK apart in the showrooms, and that was a necessity if both models were to succeed.

One could have been forgiven for expecting some radical bodywork changes for the R171 given the way SL generations were inclined to jump stylistically, but the larger two-seater was a unique beast – its lengthy model cycle making updates all the more obvious, while its fanatical following and increasingly top-end pricing put it in a niche market, allowing designers greater freedom of expression. With the mainstream SLK, a shorter lifecycle was planned for each generation, with a major face-lift keeping the design fresh in the middle of each run, although changes would err on the side of conservative within each phase. As such, it followed a traditional Benz policy of favouring evolution over revolution, which helped cars retain their resale values.

Having said that, advances were definitely made by Peter Pfeiffer's team of stylists in honing the SLK's sporting edge and propelling it further into the future, with various lines having obviously been inspired by the pair of Vision SLR models first displayed in 1999 (which duly became the SLR McLaren road car in the autumn of 2003) and the advanced Vision

The R171 SLK (foreground) was certainly striking. Even the most casual of onlookers could be left in no doubt as to its sporting intent. It is seen here with a 190SL, and a first generation version of the SLK.

SLA concept car that had appeared at the 2000 edition of the Detroit Show (a stillborn two-seater based on the A-Class with a lightweight aluminium body), as well as subtle references that gave a nod to the R230 SL, which had entered production in 2001.

Summing things up quickly, one can say that the SLK had moved on, becoming another weapon in the armoury of those looking to promote Mercedes' motorsport DNA – less sporty, more sporting. The racing flavour of the SLR was found in the pointed nose of the SLK, aping the nosecone of a contemporary

The Concept SLA show car that appeared in 2000. Wild and wacky, it does nonetheless embody a number of styling cues used on the R171 model.

Frank Knothe – former engineer, and head of SLK development until mid-2006. He was also in charge of the S-Class and SL projects at the same time, before handing over the reins to Hans-Dieter Multhaupt. Indeed, this picture shows him in the R230 SL.

Horst-Dietmar Bardehle, who was the Strategic Project Manager during the R171 model's creation. This is the official title held by the project leader, who duly reported to Knothe to keep him abreast of developments.

Formula One machine; the horizontal bars in the main grille orifice also hinted at F1 design. Meanwhile, the short overhangs employed at both ends, with flared wheelarches covering wide rubber, and the twin exhausts at the rear of the car further added to the R171's sporting credentials. As Udo Weist, one of the management team, pointed out: "We recognise that the market has definitely taken a turn toward performance."

With so many areas to cover in this comprehensive revamp, we have to start somewhere, and, seeing as the body has just been discussed, we may as well begin with a look at the revised styling ...

R171 styling

It's fair to say that the R171 was born in the wind-tunnel, with scale models based on the old car pointing the way forward on the aerodynamics package and a suitable reduction in cockpit buffeting. This work was being done as early as autumn of 1998, and, after the planners added in their engineering hard points, styling proposals were put together in earnest. Peter Pfeiffer had taken over as head of styling in April 1999 after Bruno Sacco

Gorden Wagener, who was responsible for the R171's exterior styling. Born in Essen in September 1968, he climbed through the ranks with remarkable speed, and was duly appointed head of styling on Peter Pfeiffer's retirement in 2008, thus becoming one of the youngest design chiefs in the history of the motor industry.

retired, so he was responsible for overseeing the project, although the final design has been credited to Gorden Wagener.

Beginning with the front mask, the chromed three-pointed star was now set in an extension of the central bonnet bulge: a feature that resembled the nosecone on a modern F1 car, which tapered downwards, duly blending into the upper section of the bumper moulding. It was shaped to curve back into the recess in the traditional radiator grille and provide a mounting point for the body-coloured aerofoil-style bars that sat either side of the star, further reinforcing the F1 image. Incidentally, the star motif was fixed in the lower half of its surround along with the bars, and came with a black net screen behind it to allow air through to the engine bay and set off the famous trademark at the same time; the space between the edges of the radiator grille and the aerofoils was filled with horizontal black plastic slats held in place by a series of barely visible uprights.

This page and next: Some of the early design sketches for the R171 SLK, most of them dating from the second half of 1999. One thing they all have in common is the F1-inspired nose.

S:LK

One of Gorden Wagener's final design proposals, with all the main styling features starting to show through. As it happens, there were already some very accurate computer-generated pictures of the new car appearing in magazines like *Auto, Motor und Sport* as early as the spring of 2001. But credit should also be given to Michael Plessing here, who was responsible for making the paper dreams into a production reality.

It's worth noting here that the single bar theme in the radiator grille was duly repeated in the face-lifted R230 SL of 2008, as well as the SLS AMG model that made its debut at the tail-end of the following year, albeit without the pointed nosecone approach on these two models – that was restricted to the SLR and SLK. The same single bar approach was also adopted on a number of concept cars during this period, and was also seen on the AMG versions of the C216 CL-Class, launched in 2010. As such, it became a signature piece of styling on sporting Benz models.

Meanwhile, the shape of the radiator grille opening was familiar to earlier SLK owners, although the impression of a raised lip around its outer edge was something new, created via the sharp creaseline in the bonnet that ran from the outside corners of the panel and tapered in as it moved forward to just miss the headlights. This was an idea that had been used with great success on the original R230 SL, and duly became a lot more pronounced in the 2008 face-lift to match the SLK. Something else shared by the two models was the pair of black bonnet vents, which was a new feature as far as the SLK was concerned.

On the subject of headlights, meanwhile, Xenon units – previously an option on the SLK range – were now made a standard fitment, bringing the smaller two-seater into line with

The front mask of the R171 SLK, with the Xenon projection headlights and additional body width (around 65mm/2.6in extra compared to its predecessor) giving the car a more purposeful look.

Close-up of the new nose section and headlights. These are the optional Bi-Xenon lights, by the way, distinguished from the regular version by the transparent ribs in the tail of the dipped beam housing.

its SL stablemate (the SL had adopted Xenon lighting as the norm with the introduction of the R230 model in 2001). These tapered in sharply, and swept back into the upper section of the wings, giving the car an almost hawkish look. The dipped beam light housings were pushed to the outside of the vehicle edges with the integrated front indicators set inside them, above the main beam. Headlight washer jets were covered by square lids beneath the light units when fitted, although the optional Bi-Xenon lights (with H7 projection lighting for both dipped and main beam) came with a washer system as part of the package, and cut-outs in the trailing edge of the outer light unit, which almost served as a running light when illuminated. The Bi-Xenon option also included an active cornering light function, whereby at low speeds the foglights moved in tune with the indicators or the angle of the steering wheel beyond a certain amount, thus lighting up the area in which the car was about to turn.

The shape and location of the bumper inserts was actually quite similar to those found on the face-lifted R170 model, albeit with a slightly chunkier appearance and a less rounded profile. As before, US-spec cars had a small repeater indicator unit on the trailing edge of the bumper trim (the pointier shape lending itself well to provide a stylish lens design), which also served as a mounting point for the 'Parktronic' sensors and a cover for the threaded attachment that accepted the tow-hook.

This aerial perspective gives a good view of the functional air vents in the trailing edge of the bonnet, and also shows the strong curves in the front- and rear-end of the bodywork.

Right and below: A huge amount of aerodynamic work was undertaken to ensure low drag, low lift, low wind noise, and minimal disturbance in the cockpit.

Lower down on the air dam, the overall design was vaguely similar to that of the outgoing SLK320, with two dividing vanes being angled inwards to create three separate mouths. The central mouth – directly beneath the number plate – was an air intake, covered by a black diamond-pattern grille, while those either side of it were solid plastic inserts made to look similar. Interestingly, these inserts extended further out on the R171, creating a surround for the halogen foglights – a feature that had previously been restricted to the AMG vehicles, but something that emphasised the car's width.

The lowest edge of the spoiler had a very soft profile to help the new SLK cut through the air with the minimum disturbance, while the detail work on the splitter resulted in the car's Cd being cut one point to just 0.32 (0.37 with the roof open), despite the newcomer having a frontal area that was some four per cent larger than the R170. Interestingly, thanks to the use of tiny spoilers ahead of the wheels and revised underbody panels, the engineers also managed to reduce lift by as much as 30 per cent at the front of the car, and around 20 per cent at the rear by integrating a small lip into the trailing edge of the bootlid.

From the side, the long bonnet, short deck styling and steeply-raked windscreen gave the new roadster a sporting profile that obviously contained the SLK's double-wedge bloodlines, but the larger wheel and tyre combinations (covered in the Chassis Upgrades section) under bulging arches and the angled creaseline that ran from the front wheelarch to the taillight gave the car a distinctly beefier, more masculine look.

Beginning with the nose, the front overhang was dramatically shorter, although very similar to the older model otherwise. The headlight sat proud of the wingline a touch, as before, and the bumper assembly joint was much the same in terms of positioning and styling. Even the lower part of the air dam wasn't all that different, although the bumper inserts sat at a more jaunty angle, and the tiny spoiler ahead of the wheel was more pronounced. Moving back, the fender was given a dramatic wheelarch bulge that made the old car look like a puny student standing next to his gym teacher, but the profile was kept within tasteful limits, and the panel was broken up by the aforementioned angled creaseline that somehow made the car look a lot shorter than it was by playing with light and shadow. In keeping with the design theme, the heavier side sill line and lowermost shutline on the door was angled slightly to convey a feeling of forward motion. Before moving on, we should mention the 'Kompressor' badge fitted to the supercharged cars, which was kept in the same position as earlier cars, low down on the trailing edge of the front wing.

The door itself was fairly similar to the old panel, albeit with a less rounded leading edge, and the colour-keyed door handles now sat in a larger, oval-shaped recess. Above the door, the mirrors – finished in body colour and coming with integral repeater indicators – had been carefully shaped to reduce wind noise, while the windscreen wipers were able to sit lower than before thanks to a new arm design, thus reducing drag and wind noise. While hardly visible on the R170, one could no longer see the pair of wipers at all when viewing the car from the side.

Although the SLK had pioneered the 'Variodach' metal folding roof, the design had been refined somewhat for the R230 SL, allowing it to fold faster and tighter than before, freeing up extra luggage space along the way. At the touch of a button, the fully-automatic opening and closing time was reduced from 25 to 22 seconds, while another sequence that copied that of the SL swivelled the rear window section (with a heated glass screen) allowing the mechanism to nestle closer together when the top was down, thus – in combination with a slightly taller boot profile

The 'Variodach' roof, despite having been around since 1996, still provided onlookers with a sense of awe, although it was practical advantages that brought it into being rather than marketing gimmicks.

Opposite: This series of shots of the 'Variodach' in operation, driven by five hydraulic cylinders and a single pump, also prove useful for styling reference. The ability of the bootlid to hinge at its leading and trailing edge was a key element in the mechanism.

– increasing the luggage space below it from 145 litres (5.1 cubic feet) to 208 litres (7.3 cubic feet) according to VDA methodology. In addition, the new 'Variodach' was optionally available with remote control via the car's SmartKey. From a styling point of view, the revised roof had a more rounded upper profile, and the shape of the rear and colour of the screen dressing piece helped visually lighten the C-pillar.

Continuing rearward, the wheelarch bulge was very strong over the rear wheels, its upper part touching the central creaseline, and melding into the bumper assembly, which looked quite heavy as a result. As per the front end, the lip of the arch was flat, adding strength to the panel, which was smaller than the R170 version thanks to the bootlid folding over the wings (following R230 SL practice), along with a larger bumper moulding and light unit. Again, in line with the contemporary SL, the rear light was far more rounded than the R170 design, and, while the basic bumper insert and lower valance profile was much the same as that of the early SLK, the upswept join between the bumper and combination lamp was pure SL. An aerial was fitted on the nearside wing, while the offside one played host to the oval fuel filler lid.

Around the back, it quickly became evident that the bootlid cum roof cover was actually a complicated pressing, with raised edges at the sides, making the central section sit lower until it met an integral lip spoiler on the trailing edge. This heavy creaseline, added in the name of aerodynamic efficiency, faded out at the bottom of the taillights, almost helping to visually frame the angled lamp units. As before, the third brakelight sat above the Mercedes star, with model badging off to the left. Unlike the R170, the number plate housing had no plinth above it, but it did continue to be lit from above. Interestingly, to cater for the different registration number shapes around the world, the lower section of the lid was pressed separately and joined to the main pressing via laser brazing to give a high-quality finish.

The rear combination lamps were actually quite similar to the R230 SL units, using LEDs on the taillights and brake lights to deliver faster, brighter illumination. The curvature of the lamp units made the rear bumper assembly appear heavier, although the subtle dip for the bootlid and the full-width insert helped break up the top half, while a feature line was added above the exhaust pipes to reduce bulk down below. As before, the insert curved around the car's flanks, and carried the 'Parktronic' sensors

Some clever reappraisal of the 'Variodach' mechanism allowed the rear window section to rotate and close tighter to the upper section. This freed up valuable space in the trunk, which could now boast 208 litres (7.3 cubic feet) of space with the top down, or 300 litres (10.6 cubic feet) with it up. Incidentally, the luggage cover, which needed to be in place before the roof switch would work, was now a solid moulded item rather than a flexible roller blind, marking the boot's loading limits when the top was down with greater accuracy.

The strong rear flanks of the R171 SLK, with this sunset providing ideal light to show off the car's lines.

Close-up of the latest rear combination lamp, which used LED technology for enhanced safety.

This shot of an SLK350 (chassis designation 171.456) on the move gives a perfect view of the tail-end styling. Note the twin exhaust pipes.

whenever that particular option was fitted. A small cover on the offside hid the tow-hook attachment point, while the feature line below it defined the border of an insert that continued the plain finish of the bumper moulding with a pair of cut-outs – one either side to give clearance for the pair of chrome-plated, oval-shaped exhausts. This area, the lowest part of the rear valance, was a continuation of the line found in the side skirts, and by folding in sharply, helped visually reduce bulk at the rear-end.

For those who wanted something with a more overtly sporting appearance, the AMG bodykit was once again rolled out for duty. The front apron was far more aggressive, with the bars surrounding the central intake leaning outward rather than inward, and a squared-off profile for the foglight housings. The foglights themselves, whilst still trimmed by a chrome ring, were straightforward round items rather than the stylish lights used in conjunction with the regular air dam, and this eliminated the chance of having the cornering light feature. As for the side sills, it was only really on the trailing edge, ahead of the rear wheels, that the difference was readily spotted, while the new rear valance had a stronger ridge on the sides, aft of the rear wheels, and a matching one in the rearmost part of the apron, above a plain black insert that framed the exhaust pipes. Incidentally, the kosher AMG models had a different outer edge on the front air dam, and also came with a rear lip spoiler.

Strength & safety

The first generation SLK already had an enviable reputation for body rigidity. A strong shell with a minimum of flexing was a must for any sports car, as it provides the foundation stone for the suspension, but it was all the more important in the case of the SLK – firstly, because Mercedes had a good name to uphold in its open two-seater models, from both comfort, driving dynamics and safety angles; and secondly, because the trick roof worked within some very fine tolerances, and a flimsy body would have ruined the mechanism and seals. Notwithstanding, the R171 engineering team set its sights even higher, and ultimately – thanks to advances in design know-how and an intelligent choice of materials – came up with a body that, with the roof down, displayed an incredible

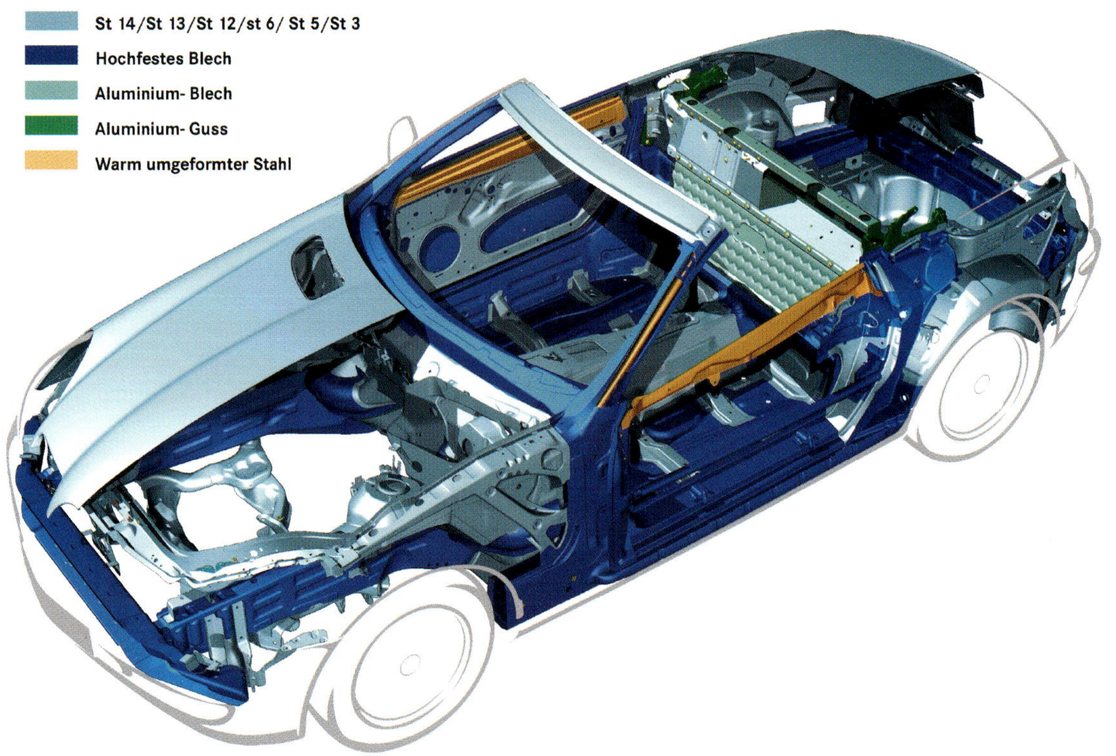

Composition of the monocoque body, with high-strength steel shown in dark blue, and regular, low-carbon steels in the lighter shade; the few hot-formed steel pieces used are depicted in orange. Aluminium sheet is shown in the light green used for the bonnet, while cast aluminium components are depicted in dark green.

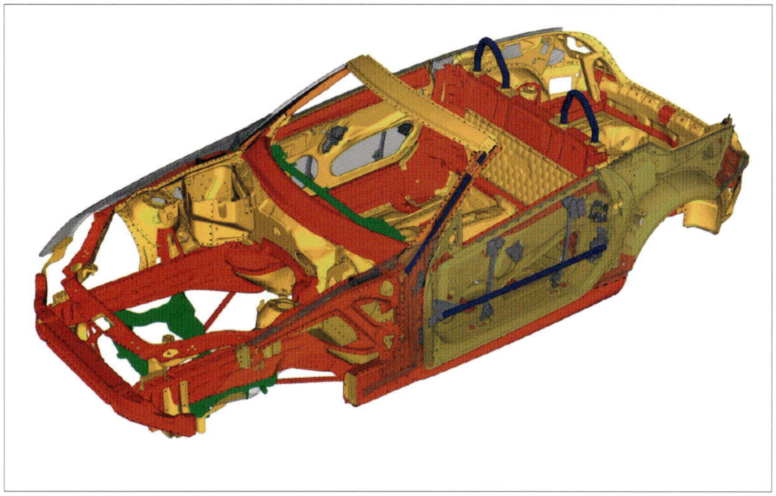
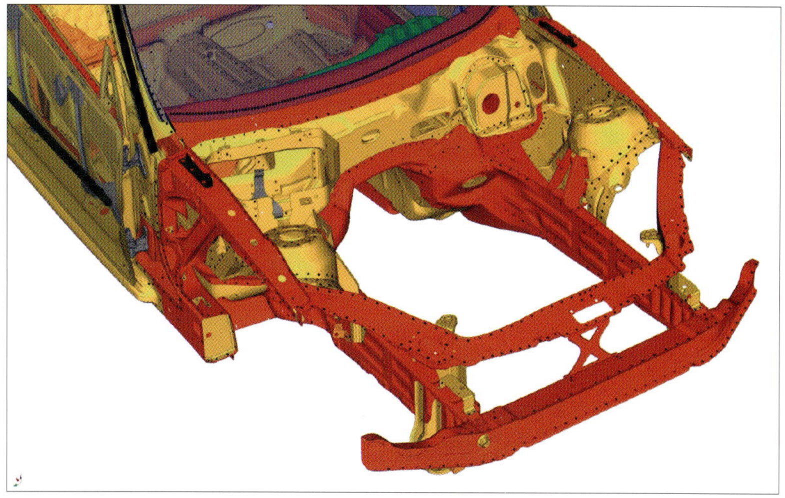
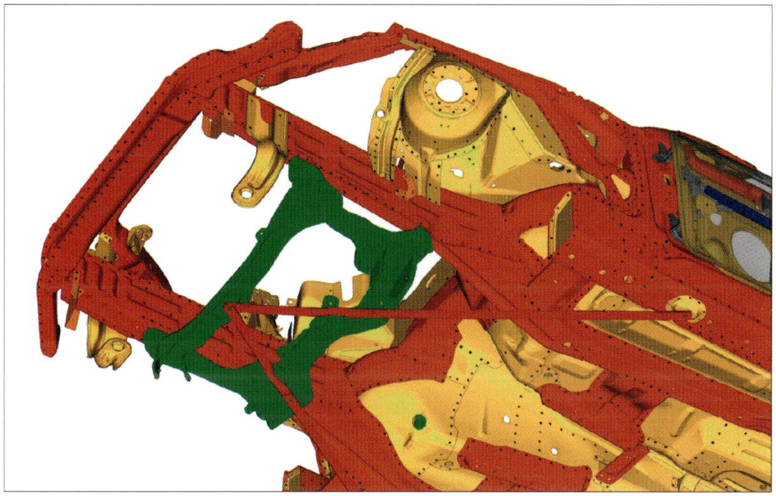
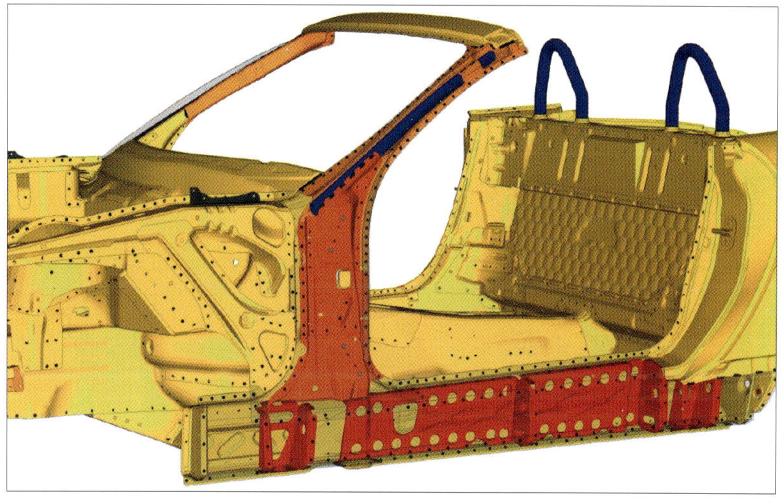
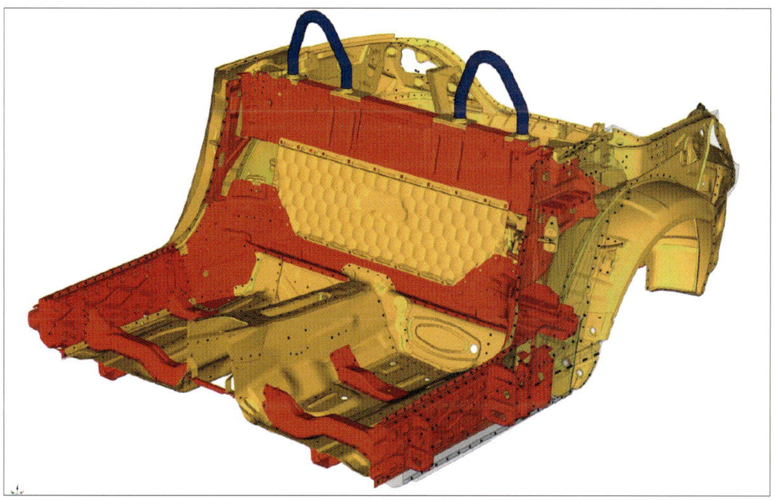

A selection of CAD/CAM images of the body construction, showing the major reinforcement areas in red, and hot-formed steel sections in blue. CAD/CAM technology allowed the engineers to prove and refine structures in a virtual environment, without having to resort to costly prototypes until the last moment.

46 per cent improvement in torsional strength compared to its predecessor, and 19 per cent better resistance to bending.

For the new SLK, the engineering team specified a far greater proportion of high-tensile steel for the shell – in fact, this type of steel now accounted for 42 per cent of the bodywork. Granted, it was more expensive than regular steel, but it allowed thinner panels for a given amount of strength, helping reduce weight, which in turn enhances handling and performance. In reality, these two aspects enhance both enjoyment and safety at the same time, as a nimble machine can avoid a bad situation with greater ease. The materials were backed up by design work that locked assemblies together into what amounted to a solid ingot of metal, and two V-shaped braces – one that ran from the front of the engine cradle to the sills just aft of the A-posts, and another attached to just below the B-posts and a single mounting point on the steel spare wheel well.

Ultimately, though, it's no good having a car that is stiff, fun-to-drive and looks pretty if it doesn't protect you in the event of an accident. As always, though, the Stuttgart engineers went well beyond the statutory requirements laid down by each country, such as the NCAP specifications in the States, and added in their own criteria based on crash data collected from decades of research with test cars and the analysis of real-life accidents.

Crumple zones, which allow the car to deform at a controlled rate in the event of a collision, are something we can take for granted nowadays, largely thanks to the pioneering work of Bela Barenyi. However, in the name of strength and safety, the front crossmember was given a reinforcing plate to laminate the component, while the pair of straight longitudinal members running back from it, which carried the engine cradle (along with mounting points for the steering and some of the suspension links), were locked into the suspension towers, and the crossmember welded to the lower part of the front bulkhead. The bulkhead itself was made up from different gauge steels to allow the panel to cope with the different levels of stress it had to contend with, enabling the engineers to reduce weight but retain strength, and was shaped in such a way as to give maximum protection to the pedal set. There was also a specially-designed

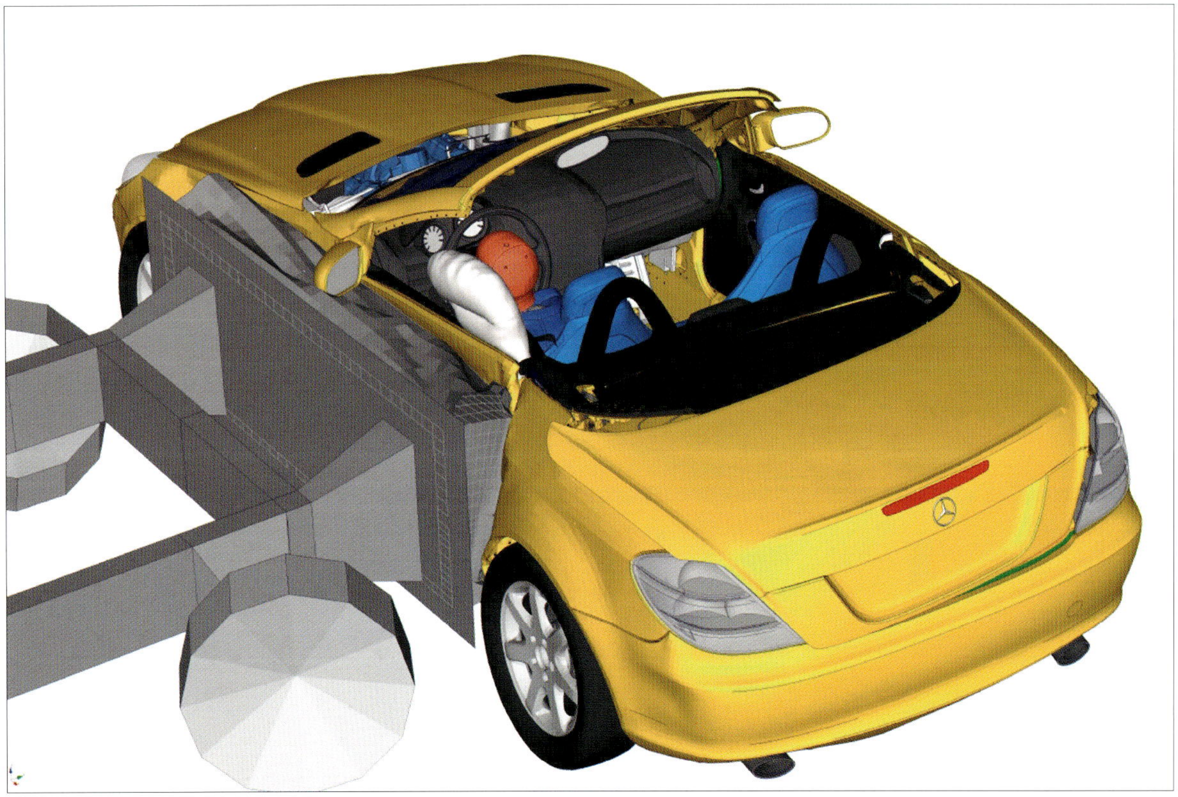

The development team in Stuttgart was even allowed to carry out early crash simulations on computers before subjecting real cars to testing.

Above and left: The new SLK being put through a punishing crash test programme. These pictures were taken in 2002.

upper crossmember assembly above the bumper blade that ran back over the wheelarches to create a two-tier sidemember that connected to the A-posts in order to take the brunt of the impact energy caused by an offset frontal accident.

The rigid passenger cell was protected by various methods. To overcome the roof-drop test, which saw the car released at a slight angle from a reasonable height so as to land on one of the windscreen pillars, and was far more severe than the statutory roll-over test, the engineers inserted oval-shaped high-tensile steel tubes, welding them into the A-post cavities. The advantage of using an oval section was that it allowed the pillars to remain slim, which increased the driver's line of vision. Anyway, combined with the hefty, heat-treated roll-over bars behind the seats, the use of these heat-formed tubes ensured that passengers were given ample survival space in the event of an accident tipping over the car. There were also side-impact bars in the doors, and a sturdy bar that ran from side-to-side underneath the dashboard, as per the R170, giving further protection for a minimal weight penalty.

The deep-section sills connected the A- and B-posts and were held firmly in place by the seat supports, which acted as crossmembers as soon as they were tacked onto the transmission tunnel, while underneath there was a continuation of the front longitudinal members beyond the side sill connections. These then strengthened the transmission tunnel and helped link the front- and rear-end structures; further bracing of the tunnel was made via a series of plates connecting the left- and right-hand sides of the floorpan.

The bulkhead between the fuel tank and the luggage compartment was made of a diecast magnesium alloy component, which weighed almost half what a piece of steel designed for the same job would have done. With the vario-roof support above it,

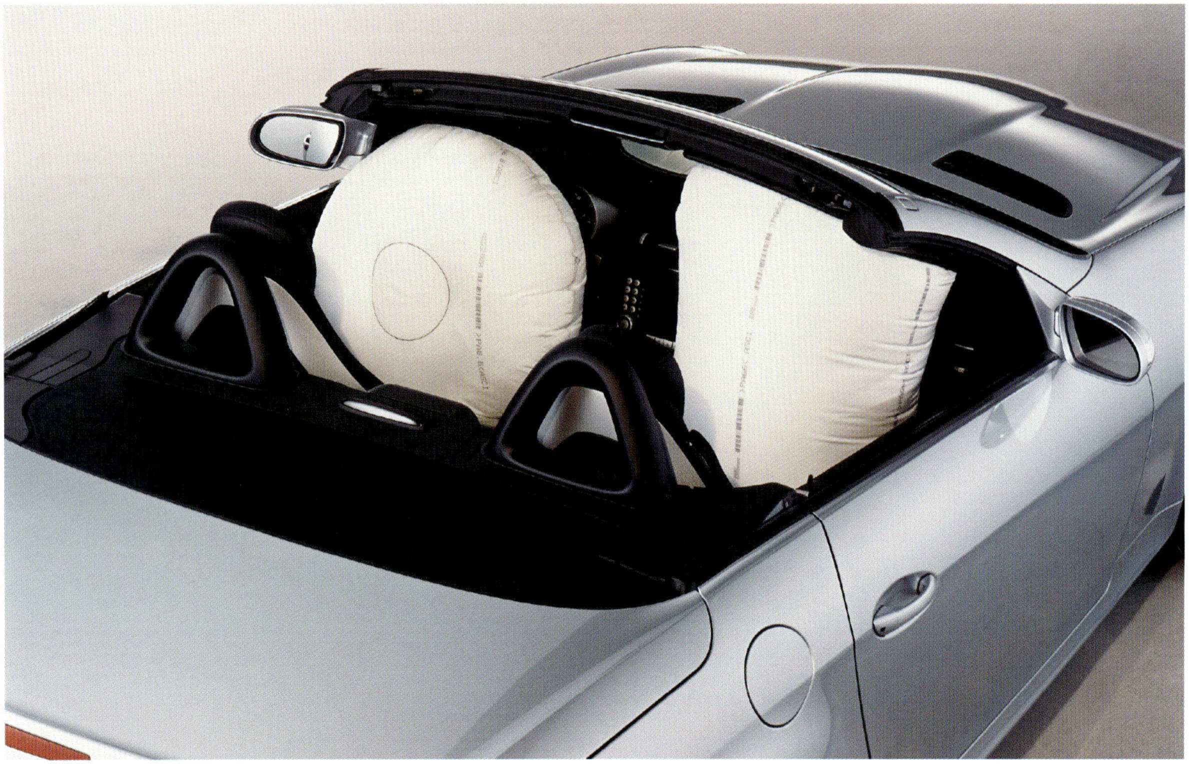

The advanced airbag system designed to protect occupants in the event of a heavy accident. The side airbags were now placed in the seatbacks rather than the door trim, while the one in the top roll was very well concealed.

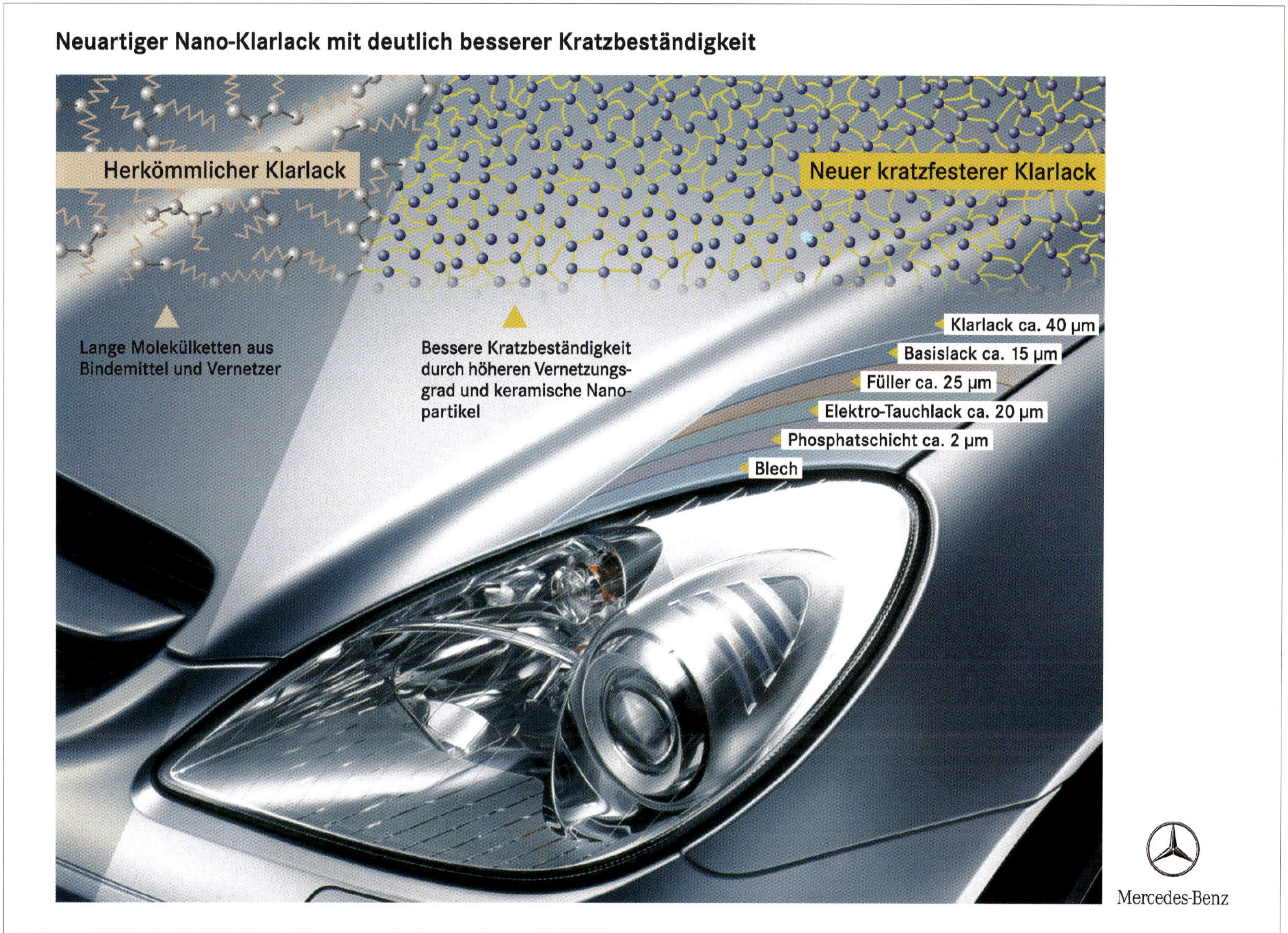

An illustration showing the latest COB paintwork advances, with the dense and strongly-bonded new paint on the right. A layer of phosphate coats the bodyshell, which is then given an electrocoat and primer. The light basecoat is then given a heavier protective clearcoat to make it scratch-resistant. Paint colours for the R171 were a lot more restrained than those fielded for the SLK in 1996.

and a full-width crossmember running underneath, this did an excellent job of bracing and protecting the rear of the passenger compartment. There was also a great deal of work done varying the thickness of the metal in this area to control the rate of deformation in an accident, allowing energy to be dispersed in the crumple zones before the passenger compartment was damaged.

The final line of defence was material selection and soft edges in the cockpit, along with the latest in airbag technology. The airbags – dual front, and revised side bags in the seatbacks rather than the door panels to shield the head and chest area – had a new, two-stage inflation facility, adapting to the severity of the accident. In reality, and somewhat ironically, there were times when the explosive force of early airbags actually did more harm than good whilst trying to protect occupants, but this new system helped avoid this problem, with sensors measuring crash intensity and roll potential in the front and centre of the vehicle allowing them to better react to the situation in hand. The same technology was applied to the seatbelt force limiters to make the most of the cushioning effect of the airbags, while certain markets (like North America) also had knee bags as part of the standard specification. All cars came with a pad in the passenger seat to detect whether or not it was being used, and the optional childseat that came with an automatic recognition facility, thus turning the airbag off, was carried over from the R170.

We can now take a brief look at protection of a quite different kind – the long-term protection of the bodyshell against corrosion, which in turn leads to a protection of investment. Aluminium sheet was used for the bonnet and in a few other areas of the body, which not only saves weight but cannot rust either, while all the steel panels were galvanized. Modern manufacturing techniques, such as the use of preserving agents in body cavities, were naturally applied, and the plastic underbody trim was used to take the place of traditional underseal. As such, they not only looked after airflow under the car, but also protected the shell from the wet, dirt and stonechips. Finally, there was the recently-introduced clearcoat paint mentioned in the previous chapter, with its special formula giving a new level of longevity. Said to have three times more scratch resistance than regular paint due to the use of minute, densely-packed ceramic particles, all 12 regular coachwork colours available on the SLK (including the exclusive Benitoite Blue shade) employed this latest paint technology. Thanks to this gambit of anti-corrosion measures, the company offered a 30-year anti-perforation warranty, as long as the car was regularly serviced by an approved dealer.

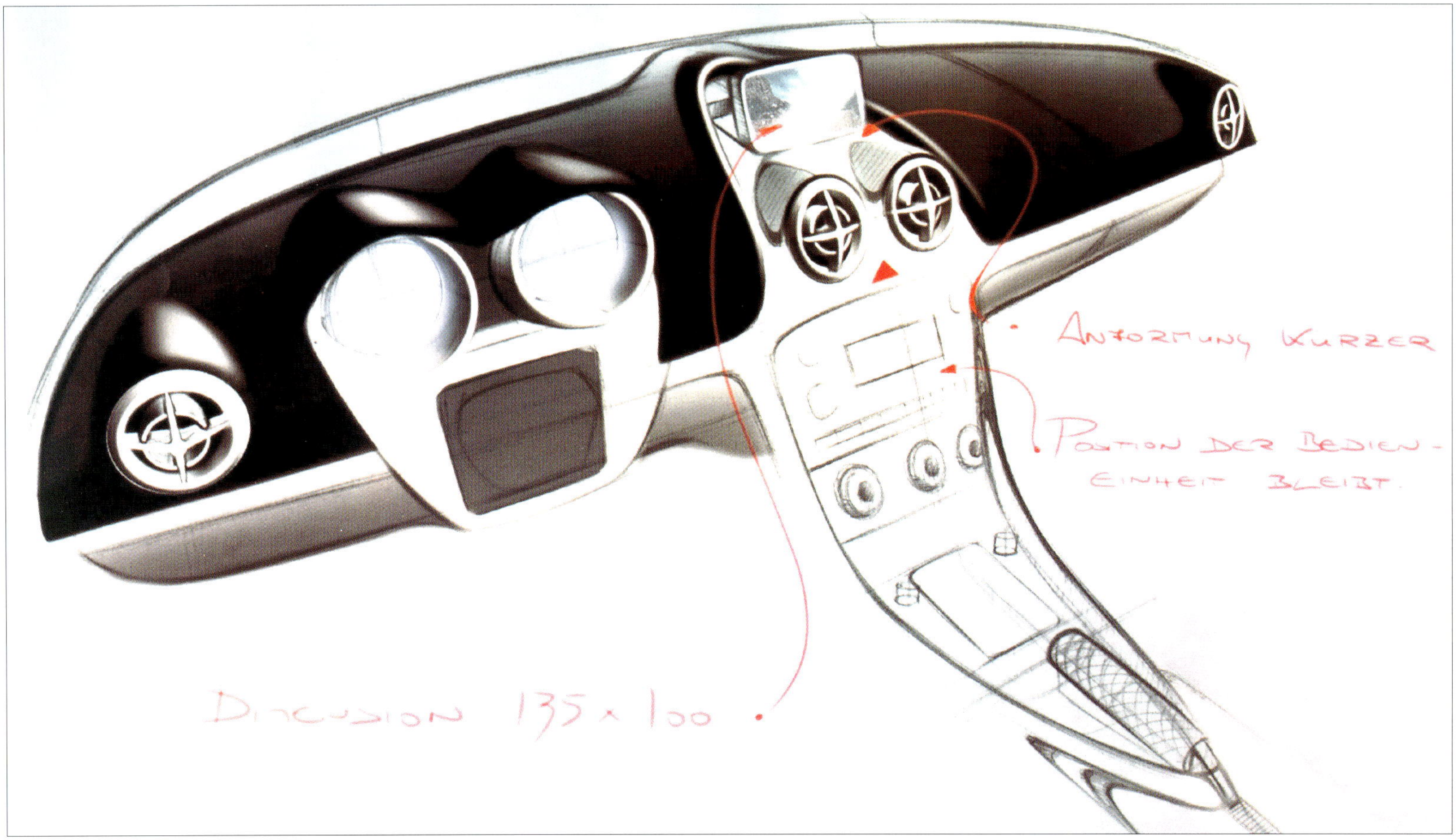

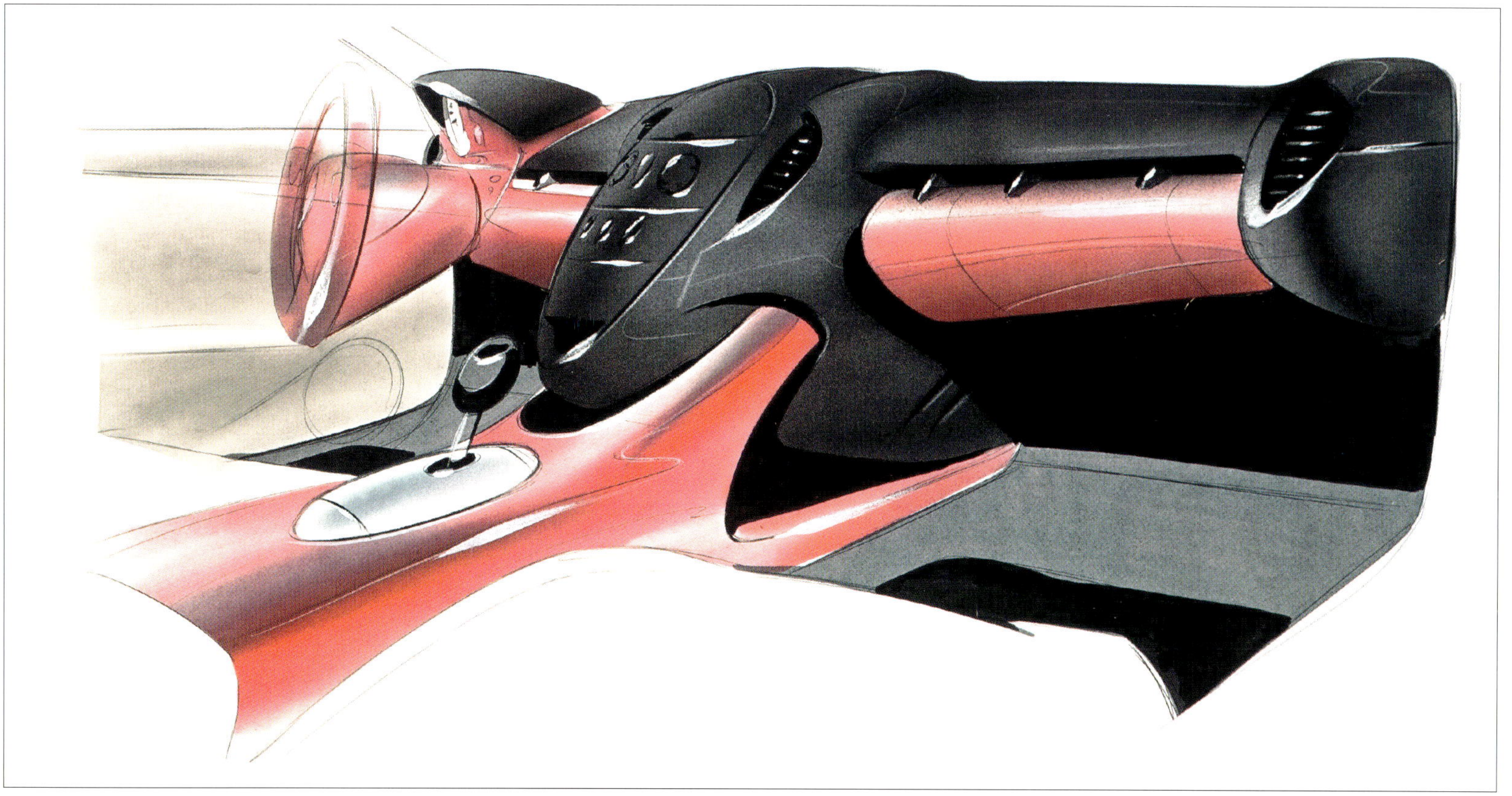

Opposite, above, right and overleaf: Some of the earliest design sketches made for the R171 interior. Several proposals featured a continuation of the bonnet slats in the dashboard's upper surface, as well as the pointed nose theme carried over into the centre console.

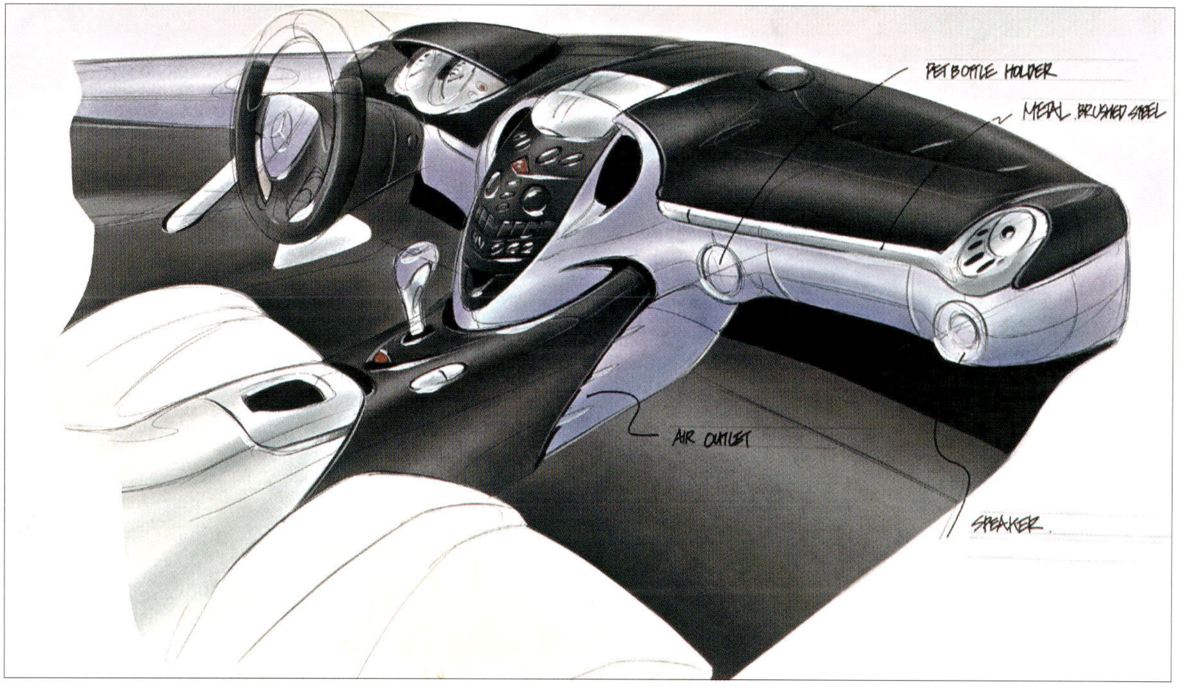

The inside story

The original R170 SLK interior had been fairly minimalistic from a styling point of view – simple and functional, with trendy colour choices bringing it alive for those who wanted something a little more adventurous. The 2000 face-lift propelled the SLK into another market sector altogether, with the emphasis quickly moving in a luxury direction. For the R171, the styling theme sat somewhere between the two – the harder attitude found in the exterior styling and drivetrain called for something overtly sporty, while market research uncovered that modern sports car buyers like to be cosseted while picking up their thrills on the open road. In reality, with heavy traffic and so many people moving over to convertibles for the first time, simply because they offered a level of practicality that was unheard of not so long ago, the days of the hairy sports car, with hard suspensions, spartan interiors and just enough luggage space for a toothbrush had long since passed.

The sporting theme was most obvious in the instrument pack, with the two main meters looming large through the top half of the 380mm (15in) diameter steering wheel. All the most important information one needs when driving was contained in these dials, styled to look like black-faced chronographs in white metal cases – road and engine speed, time, and fuel level. And although the basic layout was pretty much carried over, stronger character lines were introduced to break up the bulk of the T-shaped instrument panel, while the silver-coloured switchgear and trim elements provided a useful contrast to the darker tones on the dashboard, steering wheel and console areas.

This view of the production interior is particularly useful in placing component parts. The cockpit was roomier than before, as well as being jam-packed with the convenience features modern sports car buyers were asking for. Ultimately, the SLK could readily be used as an everyday car rather than a weekend plaything.

Klaus Busse was the person who designed the R171 interior. He is seen here with one of the sketches that formed the basis for the interior concept.

Building on the Busse proposals, most of the design work on the controls and displays was carried out by Manfred Dorn.

Looking at the interior in detail, it's easier to start with the dashboard, as that's the first thing that greets the driver once seated. The charcoal-coloured polyurethane top roll (featuring the same embossed surface texture as the integrated centre

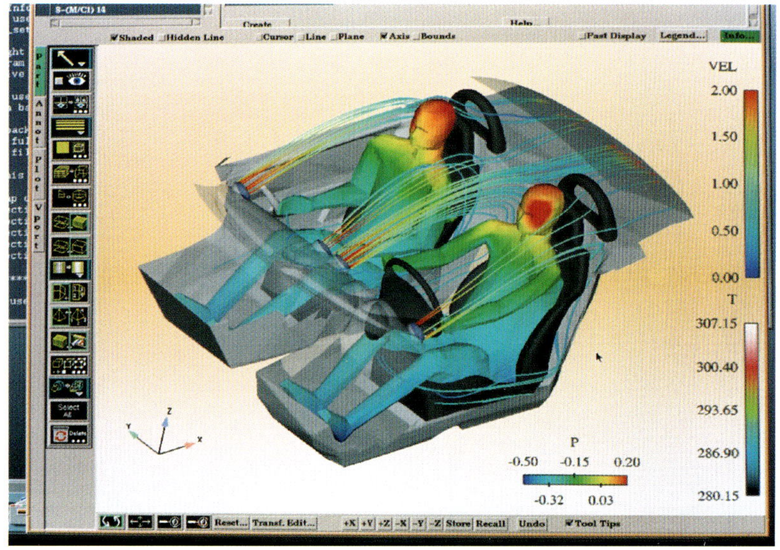

A great deal of attention was paid to increasing passenger comfort through enhanced ventilation – development work that went hand-in-hand with improved HVAC systems and the so-called 'Airscarf' feature.

console, glovebox and door casings) was angled strongly downwards from the windscreen, providing a dramatic platform for the instrument binnacle to sprout from, and broken up by a raised section in the middle that in many ways resembled the profile of the car's bonnet. There was also a pair of peaks at either end of the dash that formed the outer vent housings.

On the subject of vents, in addition to those serving the footwells, there was a full-length screen vent that dropped out of sight in a ridge beyond the injection moulded top roll, the oval-shaped outer pair we've already mentioned (with their own directional and air volume controls) with small defroster vents above them aimed specifically at keeping the side screens clear, and four vents in the centre of the dash – the two outside the centre console line being fixed, while the traditional central pair had the same controls as the outer vents, although the thumbwheel that regulated the airflow through the vents also worked on the semi-circular fixed ones. Cars with fully automatic climate control had a sunlight sensor atop the small vent in the leading edge of the bulge in the top roll, along with a thumbwheel to control air volume in the central speaker grille. However, the extra thumbwheel was done away with just before the 2008 face-

Detail shot of the dashboard, giving a view of the master lighting switch, column stalks, steering wheel buttons, and the tiny control buttons on the edge of the speedometer bezel that took the place of the usual rheostat and odometer reset spindle.

lift. It's worth noting here that the grille we've just mentioned sometimes also doubled as a monitor screen for the optional 'Parktronic' system – there were actually several variations on the theme, depending on the car's options and heating.

There were switches and buttons everywhere on the R171, although the basic control layout was much the same as the original SLK. If we use a domestic (lhd) model for reference, the master light switch and beam adjuster sat to the left of the steering column, below the vent; the mounting plinth also played host to the button for the optional headlight cleaning system.

The two main dials in front of the driver were clear, analogue items, with white pointers against a black face, and silver

The main gauge pack, with the cruise control wand and attractive ignition key showing through behind the steering wheel spokes. The 6200rpm red-line on the tachometer shows this to be a pre-production model; both the SLK200 Kompressor and SLK350 had a 6400rpm red-line in showroom guise, regardless of the transmission.

shrouds that were angled towards the centre to block out stray reflections. The speedometer sat on the left, with a clock in the lower section and a bank of warning lights above the spindle, while the tachometer and fuel gauge were on the right, with more warning lights set into the meter's face. Between the two dials was a pair of LED displays, the top one being the odometer and main display screen for the trip computer and 'Comand' system, along with an indicator for tyre pressure loss and engine coolant temperature. The visible buttons on the steering wheel spokes took care of menu selection and movement within them,

A typical centre console with the Audio 50 APS unit, seat heater and 'Airscarf' switches, and the 'Thermatic' HVAC system. This shot also gives a better idea of the moulding textures employed on the dashboard.

hands-free telephone operation, and volume control, while those out of sight behind the spokes (when fitted) gave an additional method of changing gears in the automatic transmission – rocker switches that gave both upshifts and downshifts on either side. Meanwhile, the display and trip odometer reset button was now attached to the side of the left-hand shroud, as was the dash lighting rheostat, its function now covered by a pair of '+' and '-' buttons. The lower LED screen looked after the outside temperature and a digital speedometer feature, and contained information on which mode and selector position automatic cars were in (the latter was obviously not necessary on manual machines). Incidentally, the gauge calibrations and pointers glowed light blue when the lights were switched on, matching the hue of the LED displays.

As usual, the ignition switch sat on the right of the steering column, and the horn was activated by a push on the 380mm (15.0in) diameter, leather-wrapped wheel's centre boss, or airbag casing if you want to call it that – either way, it was garnished by a chrome-plated three-pointed star. The familiar Benz multi-function wand was on the left of the column, looking after the indicators, high beam control and the windscreen wash/wipe operation. Above that was the cruise control lever, while lower down was another lever for power adjustment of the steering column, as well as the optional steering wheel heater. For those cars without this electronic wizardry, manual adjustment of the steering wheel position was made possible by releasing a handle at the base of the steering column. The bonnet release was tucked away to the left of the pedal set, with the pedals themselves being polished steel with an array of rubber studs attached – carried over from the previous generation SLK, this gave the appearance of sporty drilled pedals, but reduced the risk of the driver's foot slipping off them.

Moving across to the centre console, below the centre vents was a pop-out drawer which could be converted with ease to take a cupholder insert (some markets, such as North America, had cupholders as standard), and below that the space reserved for the updated audio or 'Comand' units – the latter with the latest thin-film transistor (TFT) screen technology, and all designed to match the rest of the car's switchgear.

There had been huge steps forward in onboard vehicle diagnostics and other electrical wiring systems since the launch of the first SLK, as well as the ease with which users could access information. The steering wheel buttons were a perfect example, along with the automatic volume control to take account of road speed and/or background noise and the integrated telephone pads on all three audio-visual (AV) units offered with the R171 model. The basic Audio 20 CD stereo, easily recognised by the CD slot being low down and the lack of a 'NAV' button on the

Close-up of the Comand APS head unit, along with the switchgear for a car fully-loaded with options below. The tray at the top was usually given a cupholder insert, with the drinks sitting above the tray base so as not to interfere with the navi screen.

control panel, offered a 4 x 25W amplifier and a CD/radio setup with presets and a scan feature. The Audio 50 APS unit added a navigation system for Europe (explaining why this option wasn't offered in States) and a colour screen, while the top-of-the-range Comand APS system – listed for the first time in the SLK – had a larger screen that enabled the owner to watch DVDs when the car was stationary, or even send SMS text messages. Thankfully, however, the bigger screen's main use was to provide a superior navigation system!

Continuing downward, there was a row of silver switches, flanking each side of the red hazard warning light switch. From left to right, the left-hand batch handled the 'Airscarf' heater, seat heater, ESP control, and central locking. On the opposite side of the hazard switch, there was a central unlocking button, a 'Parktronic' off button or a blanking piece, and seat heater and 'Airscarf' switches laid out in a mirror image of those on the left. Incidentally, there was a small light under the red triangular button, and this told occupants whether or not the passenger-side airbag is activated. It should also be noted that the most basic of cars only had two switches on each side of the hazard light switch, while some I've seen have three on each side.

Next, we come to the HVAC controls. There were actually three heating and ventilation systems used on the SLK, so the controls can vary quite a bit. Even the basic system was already pretty advanced, being automatic on the heating side of things and using four stylised rotary switches to give individual left-right temperature control, control over the booster fan speed and output position. Within these, in the centre, were silver-coloured push-button switches for turning the 'Rest' residual heat feature on, activating the air recirculation mode, defrosting the front screen, and turning on the rear screen heater. As well as having a sophisticated filter, it was also hooked up to the window controls to help keep temperatures at the right level, and automatically cancelled the air recirculation after a given amount of time to

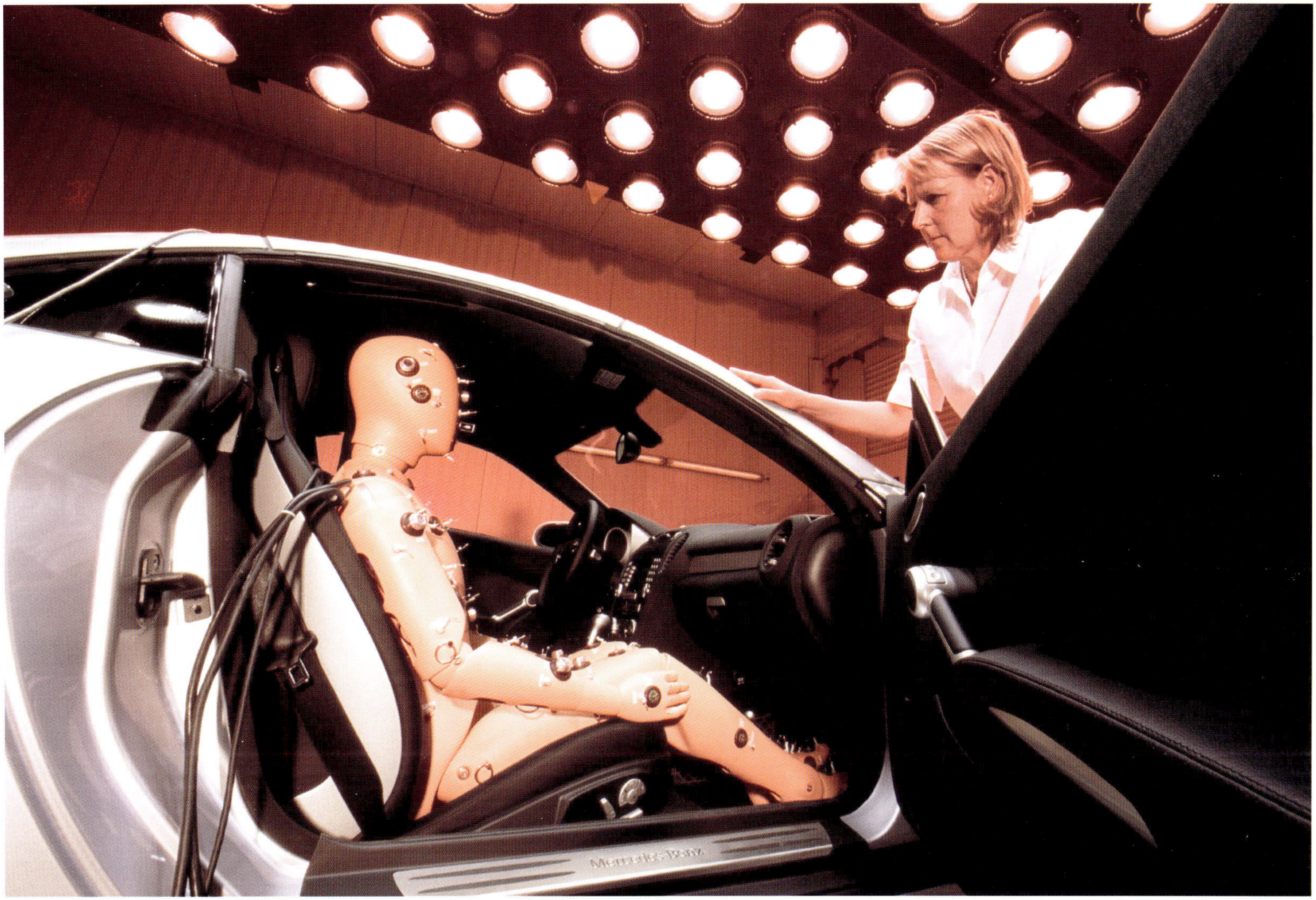

A massive amount of work went into perfecting the R171's HVAC system. This picture shows Jutta Schmidtke, the lady in charge of developing and testing this aspect of the car's design, checking test equipment in a special climatic wind tunnel.

prevent the windows fogging up and ensure an occasional fresh supply of air.

In reality, the vast majority of cars came with 'Thermatic,' as it was standard on the V6 anyway. The 'Thermatic' system added air-conditioning into the equation, with manual control over the level of cooling required in the cockpit. This looked very similar to the basic heater, but an extra function was given to the 'Rest' switch – now being used for its original purpose, and to turn off the air-conditioning when the car was running (the Mercedes system was set to run all the time otherwise, in order to combat humidity). Moving up to the 'Thermotronic' option brought fully automatic climate control, again, split left and right, with additional dew and pollutant sensors (including one in the A/C control panel) allowing the onboard processors to make accurate adjustments on a regular basis. The controls for this system were quite different, with two rotary switches for the booster fan speed and output mode, with 'Automatic' and 'Rest' buttons inside them. The other buttons, with a full 'Off' switch, and four to take

The 'Thermatic' heater and air-conditioning controls; the basic heater looked much the same, but lacked an 'AC off' marking on the switch second from the left.

The 'Thermotronic' HVAC control panel. The tray below it was often replaced by a narrower ashtray, with a cigarette lighter mounted on a plinth to its right.

the heat level up and down, were arranged above and below a digital readout telling the occupants at what temperature their side of the vehicle was set. Automatic air recirculation was a bonus, reacting to exhaust fumes and the like, and the strength of the sun's rays was also monitored to allow fine adjustments on each side of the cockpit to compensate. For techno-freaks, there was even a feature that stored settings in the ignition key!

Underneath the HVAC controls was another shallow storage box with a power socket inside, and a small coin tray below it. The owner could specify an ashtray to go inside the box, and the power socket quickly became a cigarette lighter in this case, sitting outside the narrower tray on its own plinth. Again, some markets, such as the USA, had the ashtray and lighter setup as the norm, as there was another 12V power

Interior of a manual SLK200 Kompressor (chassis designation 171.442) for the German market, with a good view of the complete dashboard, the glovebox (along with the standard silver trim above it), and the minor switchgear between the gearlever and handbrake and in the overhead control panel.

socket tucked up on the passenger's side of the transmission tunnel, above the map net. Seeing as we have made it across to the passenger side, we may as well finish off the dashboard appraisal, as there is very little else to add. Indeed, the glovebox was the main item, moulded in the same material as the dash and having a silver handle, although the trim piece above it was noteworthy, being one of the few things to offer some relief from the swathes of black plastic. This was usually a silver-coloured plastic moulding, but could be wood or leather, and came with a pair of matching inlay pieces between the air vents and the steering wheel on the driver's side. By the way, the illuminated glovebox was far bigger than before, allowing the optional six-disc CD-changer to be fitted there, and was locked or unlocked via the same central locking circuit as the doors.

Moving further back on the centre console, after the gearbox (covered in the drivetrain section) came two small knobs surrounded by a semicircle array of three buttons, in some ways aping the R230 SL styling theme in miniature. The left-hand knob adjusted the mirror position, while the two buttons either side of it selected which rearview mirror was being moved; the third button, in the middle, looked after the optional folding mirror function – particularly useful for city users. The right-hand knob was for the power roof (which was linked to the rear side windows), with various alarm functions on the buttons around its base. Then came the handbrake, and the storage box/armrest

The switches by the handbrake, but seen here on a right-hand drive car. This was one of the few instances when the controls were mirrored – left-hand drive models had the mirror switches on the left and the roof button on the right.

A picture of the basic cloth trimmed seats, complete with manual adjustment levers, although it also serves to give a good view of the storage box aft of the handbrake, and the extra one mounted upright on the rear bulkhead. Incidentally, when the headrests were raised (they are seen here in their lowest position), the space created below them was filled with a bellows trim arrangement.

between the seats, linked to the central locking and in which the telephone was mounted for those who specified one. On the R171, there was actually a second storage box, placed vertically between the seats, as well as a parcel net on the rear bulkhead for maps and suchlike.

One could be forgiven for thinking the new SLK already had more than its fair share of switches and gizmos, but there were more on the doors and the overhead console, which served as a mounting point for the rearview mirror. The stylists managed to successfully blend the door cappings with the dashboard shape and, combined with the same material and textures found in the centre console all the way back to the bulkhead behind the seats, gave occupants a feeling of intimacy and solidity. The door features were kept to a minimum, with a door release handle in the corner closest to the door mirror, and power window controls integrated into the leading edge of the door pull cum armrest – the latter finished in the same hue as the door inlay, or one of the other six interior trim colours on cars with leather upholstery. Below that was a soft map pocket, with a puddle light in its base. This left only the speakers, of which there were nine, or 11 if the optional sound system was fitted. Standard speaker positions included one underneath the grille above the central air vents at the front of the car, a tweeter in each door mirror mounting point, a pair of mid-range and woofer speakers in the base of each door panel, and one by both of the seatbelt reels on the rear bulkhead. Specifying the 380W sound system added a pair of speakers on either side of the upright storage box between the seats. As for the overhead control panel (OCP), the sensor for the auto-dimming feature on the mirror was contained in the mirror housing, but moving back along the header rail, there was a place for the transmitter used for garage door opener, the 'TeleAid' button to summon assistance (marked 'SOS' when fitted), and a bank of interior lighting switches. The two main interior lights were in the OCP, along with microphones for the hands-free telephone and 'TeleAid' system, plus the GPS antenna and light and rain sensors for high-spec models. An auxiliary reading lamp was fitted in the base of the rear view mirror on certain cars, either standard or as an option, and these vehicles also had a certain number of minor lights scattered around the cockpit that remained on to give ambient lighting that helped locate things in the dark – this is where the light sensor came into play.

Detail shot of the overhead control panel, or OCP. This vehicle has the extra reading and ambient lighting in the base of the rearview mirror.

Right and below: The inner door trim, and a close-up of the switches on the driver's-side door handle (the passenger only had window lifts for their side of the car).

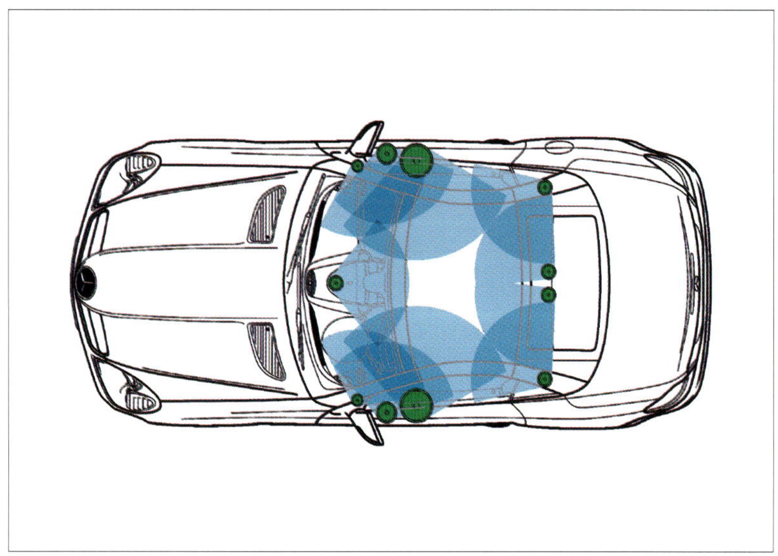

Speaker positions in the R171, with the two between the rear seats only being added if the surround sound system was specified.

Cutaway version of a leather-trimmed seat showing the frame (including the magnesium alloy bracing components), seatbelt receiver and power adjustment controls. This seat also has the innovative 'Airscarf' heating system.

And so we come to the seats, which would normally get nothing more than a passing mention. However, a lot of work went into the R171 buckets, enhancing ergonomics and long-distance comfort, so it is worth going over their features in detail. Firstly, it's fair to say the seat design looked very modern, with a pair of either cloth or leather inserts and arrow motifs inlaid between the heavy bolsters on both the lower cushion and the backrest, and an integrated headrest. The seat was built up on a glassfibre base, and duly braced at the back via a silver-painted magnesium alloy shell, that not only looked attractive but also helped reduce injuries in a side-impact situation for very little gain in weight; they also provided a solid fixing point for the side airbags.

The seats were able to fold forward, giving access to a coat hook on the back of each seat, as well as the parcel net, although the two outer seatbelt mounting points were fixed to the body – only the buckle receiver was attached to the seat, close to the transmission tunnel, although there was a strap to hold the seatbelt in a useful position before belting up. It was perhaps the headrest that held the most interest, though, as it could be adjusted up and down (manually), and also played host to something known as the 'Airscarf,' or at least the vent for it.

To reduce backdraught in the cockpit during cold weather, Mazda came up with the windblocker, but it was a big help rather than a final solution. Most manufacturers copied the principle, Mercedes-Benz included, as the simplicity and compact nature of such designs lend themselves well to lightweight open cars. For the new SLK, the Stuttgart engineers came up with something rather clever called the 'Airscarf' to augment the work of the windblocker. The optional 'Airscarf' employed a small yet powerful ceramic heater assembly, a compact blower, and a

The regular mesh windblocker, which stretched over the padded roll-over bars, and was held in place by pop-fasteners. The Mercedes engineers went a stage further on stopping drafts for the R171 SLK, though ...

Work in progress monitoring the temperature of a passenger's upper body with the 'Airscarf' installed. Thanks to good aerodynamics protecting the car's occupants from draught coming over the windscreen, the difference was quite remarkable, with or without the windblocker in place.

vent in the headrests to provide warmth to the neck and head – something that, coupled with the carefully calculated seat height and aerodynamic tweaks making the air coming over the windscreen flow above the occupants' heads, enabled SLK drivers to enjoy open-top motoring for longer periods during the winter months. The 'Airscarf' system came with three-stage heating (basically, output was judged automatically although a manual override facility was provided), and was hooked up to an ECU that automatically adjusted the boost from the integral fan according to the speed of the car and outside temperature.

The simple but effective 'Airscarf' mechanism in the back of a seat. The idea was duly adopted on the SL, too, albeit in a revised form.

As one would expect in a modern sporting machine, there was fore and aft seat adjustment (greater than before), as well as height and backrest angle adjustment. These were dealt with via three levers on cars without power controls, while those with power seats also had squab tilt adjustment, all looked after by a set of switches made to resemble a miniature seat on the seat base, close to the sills. The power seat option was usually batched together with a memory function, which allowed up to three settings on the seat, steering wheel and door mirrors to be stored on a button array next to the seat controls.

As for trim, depending on the exterior paintwork, the black cloth and six hide options gave the buyer no less than 50 recommended colour combinations to choose from, and that was before consulting the Designo catalogue, which featured another ten leather trim shades, as well as a pair of leather/Alcantara options. With a wider range of convenience features, enhanced seating and greater headroom (16mm/0.6in more than before) and shoulder room (up 13mm, or half-an-inch), the interior was more comfortable than ever, as well as safer. In reality, the revival of the lightweight sports concept by Mazda had brought about a deluge of two-seaters in virtually all market sectors. Now was the time for Mercedes to concentrate on what it was really good at ...

With a wide range of trim options, convenience features, and enhanced interior heating, ventilation and lighting, the R171 SLK's cockpit was a pleasant place to be, day or night.

Anton Waltner led the team that developed and tested the new V6.

A new drivetrain

The new SLK was able to benefit greatly from a selection of fresh technologies that had been introduced during 2003. We may as well start with the V6 engine, as this 3.5-litre unit was the mainstream powerplant for the new SLK – the other two lumps announced at the time of the R171 model's launch were more specialised, albeit for different reasons.

The basic M272 family of lightweight, all-aluminium alloy V6 powerplants was announced to the press just before Christmas 2003, and would duly find service in a number of Mercedes models, the SLK sports car being the first to benefit from the advances made compared to the older M112 lump. The key feature of this unit, when compared to the earlier M112 equivalent, was its four overhead camshafts – two per bank to operate the four (two inlet and two exhaust) valves used for each cylinder. This had a huge bearing on power output, but by adding electrohydraulic-controlled adjusters into the equation to give continuously variable timing to each camshaft, it allowed the valve timing to be adjusted by up to 40 degrees to ensure a good balance between low- and top-end performance, along with superior emissions and fuel consumption thanks to a more complete burning of the air-fuel charge – the unit could boast what amounted to an internal EGR system.

Other features included a new, more accurate HFM air mass sensor, a revised variable-length magnesium alloy intake manifold, with ECU-controlled 'tumble flaps' before the ports to increase turbulence in the airflow and help the air-fuel charge burn cleaner under partial loads, and iron-clad alloy pistons that were shaped to provide an optimised combustion chamber at TDC. The sparkplugs, looked after by individual coils placed directly onto the plugs, sat in the middle of the four valves, which each had narrower stems to help increase the speed of airflow around them.

At the same time, the cooling circuit was modified via a new electronic map-controlled thermostat to keep the engine coolant at the optimum temperature and promote faster warming-up

Display version of the M272 four-cam 24v V6, built at the same Bad Cannstatt factory as its twin-cam 18v predecessors. It was an all-aluminium alloy unit, including the upper part of the sump, with the crankcase made via high-pressure die-casting (HPDC) and featuring cross-bolted main bearing caps to provide it with extra rigidity. Whilst retaining the 106mm cylinder spacing of the M112 engine, the four main bearings were actually wider than those on the M112, supporting a lighter crankshaft, making for smoother, more responsive running.

Detail shot of the camshafts, with the intake cam driven by a duplex chain, and the exhaust cam via a spur gear. There were four camshaft position sensors linked to the Bosch ME 9.7 ECU, and four vane adjusters to give a new dimension in variable valve timing.

times, and the forged steel con-rods were made 20 per cent lighter to improve response. But it's ironic that the balance shaft – which sat between the two banks and counter-rotated at the same speed as the forged and counterweighted crankshaft to make the V6 engine run smoothly, despite its 90-degree vee – caused a few problems in service, although it was something that was quickly sorted in typical Stuttgart fashion.

In the SLK350 application (Type 272.963, or M272 E35), the free-revving V6 had a 92.9mm bore within the high-silicon alloy cylinder liner and an 86.0mm stroke, thus giving a displacement of 3498cc. With dual knock sensors allowing a relatively high 10.7:1 compression ratio, power output was quoted at 272bhp, which equates to an impressive 78bhp per litre! Not only that, it delivered 258lbft of torque, displaying an incredibly flat torque

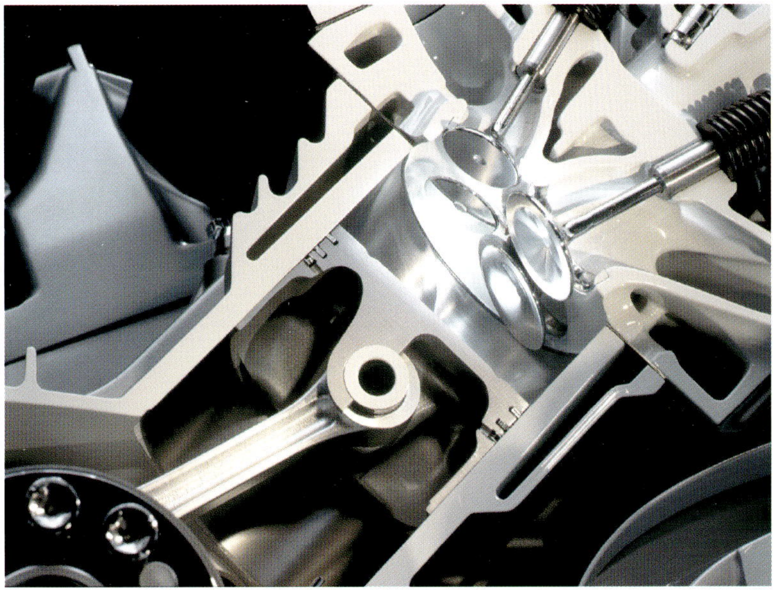

The iron-clad alloy pistons with nitrided steel rings ran in Silitec cylinder liners. The four valves above surrounded the central single sparkplug (the M112 unit had had two plugs and three valves). Incidentally, the intake valves on the new V6 were 39.5mm (1.55in) in diameter, while the exhaust valves were 30mm (1.18in) across.

curve from 2400rpm all the way up to 5000rpm to give a highly-desirable mix of mid-range punch and relaxed cruising, as well as being both cleaner and around ten per cent more frugal than its 3.7-litre predecessor used in the SL. The 16kg (35lb) weight gain was a small price to pay ...

As it happens, the car's sporting pretensions were not forgotten, and a great deal of work was done to reduce unwanted noise and tune the induction and exhaust systems to create a pleasant sound. This could only be accomplished once the emissions regulations had been dealt with, of course, with the strict EURO 4 standards due to come into force in January 2005. In the case of the V6, a secondary air-injection system helped reduce CO and HC emissions in the exhaust manifold before a pair of three-way catalytic converters (one for each bank, located close to the stainless and airgap-insulated manifolds) treated any pollutants that were left over. Each converter had two Lambda oxygen sensors working in tandem for greater accuracy in exhaust content readings straight from a cold start. Further down the stainless system, two front mufflers were used aft of the transmission, and then the pipes crossed over before the two large volume back boxes.

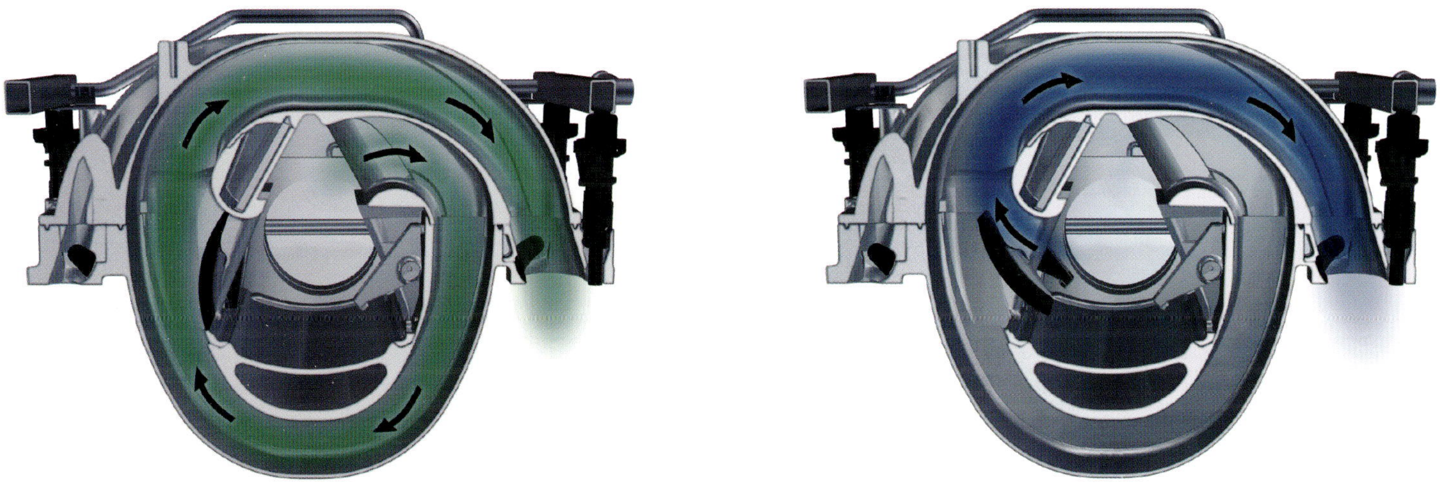

Drawings showing the way routing flaps in the intake manifold adjusted the length of the intake channels. The longer runner scenario (with the air shown in green) allowed improved torque at low revs, while opening the router flap at engine speeds above 3500rpm shortened the distance air had to travel before reaching the injectors to enhance power delivery. The dark blobs before the injectors are the electropneumatically-controlled tumble flaps, which were used at the end of each intake port to disturb the airflow at part-throttle to promote faster and cleaner burning; at higher engine speeds, they simply dropped out of the way.

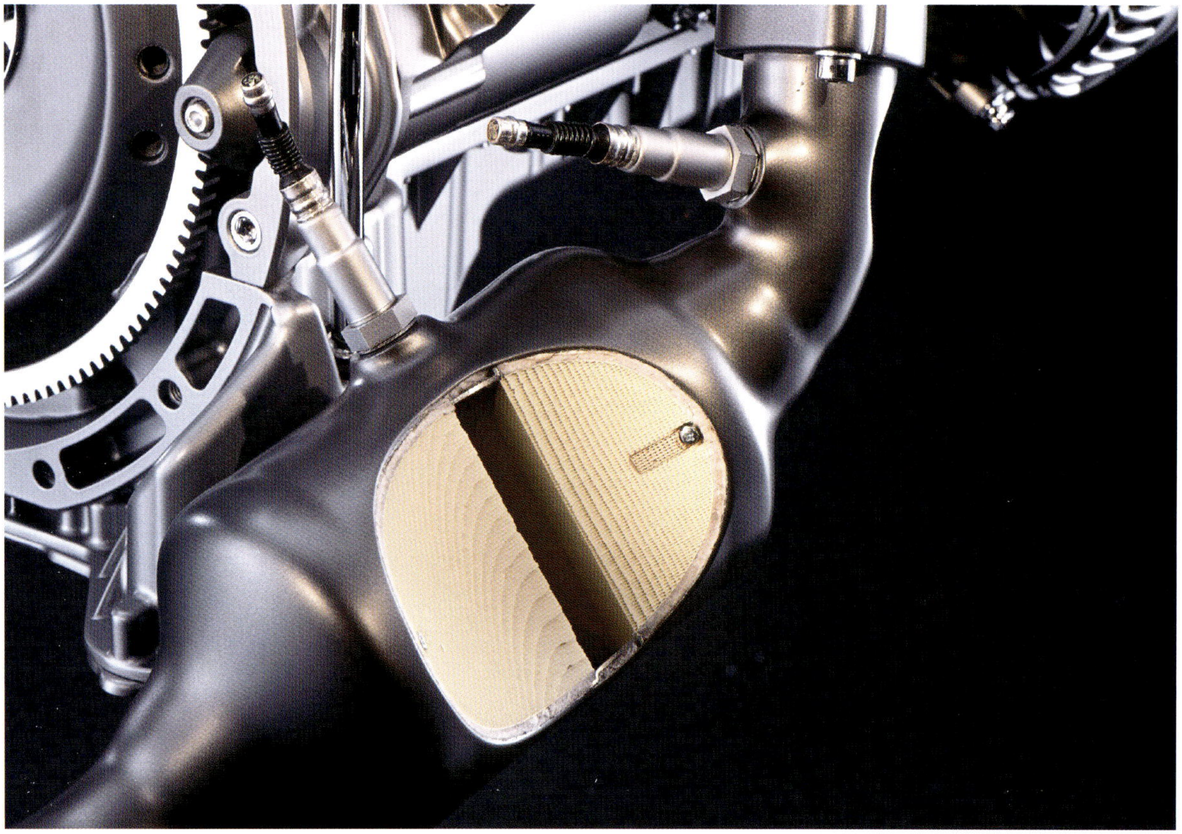

A close-up of one of the pair of three-way catalytic converters (one per bank), which featured two oxygen sensors – one upstream, and a second one mounted between the platinum- and rhodium-plated ceramic monoliths in the cat unit.

The 3.5-litre V6 installed in the SLK350.

The new V6 inherited the innovative and fast-changing seven-speed '7G-Tronic' transmission, first seen in September 2003. This compact, electronically-controlled 7AT unit was developed in-house to deliver both better performance and improved economy at the same time, achieved by a lower first gear and taller top gear, with closer ratios in-between, and even the ability to skip cogs when the black box felt this was the most efficient move. Sporting a magnesium alloy casing to save weight and a torque converter with a lock-up facility on all forward gears, in the R171 SLK350 application, the W7C700 unit (Type 722.906) as it was called, came with cogs that gave ratios of 4.38, 2.86, 1.92, 1.37, 1.00, 0.82 and 0.73, while the final-drive was set at 3.27:1.

Thanks to the Mercedes 'Touchshift' feature, when the gearshift was in the 'D' position, one could tap the lever to the left to execute a downshift, or tap it to the right to go up a gear. As well as the gate pattern guide, there was a comfort and sport mode switch (marked 'C/S') close to the ashtray (cars with the

Left and below: The 7AT '7G-Tronic' automatic gearbox and its 'Touchshift' selector. At speeds of around 60mph (roughly 100kph), the engine was able to turn over 12 per cent slower than when linked to a five-speed unit, providing a notable reduction in noise and fuel consumption. As with the 5AT transmission, one could also specify steering wheel-mounted paddle shifts as an option.

steering wheel-mounted shift paddles had an 'M' added to select a manual option, although this feature was restricted to AMG models by the time production started), with the mode displayed in the lower LED read-out in the dash.

The V6 could also be linked to a Daimler-built manual transmission with a new, fast but refined single-rod gearshift system, replacing the earlier rod and cable setup. With the SG-S400/5.3 (Type 716.664) 6MT unit, internal ratios were listed at 4.46 on first, 2.61 on second, 1.72 on third, 1.25 on fourth, a direct fifth, and 0.84 on sixth, matched up to a 3.27:1 final-drive. At 5.6 seconds, the 0-60 time was actually a tenth of a second slower that the automatic version, although both cars were governed to top out at 156mph (250kph). The advantage of the manual 'box was slightly better fuel economy and the involvement factor, which was still sought after by a lot of sports car buyers – especially when short, fast shifts were possible. As such, the manual transmission was classed as a standard fitment, with the automatic optional.

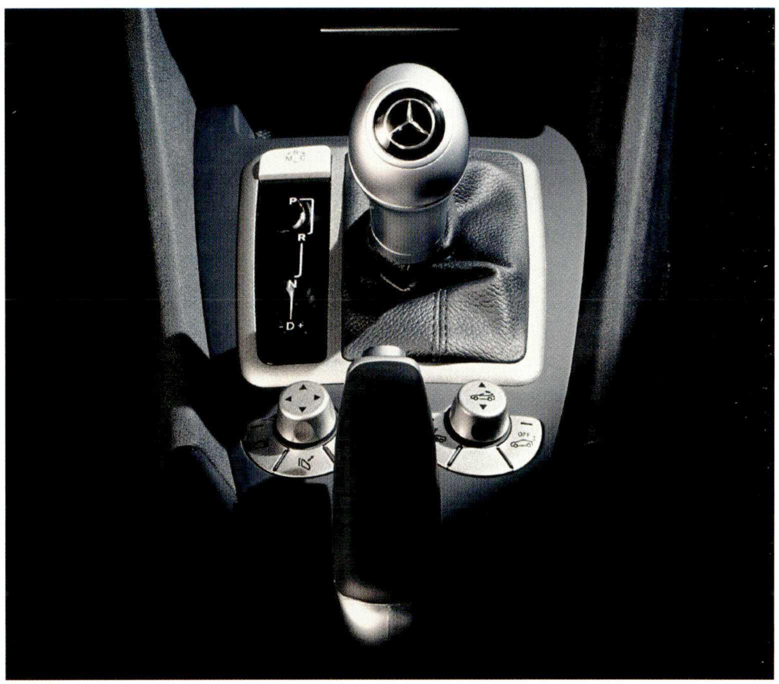

Above and right: Cutaway drawing of the six-speed manual gearbox, and a view of the standard gearlever. Note the manual gearbox shift pattern, with reverse in a different position to the R170 six-speed transmissions.

The new SLK350 was about three per cent more economical than its V6 predecessor when equipped with an automatic transmission, despite having significantly more power on tap. On the subject of economy, the R170 had gained a 60-litre (13.2 Imperial, or 15.9 US gallons) fuel tank after its 2000 face-lift. For all R171 models, a new 70-litre (15.4 Imperial, or 18.5 US gallons) steel tank with an internal pump was adopted, positioned above the rear axle for maximum protection in the event of an accident.

The other powerplant – a supercharged four – was sold mainly in Europe, where fuel is expensive and road tax is often based on engine size. Even the UK, where one used to be able to tax a Rolls-Royce for the same money as a Mini, adopted a basic sliding scale policy in 1999 and then announced a new system based on emissions in 2005. In such countries, particularly the likes of Italy and Greece, and places like Japan where anything with an engine above a two-litre threshold becomes costly to run, the option of a 1.8-litre unit was a godsend.

The engine in question was the all-alloy M271 'Twinpulse' unit, announced at the start of 2002, and first seen in cars like the C209-type CLK. There are a lot of rumours about this being a GEMA engine, brought about by the Chrysler merger, but although the launch timing and 1798cc displacement of the Chrysler, Mitsubishi and Hyundai units is close enough to raise the question, the bore/stroke relationship is quite different on the Mercedes four. One has to remember that while the Chrysler side of the business was slashing its development budget by billions of dollars at the turn of the millennium, the Mercedes-Benz brand was benefitting from a new model programme of remarkable scope. These were not simply variations on a theme, but whole new lines set to be introduced, along with revised powertrains to suit.

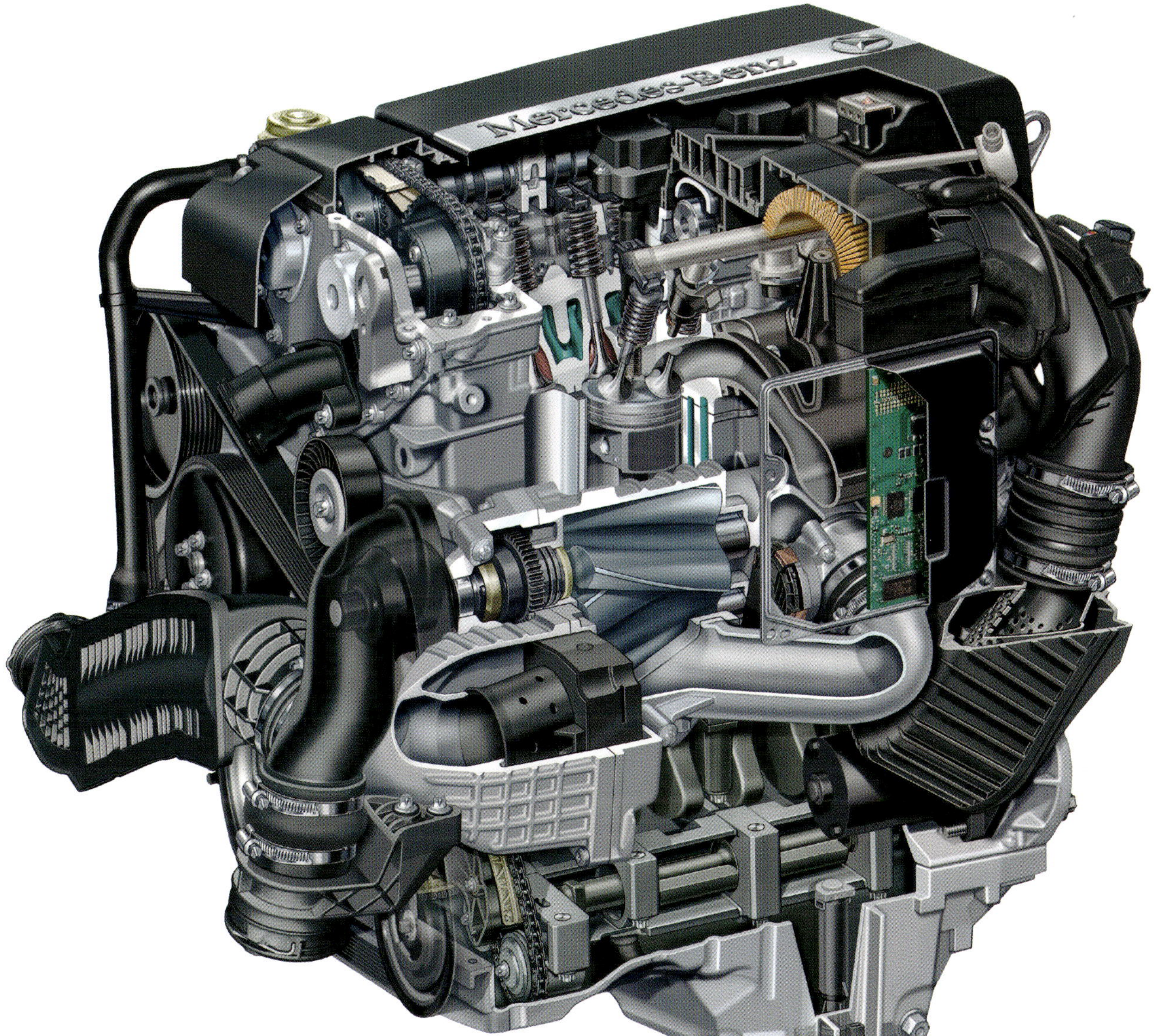

Cutaway drawing of the all-alloy M271 powerplant. Like the M272 unit, all ancillaries were driven by a ribbed belt.

Anyway, the M271 featured twin-overhead camshafts and 16 valves in its aluminium alloy head, and boasted the same vane-type adjusters as the V6 lump to provide continuously variable valve timing. Again, the main benefit was an improvement in low-end torque and top-end power, but the benefits in emissions and fuel consumption were also plain to see. Interestingly, while hardly necessary in a four-cylinder engine with a capacity of less than two-litres, the M271 was given a Lanchester balance shaft nonetheless, smoothing out inertia forces to provide greater refinement.

For the SLK, a belt-driven supercharger and intercooler was added to the spec sheet, giving the torque of a much larger engine,

The supercharged four installed in an SLK200 Kompressor model.

Display version of the four-cylinder M271 engine hooked up to a manual gearbox. Note the intercooler up front.

and all available from idling speed. This allowed the engineers to choose a taller axle ratio without hurting performance levels, and the end result of this – combined with the new technology – was an eight per cent improvement in fuel economy compared with the old SLK with an M111 unit.

As for specifics applied to the R171 application, with a bore and stroke of 82.0 x 85.0mm in the alloy block, this gave the M271 E18 ML (or 271.944) a cubic capacity of 1796cc. Combined with a 9.5:1 compression ratio and a Siemens ECU and HFM setup rather than a Bosch engine management system, the supercharged unit delivered 163bhp, along with 177lbft of torque, available in a useful band that stretched from 3000 to 4000rpm. Incidentaly, there were twin exhaust pipes out the back, just like the V6 car, and the same type of air-gap insulated manifold to allow the three-way catalytic converter to quickly reach its optimum operating temperature.

As with the SLK350, a six-speed manual transmission attached to a single dry-plate clutch came as standard. The internal ratios were the same as those found on the V6, but the SG-S270/5.3 (Type 716.631) unit was quite different in the torque rating department – the same 'box as that used in the SLK350 would have been overkill. With a 3.46:1 final-drive, the SLK200 Kompressor was capable of 144mph (230kph), and could dismiss the 0-60 dash in 7.9 seconds.

The five-speed W5A330 '5G-Tronic' automatic transmission was available as an option on the SLK200 Kompressor model, and duly given the same selector and 'C/S' mode switch as the '7G' version. The steering wheel shift buttons were also listed for those who wanted more control over the change points. The Type 722.695 gearbox, with a torque converter lock-up clutch to prevent power losses, came with ratios of 3.95 on first, 2.42 on second, 1.49 on third, 1.00 on fourth, and 0.83 on fifth. The same 3.46 back axle allowed a 0-60 time of 8.3 seconds, and while there was a minute loss on top speed, the fractionally better fuel consumption went a long way toward making up for it.

Before leaving this section, it should be noted that the R171 became the first production SLK to feature a V8 engine option, although, because this model wasn't available straight away, we'll look at it later on when we profile the AMG car in detail.

Alexander Gebhard was the man responsible for the R171's chassis development, with testing taking place on a wide range of road surfaces in all kinds of weather.

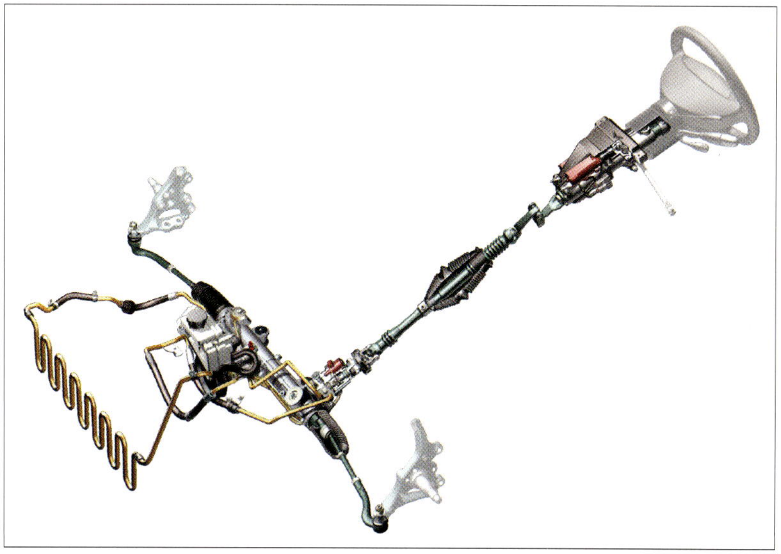

The new rack-and-pinion steering system fitted to the R171 SLK.

Chassis upgrades

The people behind the R171 concept had called for something with a more overtly sporting character. The styling had definitely moved in that direction – both inside and out – and the engines were uprated in line with the policy. But these changes count for very little if there are failings in the ride/handling balance, steering feedback, and the way the power is harnessed. As such, the whole steering, suspension and braking system was overhauled.

Starting with the steering, the old tried and tested recirculating ball PAS system was replaced by a more accurate rack-and-pinion setup. The rack was positioned in front of the axle line to encourage a mild understeering attitude as one approached the limit, which most manufacturers tend to lean towards in the name of safety oversteer can be fun in corners, but only in the hands of accomplished drivers. While not quite as good at damping road shocks through the wheel, it also saved weight, and interfered less with the body's energy absorption in the event of an accident. With manual or optional power adjustment on the column for height and reach, and an electronic steering lock linked to the ignition switch, as well as a tighter turning circle, the advantages certainly outweighed the disadvantages. The standard, regular power-assistance package could be upgraded with an optional speed-sensitive steering system, making parking manoeuvres less of a bind.

The front suspension and braking system.

The rear suspension, brakes, and rear axle setup.

The quasi-double-wishbone front suspension of the R170 was replaced by a compact three-link front end augmented by MacPherson struts. Mounted on a simple frame carrier that also supported the engine, a forged aluminium alloy torque strut ran diagonally from the front of the carrier to the hub, while a steel cross strut followed the axle line to replace the lower wishbone and provide precise wheel location. The third link was the steering's trackrod (or tie rod, as it is sometimes known), although the MacPherson strut (coil springs over twin-tube gas-filled shock absorbers) acted as a further location point, and carried a mounting point for the torsion bar linkage attached to the hefty anti-roll bar that ran in the gap between the front of the carrier frame and the steering rack. This setup enhanced handling and took out a lot of the vibrations caused by braking and minor wheel imbalance.

A multi-link rear suspension was retained, albeit in modified form, with the revised geometry and kinematics following the practice established in the 203-series C-Class and a significant increase in the track dimensions. At the end of the day, however, it was very similar to the R170 suspension, with single-tube gas shocks outside the springs, and anti-squat and anti-dive geometry included. The standard anti-roll bar, running above the suspension subframe, wasn't new either, as one had been added to the SLK spec sheet during the 2000 face-lift.

Incidentally, owners could specify a lowered and stiffer suspension setup if they wished, which in itself confirmed that the SLK had taken on a more serious sporting nature. With this option (SA 486), the body was lowered by 10mm (0.4in), along with a corresponding reduction in spring travel, and spring rates were increased by ten per cent.

On the braking side of things, while journalists had been expecting the novel electrohydraulic brakes of the SL, it should be remembered that it had been something of a PR disaster. As such, in conjunction with the need to keep the sticker price as low as possible, it was no surprise that the SLK was equipped with a regular dual-circuit hydraulic braking system with a vacuum servo.

The basic four-cylinder car came with single-piston floating calipers working on 288mm (11.3in) diameter ventilated discs at the front, and two pot fixed calipers combined with 278mm (10.9in) diameter solid discs with an integral drum for the handbrake at the rear. This was actually the same specification as that of the original SLK, although the new car benefitted from the latest ABS and Brake Assist programmes, with the ABS sensors providing information for the standard ESP electronic stability and ASR traction control systems. Combined with the new suspension, there were significant gains in directional and braking stability.

The V6 model came with the same electronic gizmos, but the disc sizes were increased, both in diameter and thickness. At the front, there were 330mm (13.0in) vented and cross-drilled discs working in tandem with fixed four-pot calipers, while at the back, the calipers were retained, but the solid discs were now

The standard 16-inch alloy wheels fitted to the SLK200 Kompressor model.

The 17-inch wheels fitted to European SLK350s, and available as an option (code SA 607).

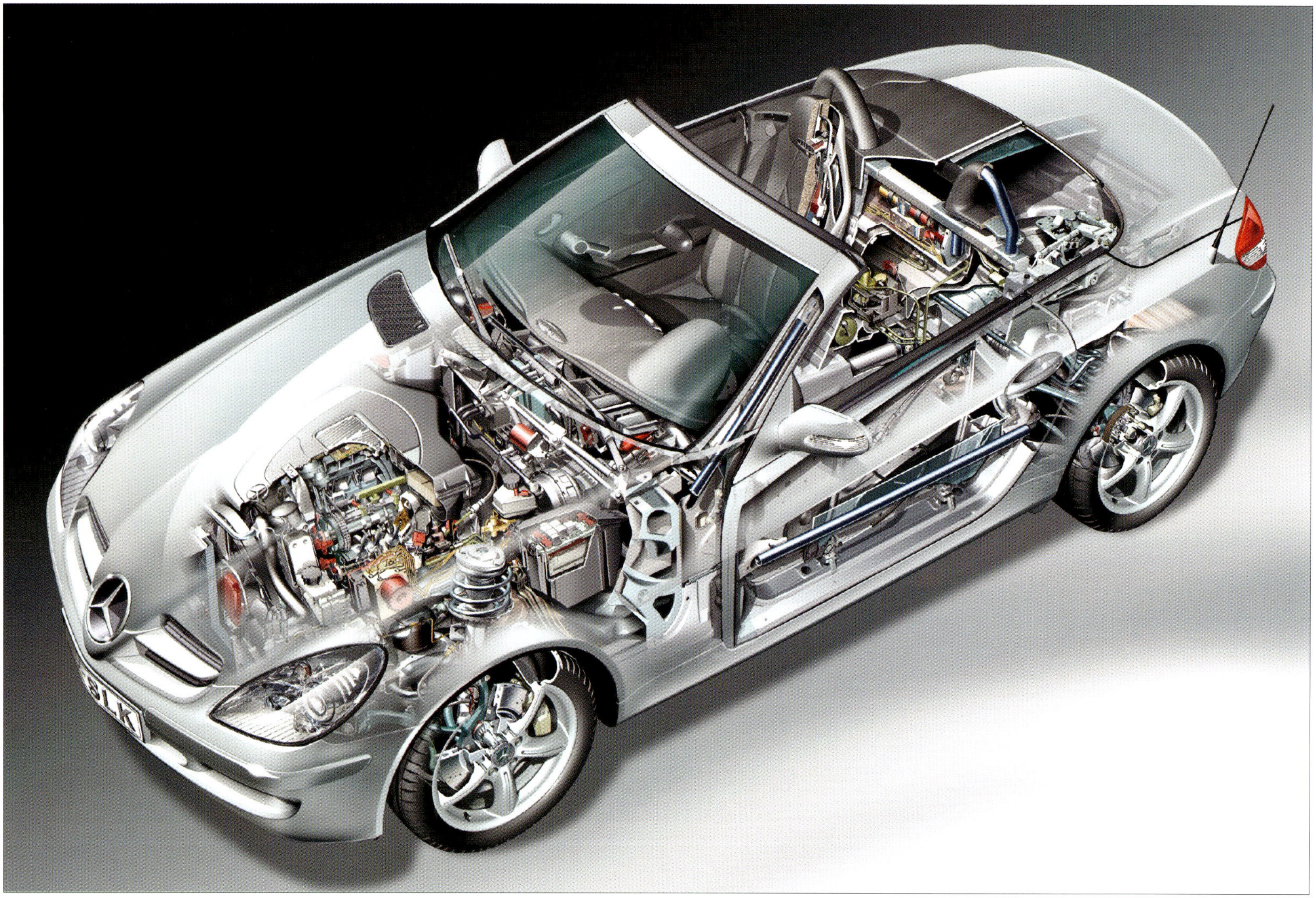

A cutaway drawing of a left-hand drive SLK350, which should prove useful in seeing how all the different components sat together under the skin.

290mm (11.4in) across. With this particular system, there was also a lot of work done on reducing weight, improving cooling, and ensuring the smooth, powerful operation of the brakes, regardless of weather conditions.

Covering the brakes were a selection of 16-, 17-, and 18-inch alloy wheels. The base car came with seven-spoke 7J x 16 rims shod with 205/55 rubber on all four corners, while the V6 model came with a staggered setup on 17-inch five-spoke wheels – 225/45 tyres on 7.5J rims at the front, and 245/40s on 8.5J rims at the rear. The latter combination was available as an option on the four-cylinder car, along with a 16-inch five-spoke design and a six-spoke version as a dealer accessory. Other 17- and 18-inch rims were available as factory options, including an AMG wheel, as well as a spacesaver spare to replace the 'Tirefit' system, winter tyres and run-flat tyres.

By the way, the latest ESP programme offered an optional (SA 477) tyre pressure loss function. The system was constantly monitoring tyre rotation speeds anyway, and this information was used to discern whether tyre pressures remained the same. Any sudden loss was quickly picked up, and a warning was flashed up on the dashboard display for the driver to check the tyres. This was not the expensive RDK feature that relayed pressure information, available on cars like the SL, but it was a useful safety item nonetheless, especially for heavy motorway users.

Testing, testing ...

As one would expect of the team behind any new Mercedes-Benz model, the testing prior to sale was extensive and exhaustive. By summer 2001, *Autocar* was showing spy shots of the R171 in heavy disguise panels, but development work had already been going on behind the scenes much earlier. This small selection of pictures gives a rough idea of the in-depth testing programmes carried out in order to get the new car reliable, practical and fun-to-drive ...

Engine testing in R171 prototypes.

Final checks on the power roof system.

A pre-production mule on a shaker rig, which could simulate several years of rough treatment in a matter of weeks.

Snowy roads provided a superb environment for testing traction control setups and refining the ESP and ABS systems.

The final series of road testing with pre-production prototypes was carried out in extremes of heat, cold, humidity, and dust, to give buyers a car worthy of carrying the hallowed three-pointed star on its nose.

The convertible version of the Chrysler Crossfire, launched at the 2004 Detroit Show. The R171 SLK was announced at the same event. (Courtesy Chrysler)

Breaking cover

Compared with the R170 SLK launch, which had a number of key events over a long period to build interest in the car, that for the R171 model was very low-key – not much different to a minor change scenario rather than the release of a brand new vehicle. Press pictures and details were handed out at the 2004 Detroit Show in mid-January, but there was no car to be seen. As it happens, the SLK-based Chrysler Crossfire Convertible was launched at the same event, with sales starting in spring as an early 2005 model. There was definitely one of those on display, and that could be the reason the little Benz was kept out of the way – to let the Chrysler model hog limelight in its native country, and deflect questions on why a new generation SLK was being launched alongside what was basically an R170 variant.

Benz enthusiasts didn't have to wait long, though, for the R171 SLK made its public debut at the 2004 Geneva Show, which opened on 4 March. The Swiss event – the 74th to be held – also

The SLK 55 AMG in its role as the FIA's F1 Safety Car, teaming up with a C-Class estate, which was the official Medical Car in the Formula One arena.

Having been heavily involved in the birth of the SLK, the launch of the R171 was a nice way for Jürgen Hubbert (seen here) to end his career as head of the Mercedes-Benz passenger car division. He officially retired in April 2005 after 40 years of service to the company. His place was taken by Eckhard Cordes, albeit briefly.

Part of the Mercedes-Benz stand at the 2004 Geneva Show, with an R230-type SL350 nearest the camera.

witnessed the first appearance of the supremely elegant C219 CLS-Class, and a face-lifted version of the 203-series C-Class. But it is the SLK that interests us here, with further publicity for the model coming a few days after it broke cover, when the FIA used an SLK 55 AMG as its safety car during the Australian Grand Prix. The SLK was duly adopted as the official Formula One Safety Car throughout the 2004 and 2005 F1 seasons, as well as in the high-profile German DTM series.

Domestic sales of the R171 SLK began on 27 March 2004, and spread throughout Europe thereafter. The next chapter looks at the early production models, and the various grades that were sold in the world's major markets ...

4

The Early Production Cars

**"Mercedes has delivered a small roadster that's not just great to own, but great to drive, too. On any given road, the new car represents such an advance over its predecessor that it's difficult to believe they're only a generation apart ..."
– *Autocar*, August 2004.**

Following on from the launch of the SLR McLaren, the 612bhp SL 65 AMG with its award-winning twin-turbo V12 engine made its debut at the 2004 New York Show, which opened in mid-April that year. It was immediately declared the most powerful production roadster in the world, but with today's crowded roads and speed cameras around every corner, one has to question where on Earth one could use such machines. They were basically playthings that could only stretch their muscles on a closed circuit. As such, with its enhanced dynamics, the SLK offered a far more practical solution for sports car enthusiasts who enjoyed the occasional early morning blast combined with stress-free wind-in-the-hair motoring ...

The gullwing-bodied SLR McLaren viewed from above. The inspiration it provided for the SLK is obvious from this angle, although the price and performance was in a different league. In reality, though, the smaller car could probably provide more fun, more of the time over a full year of motoring.

The home market

Although the SLK made its proper debut in Switzerland, a price list had been put together at the time of the Detroit Show for the dealers in Germany. This first official price list, dated 4 January 2004 and reprinted a total of four times, gives us an ideal overview of the standard specifications for the home market cars. The basic SLK200 Kompressor was priced at €28,900 at this time, while the normally-aspirated 3.5-litre model, expected in the summer, commanded €37,400; the AMG model was also listed, priced at €55,150, although customers would have to wait until the tail-end of 2004 before they started filtering through into dealerships. Accordingly, so as not to confuse things too much, the SLK 55 AMG will be looked at separately later on, with this section dealing with the SLK200 Kompressor and SLK350 only. Incidentally, as with the options that follow, 16 per cent VAT has to be added to these figures, but it was – and still is – usual for base prices to be quoted minus any taxes, as the rate can change at any time, and is something beyond the control of the works.

Continued page 107

S OA 3747

S OA 3747

This page, opposite and overleaf: A selection of press pictures showing the domestic SLK200 Kompressor at the time of the R171 launch. This manual car has the optional 639-style 17-inch alloy wheels, which came with a lowered suspension as part of a package, the Audio 50 APS stereo unit and red leather trim.

S OA 3747

SLK 200
S OA 3747

Standard features on domestic models included alloy wheels, a six-speed manual transmission, anti-lock brakes (ABS) with Brake Assist (BAS), power-assisted steering (PAS) with manual adjustment for height and reach on the column and a leather-wrapped multi-function steering wheel, the ESP stability programme combined with the ASR traction control system, sports pedals, a power roof, cruise control with a 'Speedtronic' limiter, power-adjusted and heated door mirrors with integral repeater indicators, H7 projector headlights with the Headlamp Assist system, parking lights, front and rear foglights, LED lighting units at the rear, a laminated windscreen, power windows with green-tinted glass all-round, a heated rear screen with timer, remote central locking with immobiliser and panic switch, remote boot release, black cloth trim, seat occupancy recognition, folding sports seats with height adjustment and adjustable headrests on both sides, adaptive multi-stage dual front and side airbags combined with seatbelt tensioners and two-stage force limiters, an advanced automatic heater with individual controls (including automatic window closure, as well as a 'Rest' feature to use residual heat in the engine), roof-mounted reading lights, a trip computer, an outside temperature gauge, analogue clock, audio preparation (including an aerial on the nearside rear wing and speaker covers), the 'Assyst' service reminder, a chime to warn if the lights or handbrake had been left on, stainless treadplates, soft door pockets and storage nets

Continued page 111

This page and pages 108-110: Another selection of press shots from the time of the launch. This batch shows an automatic SLK350 with its standard 17-inch alloy wheels, the Comand APS audio and navigation setup and black leather trim.

S OA 3746

S OA 3746

Shift paddles were an option that could be specified on both the 5AT and 7AT gearboxes (SA 428). Touching the rocker switch on the side closest to the driver gave upshifts, while the side furthest away looked after downshifts.

on the passenger-side footwell and rear bulkhead, the 'Tirefit' system (with an electric compressor and a can of sealant rather than a spare wheel), a hazard warning triangle, first aid kit, 12V power socket, and a cloth windblocker. The V6 car also had manually-controlled 'Thermatic' air-conditioning and an upgraded inner lighting package, as well as a larger alloy wheel and tyre combination.

Regular options included a five-speed automatic transmission for the supercharged car (SA code 423, priced at €1770), a seven-speed version for the SLK350 (427) at €1870, steering wheel shift paddles to go with the AT 'box (428) at €200, a lowered and uprated suspension (486) at €205, a tyre pressure loss warning system (477) at €55, Bi-Xenon headlights with integral washer system (614) at €825, headlight washers for the standard lights (600) at €245, a heated windscreen washer system (875) at €165, wipers with a rain sensor (345) at €95, infra-red remote control for the roof (880) at €95, power folding door mirrors (500) at €215, self-dimming mirrors (249) at €290 for a set of three, a power adjustment and memory facility for the driver's seat, steering column and outside mirror positions (275) at €795, the power adjustment and memory function for the passenger side seat (242) at €420 extra (the 275 option was a necessity), seat heaters (873) at €295, the 'Airscarf' heating system (403) at €395, an alarm system (551), which was €265, or €425 if upgraded with an interior security upgrade (882), a garage door opener (231) at €220, a heated steering wheel (443) at €250, parameter parking (213) at €195, 'Parktronic' (220) at €660, fire extinguisher (682) at €100, a suit or dress case for behind the seats (U07) at €130, fitted luggage for the boot (U23) at €170, and a luggage rack (726) at €60. One could also opt for the 'Thermatic' heating and air-conditioning system (580) on the SLK200 Kompressor for €1200 (standard on the SLK350), or plump for the fully automatic 'Thermotronic' version (581) for an additional €525, as well as the inner lighting upgrade (876)

Left and below: The Bi-Xenon headlight option (SA 614) added headlight washers and a cornering light facility provided by movement in the foglights, at least on cars without the AMG styling package. The accompanying pair of illustrations show the difference in side-road illumination on cars that had the cornering light feature and those that didn't.

The 'Airscarf' heater (SA 403) installed on a seat with Designo leather trim. Note also the Designo leather on the roll-over bars behind the seats.

found on the V6 model – this €120 package brought with it footwell lights, lights in the storage boxes, additional ambient and reading lights in the rearview mirror, lighting for the mirrors in the sunvisors, and puddle lights. With a fully-loaded car, especially one with things like seat heating, an uprated 74Ah battery (SA code 673) needed to be specified, adding €80 to the invoice, although it was already standard equipment on the V6 car (the regular battery was a 62Ah one, by the way). No-cost options (NCO) included a cupholder insert (309), and an ashtray and lighter instead of a storage box and power socket (301).

As for trim and paint options, regular metallic paint was listed at €540, while the 12 Designo Metallic shades were €1370 extra, Designo Varicolor or Mystic options were €2085, and Designo Chromaflair €4435. Regular leather upholstery was priced at €1050, with Nappa leather €300 more. The ten Designo leather hides were available in a single or two-tone colour scheme (both €2600), or matched with black or grey Alcantara for the same price. Specifying the 728 SA code brought Vavona wood trim (including the steering wheel and gearshift in wood/leather) for €750, or one could buy the trim elements only in Designo wood for €560 (W16 for Japanese ash, or W61 for the Natural Poplar veneer), or Designo leather (Y97) for €350. A leather gearshift on its own (SA code 280) was priced at €30, a steering wheel in leather and Designo wood (Y95) at €735, with a matching gearshift (Y94) at €245. There was also a steering wheel and gearshift set in two-tone Designo leather (Y96), listed at €415, and Designo Alcantara headlinings were available for €1150, coming in black (Y83) or grey (Y85). It was also possible to specify leather on the roll-over bars behind the seats (Y98), adding €550 to the invoice if regular leather was chosen, or €580 if one moved up to Designo hide.

In addition, those looking for something more sporty could order the AMG bodykit (772) at €2980. Owners of the supercharged car could go for a different 16-inch alloy wheel with a five-spoke design (606) for €275, which came with slightly wider 225/50 rubber on the back pair, or the same five-spoke 17-inch rims fitted to the V6 car as standard (607) for €825. A 17-inch ten-spoke rim (R35) wheel was listed at €925 (or €200 for

An early US-spec car with the AMG styling kit (SA 772). The front air dam gives a quick identification feature, with the central supports being quite different to those of the regular cars, while kosher AMG models had extra vents on the panel's trailing edge.

the SLK350), and another five-spoke design (639) which came with the uprated suspension package for €1080, or €355 on the V6 model. Only one 18-inch rim was listed – a five-spoke AMG alloy wheel (782), available for €2130 on the four and €1405 on the six, and again coming with the lowered suspension. There was also the option of run-flat tyres (R66) at €250, and 16- or 17-inch winter tyres (645) at a €110 premium; a spacesaver spare (SA code 669, replacing the 'Tirefit' system and luggage box) was listed as an NCO.

On the audio and communication front, there was the Audio 20 unit (SA code 523) with a radio and CD player, nine speakers and an integral telephone keypad at €650, the Audio 50 APS unit (525) with a CD-based navigation system and larger screen on top of the Audio 20 specifications for €1845, and the 'Comand APS' head unit (527) with a DVD-based navigation system, keypad and a radio/CD/DVD player combination for €2790. Buyers of one of these stereos could also opt for a glovebox-mounted six-disc CD changer (819) for €395, while the two most expensive units could be linked to a Harman Kardon surround sound system with 11 speakers (810) for an additional €650. Meanwhile, for those who preferred their own stereo choices, the nine speaker setup could be bought separately (533) for €250. As for telephones, there was a 'Handy' unit (388) for €870, although one still had to add the wiring and fitting (273) at an extra €110, or €460 if it was tied into the audio unit (386).

There was also an accessory catalogue issued for SLK users, with all manner of goodies for the car, including things like chrome door mirror covers (€230 including VAT), chrome-plated grille aerofoils (€129), rear mudflaps (€47), various aluminium-style roof-rack options, black velour floormats at €75 a set, a black seat cover for the driver's seat (€116), illuminated treadplates (€590), a clear windblocker (€299), a trunk liner (€69), a luggage net set for the same area (€30), or a shaped bag for the boot (€60), and mobile phone connections for existing users. There was also a

The 16-inch SA 606 alloy wheel option. This set of wheels was supplied with a 7J rim and 205/55 rubber for the front axle, and an 8J rim with 225/50 tyres for the rear.

The attractive 17-inch R35-style alloys.

The 17-inch SA 639 alloys, which came with a lowered suspension.

The five-spoke AMG wheels (SA 782), seen here on an SLK 55 AMG.

An alternative to the fabric windblocker was offered as a dealer accessory, but it was moved to the factory options list at the start of 2005 in Germany.

silver-painted 'Acubens' 16-inch six-spoke alloy wheel listed for the SLK200 Kompressor, which came in at just over €800 a set.

Having inherited a new flywheel and a modified driver's footrest in February, *Auto, Motor und Sport* tried a manual supercharged model in April 2004, loaded up with virtually every option available, including the 606-style alloy wheels. As such, the car was a good few kilos heavier than the 1390kg (3058lb) catalogue entry, tipping the scales at 1406kg (3093lb), while the buyer's bank account would have been about €10,000 lighter! Notwithstanding, after recording a 0-60 time of 8.3 seconds and averaging a very respectable 31mpg (Imperial) during the test, the magazine had no hesitation in awarding a five-star rating to the new Mercedes two-seater. It noted: "The SLK is – open or closed – comfortable, inspiring and agile, and, at the same time, a pleasant and well-sorted processed cruiser."

Most people seemed happy enough with the new car's styling, although it did have its critics, or at least posed a few questions. For instance, Martin Leach (ex-Ford of Europe boss) stated: "It's strange putting an F1-style nose on the SLK when they want the SLR to be unique and extreme." It was a fair point, with the R230 SL still sporting a softer, more elegant front mask at the time, but the men in Stuttgart obviously had their reasons for taking this approach. Looking back, it was probably a gamble to try and enhance the sporting image of the smaller car on the

This page and opposite: A final selection of early press pictures, this series showing a domestic SLK350 with AMG wheels, automatic transmission (including paddle shifts), Designo trim on the seats and roll-over bars, Designo black ash woodwork on the dashboard, the 'Airscarf' option, and the Comand head unit.

coattails of the Benz supercar – it would certainly add appeal in some quarters, especially with younger buyers, while the marketing folks looking after the SL didn't have to resort to such tactics, being able to rely on a strong customer base that was less easily swayed away from the marque.

Anyway, the 1465kg (3223lb) V6-engined SLK350 eventually made it into domestic showrooms in June once full-scale production started in May, lining up alongside a new A-Class model, while the AMG version of the SLK finally put in an appearance in September, just in time for the 2005 season. More powertrains were expected during the year, but firstly, it's time to take a detailed looked at the long-awaited SLK 55 AMG ...

The AMG variant

The SL had benefitted from an AMG model for some years, the earliest versions dating back to the R107 series, long before the tuner became part of the Daimler-Benz empire. As for the SLK, the addition of the SLK 32 AMG grade in 2001 brought a whole new sporting dimension to the smaller two-seater, and naturally there were a lot of punters anxious to see how the R171 version would fit into the line-up.

Having been announced alongside the regular models at the start of 2004, as well as taking a highly visible role on the F1 stage, people had a very good idea of what to expect. But TV appearances and paperwork issued nine months before sales started are one thing – the availability of a production version, and the way it slotted into the rest of the contemporary Mercedes-Benz programme, is something quite different.

The R230 SL employed a 5439cc V8 in supercharged form to give 476bhp and 516lbft of torque. This was fine in a heavy flagship model, but would hardly have suited the lithe SLK. But looking back in history a little reveals that the R129 SL had employed a normally-aspirated version of the same powerplant (the Type 113.985), and rather than repeat the R170's supercharged V6 philosophy, the folks at AMG decided to revive the proven NA V8 formula for the new car. As such, the R171 had a lot less power than its then-current SL stablemate, but became the first SLK to feature an eight-cylinder engine, as well as the first in its showroom class to adopt V8 power. Considering that the first six didn't arrive until 2000, progress was certainly rapid within the SLK line.

Above and opposite: A dramatic set of pictures used to introduce the SLK 55 AMG (chassis code 171.473), which went on sale in Germany in September 2004.

S MA 5540

AMG
S MA 5540

The latest 5.4-litre AMG engine used in the SLK 55 AMG model. Note the plate beyond the three-pointed star, which carried the engine builder's name.

The SLK 55 AMG was launched at €55,150 plus tax (€63,974 inclusive), which was almost twice the price of the entry-level SLK200 Kompressor model. The main component in justifying this huge difference was naturally the handbuilt engine, although – as one would expect – it was a fully-engineered car, with each and every part designed by AMG technicians to match the enhanced performance and then tested extensively, both on the road and at the punishing Nürburgring.

The engine provides us with as good a place as any to start, though, and the specifications were recognisable to all followers of Mercedes-Benz lore. Like its brethren, the M113 E55 AMG (Type 113.989) all-alloy 90-degree V8 had a 97.0mm bore and a 92.0mm stroke to give a cubic capacity of 5439cc, although the stylish new top cover gave the powerplant quite a different impression.

Below the cover, however, most of the hardware was familiar. As with the other M113 and M112 sister units from the past, the three valves per cylinder were activated by a single overhead camshaft on each bank, while the two-stage variable length intake manifold and twin-plug ignition were also constant features. In this application, an 11.0:1 compression ratio was

The calibrations and 'V8' logo on the AMG's instrument pack left little doubt that there was something special lurking underneath the bonnet. Note also the darker gauge hood arrangement on the AMG cars.

specified, and the fuel-injection was controlled by a Bosch ME 2.8 black box. It also came with an oil cooler and a stronger fuel pump with an increased delivery rate to deal with the added performance, while the tuned stainless exhaust system sported a pair of catalytic converters near the manifolds, and another pair just before a single central muffler, before the pipework split again into two large backboxes with dual, chrome-plated tailpipes sprouting from each of them.

According to the catalogues, the AMG unit delivered 360bhp DIN at 5750rpm, which was 6bhp up on the old supercharged V6, and 376lbft of torque – 15lbft down on the earlier R129 unit, but a figure that represented an increase of 44lbft over the last AMG SLK powerplant. The red-line was marked at 6400rpm on the unique tachometer, and while the torque curve wasn't particularly flat, it was certainly meaty, and the standard 7AT gearbox made the most of it at all revs.

One huge advantage of having less power and torque to handle was the ability to use the W7C700 seven-speed '7G-Tronic' automatic transmission (Type 722.907), which was matched with an 'AMG-Speedshift' feature on the AMG model. There was no manual gearbox option, but the shift selector had a manual mode added, which allowed the driver to hold onto gears (regardless of engine revs or kickdown), duly called up via the 'Touchshift' lever or the dedicated steering wheel-mounted shift paddles. Unlike the regular models, in which the same button was used to go up and down through the gears, the right-hand paddle executed upshifts, while the left-hand one looked after downshifts on the AMG car.

Torque converter lock-up was provided on all forward gears to reduce power losses, and the gearbox's software was modified to give up to 35 per cent sharper reactions, including an active braking downshift. With the same internal gears as the optional 7AT unit on the SLK350 and a 3.06:1 final-drive, the engine and gearbox came together to endow the 1540kg (3388lb) SLK 55 AMG with a 0-60 time of 4.9 seconds and an electronically-governed top speed of 156mph (250kph).

Naturally, to keep things in check, the suspension and braking system was suitably uprated. Stiffer spring and damper rates were

The rather special braking system used on the front-end of the SLK 55 AMG. Although ceramic brakes had already appeared in the Mercedes-Benz line-up via the 'F1 Limited Edition' CL 55 AMG model of May 2000, a steel friction area is much better for road car use. In this case, an alloy bowl was used to save weight in this composite disc setup.

The standard multi-spoke alloy wheels assigned to the SLK 55 AMG. This shot also gives us a good view of the vents in the side of the front spoiler.

specified, along with beefier anti-roll bars at both ends. The ESP and ASR programmes were also tweaked to give a more sporting driving experience, as well as enhanced traction off the line. Composite disc brakes were employed up front, 340mm (13.4in) in diameter, and coming ventilated and cross-drilled, like the one-piece 330mm (13.0in) versions at the rear of the car. Six-pot alloy calipers were called up for duty at the front, with four-pot items and a handbrake mechanism at the back; the Brake Assist system was duly tuned to suit. Finishing off the chassis package was a set of silver-painted 16-spoke AMG alloys. The front axle had 225/40 tyres mounted on 7.5J x 18 rims, while an 8.5J wheel was used at the back, shod with 245/35 rubber. Buyers were able to request the SA 782 18-inch AMG alloys as a no-cost option, which came with the same rim widths and tyre sizes.

As far as the body was concerned, the optional 772 styling kit formed the basis for the AMG transformation, with the same side skirts and rear valance being employed – even the narrow body-coloured strip between the exhaust pipes was carried over. However, while the front spoiler looked similar, it gained extra vents in the sides, beyond the fixed foglights (a chrome trim ring

A better shot of the front apron, as this also shows the black-painted bars in the main grille, and a glimpse of the gills that were added to the bonnet vents near the windscreen. It gives us a clear view of the fixed foglights, too, and one can just make out the lower grille insert pattern.

A close-up view of the AMG car's bonnet vents.

The tail-end of the SLK 55 AMG, with its darkened light lenses, rear lip spoiler and impressive exhaust pipe arrangement. The spoiler on the bootlid reduced lift over the back axle by as much as 36 per cent. Note that series-production cars had a square tow hook cover above the offside exhaust pipes.

was retained for these, by the way), which were actually for the oil cooler installation, and a lip spoiler was added to the trailing edge of the bootlid, which didn't come in the styling package. Other refinements included gloss black-painted aerofoils in the main air intake, a different pattern grille in the lower intake, darker rear combination light units, a darker third brakelight lens, and small, silver-coloured gills added to the bonnet vents, aping those found on the SLs.

Moving inside, the driver was greeted by stainless treadplates with 'AMG' script on them, an AMG steering wheel with a leather-wrapped ergonomic rim and shift paddles, an AMG instrument cluster with darker shrouds, red needles and unique calibrations (including a 320kph speedo, or the equivalent), a leather AMG gearshift, and Nappa leather trim on the seats, door linings/furniture and the storage box between the seats. The AMG sports seats, incidentally, came with heavier side bolsters with an Alcantara section to hold the shoulders firmly in place, and a more traditional insert pattern, complete with the AMG emblem in the backrest.

Manual air-conditioning and the interior lighting package were also included in the price, as well as seat heating, although the 'Airscarf' feature was still only available as an option. Actually, it's fair to say that there wasn't that much in the way of options for the AMG model. Apart from paint, audio and phone choices and the things already mentioned, one could upgrade by opting for the Bi-Xenon lights, headlight washers, the tyre pressure loss warning system, parameter parking, the heated windscreen washer setup, wipers with rain sensors, 'Parktronic,' the fully-automatic version of the air-conditioning system, infra-red remote control for the roof, auto dimming mirrors, folding door mirrors, an alarm, power seats and column adjustment with memory, Designo two-tone leather trim, Designo wood or leather minor trim components (including a Designo wood/leather gearknob), an Alcantara headlining, leather-trimmed roll-over bars, a garage door opener, fire extinguisher, fitted luggage, a roofrack, or a spacesaver spare – there was basically nothing else, except for a few dealer accessories.

Not long after the launch of the new M-Class, there was a slight price increase at the end of January 2005, taking the domestic SLK200 Kompressor up to €29,500 plus tax, the

Continued page 127

This page and opposite: A selection of shots showing a domestic SLK 55 AMG from the time of its launch. This car has the standard alloy wheels, red leather trim, and the Comand APS unit. All AMG models came with black seat surrounds, with the inserts providing buyers with a certain amount of individuality (Europeans had the choice of black, red, grey or beige inserts, but Americans had to do without the latter). Note also the standard aluminium dash trim, although European buyers could choose Designo wood or leather (the 728 Vavona wood option was not available) if they wanted.

Colour & trim guide

There were very few changes on the paint and trim side of things, so it's easier to chart them in one block for pre-face-lift cars. Please remember it was still possible to order certain paint and trim outside these catalogue options, but the list below (based on the domestic market) certainly covers the vast majority of vehicles.

Standard paintwork options

Black (040), Fire Opal, aka Mars Red (590), and Alabaster White (960). Alabaster White was replaced by Calcite White, aka Arctic White (650) in August 2006, in time for the 2007 season.

Metallic paintwork options

Obsidian Black (197), Jasper Blue, aka Orion Blue (345), Tanzanite Blue, aka Capri Blue (359), Amber Red, aka Bernstein Red or Firemist Red (548), Cubanite Silver, aka Pewter Silver (723), Tellurium Silver, aka Diamond Silver (762), Iridium Silver (775), Andradite Green, aka Everest Green (816), and Benitoite Blue, aka Caspian Blue (950). Amber Red was replaced by Thulite Red, aka Storm Red (541) in May 2006, along with the substitution of Andradite Green for Periclase Green, aka Jade Green (300).

Interior trim options

Black 'Sienna' cloth (081); regular leather in Black (871/801), Universe Blue (872), Orient Beige, aka Beige (875/805), Dusky Red, aka Red (877/807) and Alpaca Grey, aka Ash (878/808), and 'Nappa' leather in Tobacco Brown, aka Brown (844/864), Black (851/861), Orient Beige, aka Beige (855), Dusky Red, aka Red (857) and Alpaca Grey, aka Ash (858). From September 2004, one could also specify 'Designo' leather in Black (X11) and Classic Red/Black two-tone (X83), and 'Designo' leather combined with Alcantara in Black (X20) and Alpaca Grey (X21). The optional wood trim came with a choice of Vavona plus, from September 2004, 'Designo' Anthracite Tamo or 'Designo' Natural Poplar veneers. Universe Blue leather was dropped in May 2006.

NB. The black, beige, red and grey 'Nappa' leather shades were reserved for the SLK 55 AMG model until the 2007 MY, when black 'Nappa' was made available on the non-AMG grades, too (in this case, the 861 code was used, although 851 was retained for the AMG car); the red and grey hides came in two-tone colour schemes matched up with black on AMG models. There was also a change in the codes on regular leathers for the 2007 season, with 871 becoming 801, 875 becoming 805, 877 becoming 807, and 878 becoming 808. At the same time, the 844 code was changed to 864 to bring it in line.

Martin Bremer was responsible for selecting the various exterior and interior colours for the new SLK.

Some of the German accessories available in 2005. This page is particularly useful for alloy wheel identification.

SLK350 to €38,100, and the AMG model to €56,200. Costing a fraction over €1000 more than before, it was the AMG car that took the hardest hit during the price hike, although, to be fair, the increase was still below the rate of inflation nonetheless.

A few of the options were given different prices at the same time, with paintwork going up by between €30 and €105, for instance, and leather trim between €20 and €50 depending on which hide was chosen. Smaller increases were applied to the headlight washers, 'Thermotronic' air con, power seat function, Designo dash and roll-bar trim, the leather and leather/wood gearshift options, automatic dimming mirrors and garage door opener at €5 more; Bi-Xenon lights, the three audio units and sound system upgrade, 'Parktronic,' the leather/wood steering wheel, inner lighting package, seat heating, Alcantara headliner and roof-rack at €10 more, and the two automatic transmission options for the four- and six-cylinder cars at €20 more. It should be noted that the cost of alloy wheels also went up by €5 or €10 a set at this time, although the price of other wheel-related options remained unchanged. Finally, the mobile phone was €30 more expensive, with the wiring interface adding an extra €10 to the invoice compared to before. The only new items were a transparent windblocker and an aluminium base to suit the roof-rack, both of which had previously been offered as accessories. Given the SA 283 option code, the windblocker was priced at €255, while the rack attachment (SA 721) was listed at €350 plus tax.

On the subject of accessories, the list had blossomed over the course of a year. Prices increased across the board by a fraction, but black velour floormats were now joined by a heavily ribbed nylon mat set, and an uninspiring rubber set. The dedicated childseat had actually been around for some time, as had the replacement bulb set, but a 'Cleanbag' litter holder was made available for €37, along with a baggage strap set for €15, a chrome light surround for €19, and a chrome mirror base €119 for those who went for the existing chrome housing. For the more adventurous, there was a front lip spoiler for €305, a rear skirt for €254, and more alloy wheels to choose from – the 17-inch 'Elarneb' six-spoke rim at about €2000 a set, the darker-coloured 18-inch 'Sadachiba' five-spoke rim at €2440 a set, and the 18-inch 'Alresha' multi-spoke rim at around €2400 a set.

There had already been quite a few small changes made to the R171 SLKs, with the four-cylinder model gaining a new water pump in June 2004, a fresh exhaust manifold in the following month, and a revised Lambda sensor in August. The ECU was tweaked a couple of times during the autumn as well, and then again in January 2005, alongside the ESP control unit. The crankshaft was also modified a couple of weeks later, in February. The SLK350, meanwhile, inherited a new timing chain tensioner mechanism in September 2004, new cylinder heads in December, modified cylinder head gaskets in February 2005, and a fresh water pump and thermostat a month later, when the first of two timing casing modifications took place close together. All cars had been given a different windscreen almost a year earlier, in June 2004.

A fourth model

No sooner had the new price list been issued than another one was needed, for the 2005 Geneva Show played host to an additional SLK280 model, as well as a face-lifted C209 CLK series, a new B-Class, numerous C- and E-Class models, and the

This page and opposite: Selected images from the German catalogue issued in the second half of 2005, which includes the SLK280 (registration S-OE 6513). The international catalogue was basically the same, except for one double-page spread that avoided the grey trim shown here, and used a car with a red interior instead.

The 2005 Geneva Show had diesel versions of the SL and SLK on display, giving us a glimpse of the future. This is the SLK320 CDI Tri-Turbo, which was powered by a V6 diesel with three turbochargers – one on each bank close to the exhausts, and a third, larger one placed in the vee between the two banks. According to engine loads, the larger turbo gradually took over the lion's share of the work. It was a stunning blend of high-performance (0-60 in 5.3 seconds) and fuel economy.

Maybach 57S. This was certainly a busy period for the company, as a few weeks later, the new R-Class was launched at the New York Show in the States; like the B-Class, this model had first been shown as a concept car at the 2004 Paris Salon.

As it happens, the prices were unchanged on the existing three-car SLK line-up, the latest three-litre V6 (chassis code 171.454) simply filled the gap between the two non-AMG models, being listed at €33,950 plus taxes.

Despite the reference implying something smaller, the SLK280 employed the M272 E30 engine (Type 272.942), which was basically the same as the 3.5-litre unit used in the SLK350, except the 88.0mm bore and 82.1mm stroke measurements, which gave a displacement of 2996cc. With an 11.1:1 compression ratio, maximum power was quoted at 231bhp at 6100rpm (300rpm short of the red-line), while 221lbft of torque was developed at 3500rpm.

The SLK280 had the same gear ratios as the SLK350 on both gearboxes, and the same 3.27:1 final-drive, although the code numbers were different for the smaller-engined car – the six-speed SG-S400/5.3 manual gearbox was the Type 716.669, while the seven-speed W7C700 automatic transmission was the Type 722.999 model. Tipping the scales at 1440kg (3168lb), the SLK280 was around nine per cent more frugal than its V6 brethren, yet sporting the same governed top speed and being less than a second slower in the 0-60 dash.

As for equipment, only the wheels and braking system were different to the SLK350 – the rest of the specifications were the same as the other V6 car. Basically, the alloy wheels were the 16-inch SA 606 five-spoke rims that had been offered as an option on the SLK200 Kompressor model, while the brakes were unique to the SLK280. The front discs were ventilated and 300mm (11.8in) in diameter, which was a size between the existing specs on the non-AMG models, served by a single-piston caliper, while those at the rear were the same as those found on the four-cylinder car.

Options were also identical to the SLK350, apart from the alloy wheels, that is, with the 606 rims as standard, and the 17- and 18-inch rims available slightly cheaper than they were on the four-cylinder model. Incidentally, the only change applied to the option list was a price increase on the CD-changer (up by €20), and the accessory list was basically the same, too, with an iPod interface kit and fixed phone installation being the only newcomers.

Soon after production got under way, several changes were implemented on the two V6 engines. The timing chain case was modified in May – a couple of months after the first revision to this component, and new intake and exhaust valves were adopted in the same month. There was also a minor change to the casing for the manual transmission, and a new clutch was fitted from June 2005 onwards.

As for the four-cylinder engine, it gained a new dipstick design in June 2005, along with a fresh wiring harness. In the same month, all cars gained modified front wings, and a different A-pillar pressing incorporating part of the sill.

The American market

The Americans only had two grades to choose from initially – the SLK350 and the AMG model. At the end of the day, the cost of fuel was hardly an issue in the States, being $1.65 a gallon (or 43 cents a litre) at the time of the R171's announcement, which wasn't all that much different to 1990 prices. Interestingly, though, the cost of regular petrol rose steeply thereafter, which would explain why the smaller-engined SLK280 was such a hit the moment it became available.

Anyway, the R171 SLK went on sale in September as a true 2005 Model Year vehicle, enabling the US marketing men to make the most of the undeniable fascination attached to the AMG variant, which followed soon after in November. As such, given the stream of media attention following the Detroit Show at the start of the year, the lead-up to sales was almost as long as the R170 one had been!

The cars sold in America were much the same as their European counterparts, with the minor lighting differences we've described before (the extra amber running lights on the trailing edge of the front bumper being easy to spot) and revised calibrations on the speedometer to suit road markings (the SLK350 had a 160mph speedo, while the AMG car had a 200mph one, even though the electronic limiter made this seem frivolous) being the main items. Wheel specifications and standard equipment levels were also subtly different, as were the various option packages, so we may as well go through the whole list to clarify things.

A six-speed manual gearbox was standard on the $46,250 SLK350, with a seven-speed automatic transmission adding $1390 to the invoice. The 7AT gearbox with 'AMG -Speedshift' was standard on the $60,500 SLK 55 AMG, as in other markets, with no manual option available.

All cars came with projector headlights with an 'Auto' setting, front and rear foglights, ABS with Brake Assist, power steering,

Cover from the first US catalogue.

One of the first R171 press pictures released in the States. Note the standard wheels for the SLK350, and the running light arrangement, which was unique to the North American cars.

ESP and ASR, programmable night security illumination, heated windscreen washer nozzles, a heated rear window with timer, power windows with tinted glass, heated power mirrors, manual air-conditioning with the 'Rest' function, a cloth windblocker, additional knee-level airbags, leather upholstery, a multi-function leather-wrapped steering wheel and leather gearshift, a SmartKey with integrated engine immobiliser and remote control keyless entry controls, cruise control, the Audio 20 radio/CD unit, cupholders, velour floormats, stainless treadplates, an ashtray and cigarette lighter, an alarm, the 'TeleAid' system, and a spacesaver spare.

The 268bhp (SAE) V6 car had 17-inch ten-spoke wheels, while the 355bhp (SAE) AMG machine added the full AMG bodykit and detailing, 18-inch monobloc 16-spoke alloy wheels (the 782 five-spoke rims were available as a no-cost option), a lowered suspension, variable-assistance PAS and power adjustment (with memory) on the column, shift keys on the ergonomic steering wheel, auto dimming mirrors, remote control for the roof, the upgraded interior lighting package, Nappa leather trim, heated sports seats with power adjustment and memory settings, and aluminium dash trim and AMG gauges.

Individual options for the V6 model included the AMG's sports suspension ($420), run-flat tyres with a pressure loss warning system ($250) and heated seats ($680), while the AMG car had the 'Airscarf' at $350 (it was only available as part of a package for the SLK350); a CD-changer was listed for both cars at $420.

As for packages, the $4000 AMG Sport Package (SA 321) could be bought for the V6 model, bringing with it the basic AMG bodykit, a 17-inch version of the familiar five-spoke AMG alloys, an uprated suspension, and steering wheel shift buttons on automatic vehicles. The $1125 Comfort Package (standard on the SLK 55 AMG) came with eight-way power seats and power steering column adjustment, combined with a memory function for these and the outside mirrors; the $950 Heating Package added heated seats and the 'Airscarf' option, while the $700 Trim Package (also for the SLK350 only) contained Vavona wood components to enhance the appearance of the steering wheel, handbrake, dashboard and door handles.

Packages suitable for both SLKs included the $975 Lighting Package, which contained Bi-Xenon headlights and heated

Continued page 136

headlamp washers, as well as cornering lights on cars with the regular front spoiler. There was also an Entertainment Package with the 'Comand' head unit linked to a surround sound system and a CD-changer; for a further $1200, this $1600 set could

Above, opposite and overleaf: The 2006 US brochure basically used the same artwork inside as the 2005 version, with the specifications pages changed to suit. Among other things, this selection of shots show an SLK350 with the AMG Sport Package, a manual SLK350 with Vavona wood trim, and a good view of the kosher AMG car.

PAGE 6:7
SLK 350
EXTERIOR
365 first drives per year.
Every day holds great promise, especially when it starts with the invigorating rumble of 268 horsepower through a sport-tuned dual exhaust. Slip the 6-speed manual into first, notice the smooth precision as you ease out the clutch, and marvel as the wide powerband of the SLK 350's 3.5-liter DOHC V-6 presses you firmly into your seat. A quick tug of the short-throw shifter and the momentum continues to build. A corner is quickly dispatched by a tap of race-bred front brakes with 4-piston calipers and the bite of staggered-width 17" multispoke alloy wheels wearing high-performance tires.[1] Then aim for the horizon and marvel as the 4-wheel independent multilink suspension fluidly responds to every twist the road presents. For those who believe in seizing the day, there's no better place to grip it than the leather-wrapped wheel of the SLK 350.
1 Z-rated tires are optimized for performance driving and may provide reduced ride comfort, increased tire noise, substantially increased treadwear and greater susceptibility to damage compared with H-rated tires.
SLK 350 shown in optional Iridium Silver metallic with optional AMG Sport and Lighting Packages.

PAGE 16:17
SLK-CLASS
HANDLING
The last time you pulled .94g you had to wait two hours in line.
Welcome to Driverland, conveniently located anywhere an SLK is found. The fun starts almost immediately, because as impressive as ultimate cornering grip may be, it's how an SLK gets there that's equally important. The accuracy of rack-and-pinion steering lets you point its Formula One-inspired nose exactly where you want it. A near-ideal front-to-rear weight balance delivers the same thrill whether diving in for that late apex or unwinding the wheel as you accelerate out. Outstanding torsional rigidity helps the 4-wheel multilink suspension work with razor-sharp precision, allowing the high-performance tires[1] to be pushed eagerly into every corner. And with our standard ESP stability control, you can explore the SLK's awe-inspiring handling with confidence-inspiring poise.[2] It all adds up to an experience that only the SLK can provide – turning rubber, metal and tarmac into your own personal theme park with one of the world's most exhilarating rides.

PAGE 10:11
SLK 350
INTERIOR
0
afterthoughts.
In the SLK, form doesn't just meet function – they engage in a passionate relationship. The prominent speedometer and tachometer reside in dramatically angled tubes that add style while helping to reduce glare – especially important in a roadster. The 3-spoke multifunction sport steering wheel puts numerous controls at your fingertips – vital when spirited driving is the priority. A door pull that is a piece of modern architecture is home to seamlessly integrated power window switches. Sport seats with leather upholstery reveal Silver-painted magnesium seat frames chosen for both their light weight and exceptional strength. Intuitive seat-shaped controls adjust the optional power seats. Everything lies within reach, and begs to be touched.

PAGE 22:23
SLK 55 AMG
PERFORMANCE / EXTERIOR STYLING
AMG
355
hp
period.
Affordable exotic. The term gets thrown around, but does any vehicle truly live up to it? For your consideration, we offer the SLK 55 AMG – perhaps the most affordable car worthy of the label. With a handcrafted 5,439-cc V-8 pumping out 355 hp and 376 lb-ft of peak torque and the first 7-speed automatic ever offered on an AMG model, you can reach 60 mph in a scant 4.9 seconds! Bend curves to your will with an AMG-calibrated suspension and feel the arresting performance of 6-piston composite front calipers grasping perforated 13.4" brake discs. After you've admired the unique AMG-design lower bodywork, the subtle rear lip spoiler, the AMG multispoke 18" wheels with high-performance tires and the sophisticated growl departing the four polished stainless-steel exhaust tips, you might just decide this is the only exotic you'll ever need – at any price.

PAGE 24:25
SLK 55 AMG
COCKPIT
AMG
Your brain runs at 200 mph.
Can your car measure up?
The more time you spend inside the SLK 55 AMG, the more you realize how much thought went into it. Your immediate impulse for manual mode shifting is met by ideally placed fingertip controls on the thick-rimmed, leather-wrapped steering wheel. Your cognitive center's demand for information is fed by the rapid sweep of red indicators across a 200-mph speedometer1 and 7,000 rpm tachometer. Your brain's pleasure center revels in the touch of supple two-tone Nappa leather with Alcantara trim on AMG sport seats. It's the perfect environment for those who like to think fast.
1 Obey all speed laws. Top speed electronically limited to 155 mph.

PAGE 28:29
SLK-CLASS
INNOVATIONS: AIRSCARF
72° of freedom.
If you drive a convertible, you know it – that point when it gets too late in the day or in the season, and the top must come up. It's like being told to go inside when you still want to play. That's why Mercedes-Benz created AIRSCARF. A soothing stream of heated air to your neck, head and shoulders helps take the bite out of chilly top-down conditions. With individual 3-stage temperature controls and airflow that automatically adjusts to your driving speed, it's never been more fun to stay out late.
SLK 350 shown in optional Iridium Silver metallic with optional AMG Sport and Lighting Packages.

be upgraded to include a DVD-based navigation system. Finally, there was the Premium Package, with automatic air-conditioning, speed-sensitive parameter parking steering, rain sensors for the wipers, auto dimming mirrors, remote control for the top and windows, upgraded interior lighting, and a garage door opener. Because so many of these things were already included on the AMG car, this package was listed at $750 on that model, instead of the normal $1450.

With the exception of Cubanite Silver (aka Pewter), the coachwork colour palette was the same as the one in Germany, even if the names used were different. As for interior trim, again, the five regular colour options were there, although there was no cloth trim or brown Nappa hide listed; AMG buyers had the choice of black, beige, black/red or black/grey Nappa upholstery. The only wood trim available was the Vavona option, unless one ordered one of the three off-the-peg Designo models.

These Designo models followed an established pattern as far as the States was concerned, being offered on both cars as a $7950 package. The Espresso Edition (code 181) brought forth Designo Black Mocha paintwork, a black interior with Designo Sand Nappa leather and Natural Poplar wood trim, Sand Nappa hide on the roll-over bars, and black Designo velour floormats. The Graphite Edition (235) was much the same, with Designo Graphite paint replacing the Mocha shade, and Designo Graphite Nappa leather taking the place of the Sand-coloured trim components. The Chablis Edition (263) did the same thing, employing attractive Designo Chablis gold metallic paintwork and Designo Chablis Nappa leather in this case. All three Designo models required the heated seat option to be fitted.

Naturally, dealers were more than happy to top up the extras list, offering things like car covers, chrome mirror housings, telephone and satellite radio connections and so on, as well as some attractive alloy wheels – the 'Sadachiba' 18-inch rims and 17-inch SA 639 alloys were illustrated in the main catalogue.

So, what did the press think? After testing an early SLK350 for *Car & Driver*, Tony Quiroga reported: "Our SLK350 had a precise and rewarding six-speed manual. The shifter feels like the love child of a Honda S2000 and BMW M3. There's a slightly rubbery feel as in the M3, and the throws aren't quite as short as the S2000's, but the effort is light and positive. Shift as fast as you like, because the gearbox synchros feel unbeatable. Pedal placement is good, although the smaller-shoed will wish the brake pedal was just a bit closer to the accelerator to facilitate heel-and-toe downshifts. It's easy to match revs in the SLK, as the engine responds instantly to accelerator contact, and, unlike most modern engines, the SLK loses revs quickly. The engine has a willing personality that is perfectly suited to a manual transmission – you'll definitely not regret choosing it over the automatic.

"Even with staggered gumballs, the SLK resists understeer unlike any other Mercedes. At low speeds, power oversteer is readily available, and at higher speeds, you'll find some reassuring understeer, but it's never of the terminal variety. Grip is plentiful at 0.87g, and roll is kept in check. The ride is now sports car stiff, but the SLK will absorb large impacts without jarring the occupants. Toss it through a few corners, and it immediately feels smaller than its predecessor, despite its larger dimensions.

"Top down, wind rushes over and around the large windshield. To avoid buffeting from the rear, Mercedes throws in a see-through fabric shroud that attaches to the two roll hoops. But the shroud muddies visibility as effectively as it blocks the wind. After only a few miles with it attached, we decided to remove it, as looking through the rearview mirror made us think we had developed cataracts. Another annoyance with the SLK stems from the dimly-lit radio and climate control readouts. With the top down, even a small amount of sunlight makes the display unreadable; brighter lighting would fix that ... Controls are straightforward, and the overall [interior] design is original and satisfying.

"The SLK will likely continue to be purchased for its appearance and cachet rather than for its newfound sports car soul, but for those who seek a dynamically satisfying performer, the SLK will not disappoint."

Tony Swan chipped in with: "This second generation SLK is a whole order of magnitude better – better-looking, better on the road, a real grown-up GT. It makes the original SLK look like little more than an appealing novelty."

And at *Motor Trend*, Todd Lassa noted: "The car's 3.5 V6, stout chassis, and well-balanced suspension make the SLK an ideal sports car for mountain road drives. It's crisper and sharper in every input versus the old SLK320. Quick, precise steering with good feedback and light feel is largely due to a switch from recirculating-ball to rack-and-pinion. The short-throw six-speed manual has a snicky, quick action, making it one of the best gearboxes in the sports car biz, replacing what must have been among the worst. Ride and handling are well-refined, without much compromise to either. You feel bumps and expansion strips on the highways, but there's enough compliance to keep them from being uncomfortable. And in mountain curves, the suspension rolls just enough to lean into a hard bite, giving your backside time to warn your hands to respond to oversteer."

The same magazine brought together an SLK 55 AMG and Porsche Boxster S in early 2005. It stated: "Mercedes estimates the SLK55 will hit 60mph from rest in 4.9 seconds, but we clipped off 0-60 runs in 4.5. The handbuilt V8 sounds glorious, exhaling through its four stovepipe-size exhausts. This motor gurgles out a tanker-load of torque, and the close-ratio seven-speed gearbox ensures that it's always in the fattest part of the rev range. The rpm fall-off after each shift is minimal."

However, the added weight and bulk of the engine meant that the old V6-engined AMG model was quicker through the slalom, and the Porsche was much faster, both through the slalom course, and out on the track, too. A test note read: "The SLK55's chassis is more than up to the job, but it feels as it if needs wider tyres." But ride quality had come under fire in other SLK 55 AMG road tests, which raised a question mark over adding extra rubber. On saying that, those involved in this particular test were happy enough with the NVH levels, and praised the AMG when tootling along in the countryside.

Although only 1000 AMGs were imported by the US distributors in the first season, adding rarity value, the *Motor Trend* team still went for the Porsche: "[Nothing], however, diminishes the SLK 55 AMG's considerable, iron-pumping appeal. If the Boxster is an X-Acto knife, this Maximum Strength SLK is a designer meat cleaver. And, man, does it cleave, especially in a straight line, though there's an extra layer of insulation between it and the driver as compared with the Porsche. The Benz's edgier visual statement, trick retract-o-top, faultless high-speed stability, symphonic exhaust notes, industry-leading transmission and AMG-level of exclusivity earn it a bunch as a first-class choice for a fast cruise across the country – or a slow one, down the Sunset Boulevard."

Before moving on, it's worth quoting a couple of paragraphs from a *Car & Driver* test that brought together the SLK350, Porsche Boxster S, Chrysler Crossfire SRT-6 and Chevrolet Corvette, in which the Mercedes came third. "My, what a difference a generation makes," the magazine said. "After putting its old parts out for the scavengers, the SLK receives a chassis that is light on its feet, tight in the structure, and immensely responsive to a driver's whims.

"Lapping up the open road, the SLK demonstrates resolute body control but no brittleness to the ride as you'll find with the Crossfire. The nose cuts its arcs with go-where-she's-aimed steering, the brakes working hard and progressively as we ground them to squeaking slivers on the track. A lot of horseplay slips past the stability-control computer before it intervenes. Suddenly, Mercedes makes sports cars!

"So why the third place? The Corvette has overwhelming firepower, plain and simple. A few complained about confusion with the SLK's button-dense dash. And all drivers felt the Benz's big steering wheel was hiding something, losing a few bytes of scrub data to a slightly cushy mechanism. We might not have noticed were the Boxster not along to demonstrate perfectly organic steering. However, as an everyday please-me machine, the new Benz earns a solid silver star."

When the 228bhp (SAE) SLK280 arrived Stateside in July, classed as an early 2006 model, the vast majority of the standard equipment was the same as that listed against the SLK350. However, it came fitted with 16-inch five-spoke aluminium alloy wheels instead of 17-inch rims, and the less exotic braking system adopted on the three-litre cars in Europe. At $42,900, the SLK280 was $4050 less than an SLK350, and an incredible ten times cheaper than an SLR! In fact, although $61,500 may seem a lofty price for the 2006 SLK 55 AMG, it was still below the S-Class entry point, so certainly offered good value-for-money for sports car enthusiasts.

A few option prices changed, including the cost of the Sport Package increasing by $40, the 7AT gearbox going up by $20, and the run-flat tyres, Heating Package, 'Airscarf' heater, Trim Package, heated seats and CD-changer by $10. The lowered suspension option was deleted, while other packages were realigned, with the Comfort Package now costing $1300, but including the speed-sensitive PAS and auto dimming mirrors as extra items. These had previously been part of the Premium

The Carlsson CK20, based on the SLK200 Kompressor. As always, the Mercedes tuning business was thriving ... (Courtesy Carlsson)

Package, which was reduced to $1200 as a result. Likewise, the CD-changer was taken out of the Entertainment Package, but even this couldn't prevent a $100 price hike on this popular option; an iPod integration kit was offered as a new accessory to suit, while the hands-free communication setup cost a hefty $925.

The big news, however, was the availability of the $6800 AMG Performance Package (SA 030) for the SLK 55 AMG, which came with uprated brakes and suspension, 18-inch AMG alloys, a sports steering wheel with Alcantara accents, carrbonfibre trim, and a new limiter to allow a higher top speed. Dealers were quoting an October delivery, although strangely it was not featured in the catalogues, only in price lists. A similar kit was duly sold through official dealers in Europe for the 2007 season.

The only other major change for US buyers was the loss of the blue leather trim option, although brown Nappa took its place on the colour charts, priced at $400. In addition, while Orion Blue and Everest Green were dropped, the Pewter shade was added to the coachwork colour options.

The rhd markets

The right-hand drive market had always revolved around the UK. In an interesting development, the EU opened up the possibility of ordering a car abroad and having it built with rhd, and then shipped to Britain. It was a kind of grey market, but a higher surcharge in mainland Europe soon curbed the practice. With faster deliveries than the days of yore (but still a 12-month waiting list), there was little point in going beyond a UK dealer for British residents.

The R171 was listed in the British Isles from July 2004, with the SLK200 Kompressor commanding £27,470 (a touch more than the expected £27,000, and a couple of grand up on the equivalent R170) and the SLK350 priced at £34,270. Automatic transmission was £1450 extra on the four-cylinder car, or £1770 on the six, although air-conditioning and the Audio 20 unit were fitted as standard. Popular options included Bi-Xenon headlights at £710, AMG alloys at £1820, leather trim at £900, the 'Airscarf' heater at £340, remote control for the roof at £90, and a CD-changer at £350.

Autocar tried a manual four-cylinder model for size, and having recorded a top speed of 142mph (227kph) and a standing-quarter time of 16.2 seconds, found that: "This new Mercedes will be a revelation to drivers used to the previous generation. Whatever the road, the new SLK displays a level of agility and composure that really impresses." Mid-range performance was more than acceptable thanks to the boost from the supercharger, but it was the chassis that wooed the testers, especially the supple ride.

While there were plenty of other open cars in this price range, such as the Honda S2000, Lotus Elise 111R, BMW Z4 2.5i, Alfa Romeo Spider and Audi TT Roadster, as well as the significantly cheaper NB-series Mazda MX-5 to consider, the magazine concluded: "Mercedes has created a package so complete that, for many potential buyers, finding a reason not to choose it over the competition will be difficult."

As it happens, the £50,530 AMG model was also listed from the off, although it wasn't actually available until February 2005. Four months later, the line-up was completed by the SLK280. Priced at £30,975, it slotted into a Mercedes range that started at £13,655, and bracketed the other two SLKs – now listed at £28,045 and £34,930 respectively. Prices increased by £25 across the board at the end of the year, but it was hardly a painful hike, especially when fuel was at a record high. If one could afford the 88p asked for a litre of unleaded in the summer (£4 a gallon), £25 was a drop in the ocean! The relatively good 25.4mpg average recorded by *Autocar* when testing the SLK200 Kompressor would have been welcomed, that's for sure.

As for Japan, the venerable Jack Yamaguchi went to the press launch in Majorca on behalf of *Car Graphic*, and declared himself happy with the sophisticated looks of the car. He also enjoyed the mountain roads, praising the six-speed gearbox and the good ride/handling compromise offered by the sports suspension and 17-inch wheels, and was surprised by the amount of oversteer available before the ESP kicked in. He was less than enamoured by the confusing abundance of switches, however.

The R171 arrived in the Land Of The Rising Sun just in time for the 2005 season, with the same line-up as America. The SLK350 (automatic only, but available in lhd or rhd guise) was listed at 6,720,000 yen, with the AMG model (AT and lhd only) priced at 9,597,000 yen. Although both were significantly

Japanese advertising showing the contemporary CLK series – a four-seater alternative to the SLK.

more expensive than their R170 predecessors, for the record, contemporary Mercedes prices ranged from 2,373,000 yen for the basic A-Class car all the way up to 27,405,000 yen for the mighty SL 65 AMG in Japan, while competitors like the BMW Z4 commanded between 4,179,000 and 5,900,000 yen, depending on the grade, which was much the same as the cost of an Audi TT. The Porsche Boxster was perhaps closest in pricing policy, with the entry-level machine carrying a 5,775,000 yen tag, and the automatic S a 7,455,000 yen sticker price.

Above and below: A special effort was made to celebrate ten years of the Designo brand at the 2005 Frankfurt Show. This SLK features Designo paint and trim.

Heading south to Australia, the new car was priced at a similar level to its predecessor when it was released in August 2004, with the SLK200 Kompressor at $83,800 in six-speed manual guise, or $86,900 with a five-speed automatic. The manual SLK350 was $109,400 (quickly revised to $110,900), while the seven-speed automatic version was priced at $112,500. These four- and six-cylinder variants were duly joined by the 7AT-equipped SLK 55 AMG in January 2005, which commanded $161,900 at a time when the Porsche Boxster ranged from $107,400 to $132,500 and the cheapest Benz SL was around $210,000.

The 2006 MY proper

The Mercedes-Benz stand at the 2005 Frankfurt Show had a lot of exhibits focusing on hybrid technology and the AMG brand, especially seeing as the latter had only just unveiled its new

6.2-litre M156 V8 engine. This high-revving 510bhp NA unit started finding its way into cars during the autumn, and duly went on to win several awards. The show also witnessed the public debut of the all-new W221 S-Class, featuring all manner of leading edge technologies, along with a new M273 32v V8, and a special feature to celebrate ten years of Designo customizing.

Jürgen Schrempp stepped down as Chairman of the Board of Management at DaimlerChrysler AG at the end of 2005, with Dr Dieter Zetsche taking his place at the helm from the first day of 2006. Zetsche, it will be remembered, was one of the key figures in getting the SLK project rolling. Shortly after he took up his new position, the new GL-Class SUV was launched at the 2006 Detroit Show, along with the eco-friendly 'Bluetec' diesel powertrain.

Meanwhile, the engineering team at Mercedes kept updating parts as and when, with the four-cylinder SLK gaining a new ECU, cylinder head and rocker arms in August 2005, along with a fresh set of valves. The supercharger was modified in the following month, while January 2006 brought with it another ECU change, followed by the adoption of a new accelerator pedal assembly.

With all cars having gained a new set of plastic trim pieces behind the roll-over bars (to cover the roof mechanism), February saw the release of another price list for the SLK, although there wasn't much to write home about: The cost of the SLK200 Kompressor and SLK280 rose by €200, that of the SLK350 by €250, while the sticker price went up by €550 on the AMG grade, although the parameter steering feature became a factory fitment on the AMG car (as in the USA), which covered a lot of the price hike on that particular model. This saw the SLK range now starting at €29,700, with the flagship SLK 55 AMG commanding €56,750, or €65,830 if one includes tax.

There were nonetheless a few hidden costs, such as the interior lighting package moving from the standard specification list to the options list on the SLK280, while the windblocker became a €70 option on all cars. In addition, the ashtray was a €25 extra instead of a no-cost option, and likewise the cupholder insert went from NCO status to a €30 option; the spacesaver spare also became a €50 option.

The cost of a few regular options increased, too. Headlight washers, seat heaters, automatic dimming mirrors and the rain sensor went up by €5; the 'Thermotronic' air-conditioning, 'Parktronic' system, winter tyres, Designo trim for the roll-over bars and dash, the two APS audio units, speaker set, folding mirrors and fire extinguisher all went up by €10, and the Alcantara headliner by €15. Metallic paint cost €5 more, except the Designo shades, which each went up by €50. The price of a mobile phone also increased a touch, along with its installation bill. Only a couple of items escaped a modest hike on the accessory listing, although the chrome grille bars went down in price by over €30 once tax had been added, which was a very unusual scenario.

2006 Geneva Show premieres included the CLS 63 AMG and CLK 63 AMG models, as well as a face-lifted version of the R230 SL. In the following month, the face-lifted 211-series E-Class made its debut in New York, and yet another price list was issued for the SLK. Careful inspection revealed the addition of a 'Racetimer' feature on the AMG car, and a new chrome key for all cars, which was far more attractive than the old black plastic one. The 7G-Tronic Sport gearbox with a manual mode switch and proper shift paddles was added for the V6s at the same time, priced at €2120, although the SA 427 and 428 option code numbers were retained. As it happens, the cost of the shift buttons actually went up by €30 in April. Furthermore, in addition to the adoption of a new centre console lid (the one between the seats had gained something of a reputation for coming loose), May 2006 saw a couple of paintwork changes, and the end of the blue leather option.

There were also more mechanical changes, such as a new intake manifold and vacuum pump for the SLK200 Kompressor model in May, as well as a new wiring harness for the engine. As it happens, the V6s had been given a new wiring harness at the end of 2005, and inherited new front pipes for the exhaust system in May 2006, plus redesigned ignition coils a month later. In addition, the SLK350 was given fresh front brake calipers and pads in January, and a new differential unit in March.

The season was rounded off with the 150-off Mercedes-Benz SLR McLaren 722 Edition going on sale in July 2006. Handbuilt by McLaren, it had 650bhp on tap. A few days later, the AMG Performance Studio opened for business, providing greater individuality for customers, as well as marketing limited run models – the SLK would actually provide the basis for the first ...

An SL350 from the time of the 2006 face-lift. Although the powerplant was similar to that of the SLK, the pricing policy took the SL into another world.

The SLK Black Series

As it happens, the AMG Performance Studio's SLK 55 AMG Black Series model was fairly straightforward to produce, as most of the main components had already been created for a run of 35 cars built for a Far East investor. These special machines were not road-registered – they were simply built to allow a select few the chance to drive something exotic at certain motorsport events, the first being the 2006 Malaysian Grand Prix, held in mid-March that year. While the engine was untouched, the brakes, suspension and the various oil cooling systems were modified to suit track work in a hot environment, and the transmission was setup to enhance manual shifting. The regular folding roof was replaced by an unpainted carbonfibre hardtop with a plastic rear window, which saved around 25kg (55lb), while a set of ultra-lightweight 19-inch multi-spoke forged alloys, modified exhaust, and carbonfibre shell seats and door linings easily cancelled out the weight of the larger fuel tank, rollcage and fire extinguisher; overall, a weight reduction of 37kg (82lb) was possible. With the

The limited-run Asian racing model that formed the basis for the Black Series model – officially, the first AMG Performance Studio creation.

Above and left: Early press pictures of the SLK 55 AMG Black Series variant, with the interior shot showing the velour seat trim option. Note also the heavier shift paddles on the steering wheel, adopted on all Sport transmissions.

battery moving to the boot and the weight saved in the roof area, the vehicle was much better balanced, too, with a significant shift in the car's centre of gravity.

The €107,300 (including tax) Black Series model, available from July to help promote the newly-opened Performance Studio, essentially brought together all the experience gained in fielding the US Performance Package and the Asian racer, and then had a little spice added with some modest engine tuning thrown in.

The main features were the fixed carbonfibre roof (with the centre section finished in such a way as to highlight the material),

The stuff that every racing driver's dreams are made of: carbon fibre. If you wish, we can include a whole package's worth of it! The interior package comprises the instrument cluster tubes, the surrounds for the buttons on the steering wheel, the door sill panels with AMG lettering, as well as the selector lever bearing the AMG emblem.

By opting for the exterior carbon-fibre package, you will find the exclusive material adorning the crossways fins in the radiator grille, the exterior mirror housings and the AMG spoiler lip on the boot lid.

An interesting page from the SLK 55 AMG Black Series catalogue, stating that if the buyer opted for the Carbon Exterior Package, the mirror housings, grille aerofoils and rear spoiler came in this exclusive material.

Above, left and opposite: Detail shots of the Black Series, including the 400bhp V8 engine, gearshift, front air dam and wheel design. The final picture is ideal for showing the lightweight carbonfibre hardtop.

the 19-inch wheels off the Asian special covered by wider, carbonfibre wings at the front (complete with unique air outlets on the trailing edge), a more aggressive front air dam with the foglights being replaced by grilles to feed the additional transmission oil and PAS oil coolers (a stronger power steering pump was fitted), carbonfibre vents on the sides of the front spoiler to suit the engine oil cooler, an adjustable suspension, the larger brakes sold in the Performance Package, and a brace bar in the engine bay. It's worth noting that the alloy wheels (8.5J with 235/35 tyres up front, and 9.5J shod with 265/30 rubber at the rear), despite being larger, were actually 4kg (9lb) lighter than the regular 18-inch AMG rims; Pirelli P-Zero Corsa tyres could be specified as a no-cost option, incidentally. Inside, there were lightweight bucket seats trimmed in leather or black velour (minus the airbags to save weight), carbonfibre trim on the dashboard, doors and handbrake, a black rooflining, and a new leather/Alcantara steering wheel.

New intake manifolds and filters, a modified exhaust manifold and revised valve timing released a few extra horses, with the engine now developing 400bhp at 5750rpm, and 384lbft of torque at 3750rpm. Weighing in at 1495kg (3289lb), which was 45kg (99lb) lighter than the stock vehicle, with the Sport gearbox and its manual modes, the 5.4-litre NA machine could dismiss the 0-60 dash in 4.5 seconds before going on to a top speed of 175mph (280kph).

Reliable road tests are few and far between. The UK's *Top Gear* was not impressed, that's for sure, and even went so far as to call the Black Series machine "pointless." Indeed, other tests have stated that the standard car was already hairy enough, as well as pushing the limits on traction and comfort. But whatever the reality of the situation, with modern road conditions being what they are, there will always be a market for highly-tuned exotics – the Black Series had just as many fans as critics.

Rhd recap

Prices were carried over for the UK 2006 Model Year, with the SLKs ranging from £28,070 to £50,555. For reference, the SL350 was £61,600 at the start of the season, and duly went up to £62,885, which tends to point towards the SLK350 offering very good value. For those that like collecting figures, the SLK 55 AMG Black Series was available for £73,350, which was about the same cost as an SL500.

A little while later, Mercedes-Benz UK increased its SLK prices for 2007, with the SLK200 Kompressor now listed at £28,750, the SLK280 at £31,775, the SLK350 at £35,780, and the AMG car at £51,580. This was at a time when the Porsche Boxster was priced at between £33,000 and £44,000, depending on the grade.

There had been no change to the Japanese SLK line-up, including pricing, until the end of 2005, when the SLK280 augmented the range. Coming with an automatic transmission and right-hand drive only, this was introduced at 6,090,000 yen, while the cost of SLK350 motoring increased to 7,140,000 yen. At the same, the AMG model was given a 10,101,000 yen sticker price – up nearly half-a-million yen from a year previous. By the spring of 2006, the SLK200 Kompressor (AT and rhd only) had also joined the Japanese line-up, priced at 5,460,000 yen, which was about the same as a C230 estate.

Mercedes-Benz Japan started rounding figures off in the spring of 2007, with the SLK200 Kompressor now listed at 5,520,000 yen, the SLK280 at 6,150,000 yen, the SLK350 at 7,220,000 yen, and the SLK 55 AMG commanding 10,200,000 yen.

The SLK280 was introduced to the Australian market in August 2005, although its sticker price had already increased by the time the traditional 2006 Model Year got under way. For 2006, the SLK200 Kompressor was listed at $85,300, or $88,400 in automatic guise, while the new SLK280 was $97,900, and the SLK350 $13,000 more (an automatic transmission added $3500 to the invoice on both of these grades). At the top of the range, there was the SLK 55 AMG, which was $163,400 – almost double the cost of a basic entry-level model. At least these prices were carried over for the 2007 season.

The 2007 season

The 2007 Model Year saw the base price on all SLKs rise by €200, taking the entry-level model to €29,900 plus tax, while the flagship AMG variant was now priced at €56,950. The SLK 55 AMG gained some proper, much larger aluminium shift paddles at this time, which were far easier to use than the earlier versions. There was also a new option for the AMG model – the €4500 Performance Package (SA P30), which, although a year behind the US release date, added larger 360mm (14.2in) diameter composite brakes for the front axle, 18-inch five double-spoke AMG alloys (featuring 7.5J rims with 225/40 tyres up front, and 8.5Js shod with 245/35 rubber at the back), uprated suspension tuning, a new steering wheel in black leather and Alcantara, and carbonfibre trim pieces.

The regular line was not overlooked, though, gaining a new Sport Package (SA code 952) that brought with it 18-inch alloys with a six double-spoke design and special centres (the same rim and tyres sizes as those specified in the Performance Package were used), larger brakes with cross-drilled front discs and 'Mercedes-Benz' lettering on the calipers, and the lowered sports suspension, although quoting the SA 485 code allowed the owner to retain the stock chassis setup; there was also a sports air filter for the V6s, giving an altogether throatier noise. As for

An SLK 55 AMG with the P30 Performance Package.

This page and overleaf: A domestic SLK200 Kompressor model with the Sport Package. Note the red stitching on the upholstery, and the sporty red seatbelts. The steering column-mounted shift paddles, like those of the AMG model, were much improved on the regular cars, adopted on the production line in June 2006 in time for the 2007 season.

S CR 5396

the cosmetic side, there was a darker surround on the headlights, an AMG boot spoiler, red stitching on the leather steering wheel and gearshift, as well as the seats and door furniture, a black headliner, red seatbelts (the U17 code brought back black ones), red edging on the velour floormats, red pointers on the instruments, black dash trim surrounding the steering column, and a carbonfibre style insert for the passenger side. The Sport Package cost €1390 on the SLK200 Kompressor, €150 less on the SLK280, and €990 on the SLK350. Opting for this package also made the AMG 782 alloys cheaper – the cost was reduced to €600 a set, which meant a saving of over €800.

Other than a different Bluetooth telephone connection offered by dealers, there were no other changes to the factory options or accessory listings, both in terms of the various goodies available and their prices. There were a few revisions on the colour charts, however, with Alabaster White being replaced by Calcite White (or Arctic White), while the code numbers were changed on the leather options. In addition, black Nappa leather became available on the non-AMG cars, augmenting the existing brown Nappa hide option. There was also a new 'Alarm' warning sticker for the window, and the power seat switches were modified.

In America, too, with new red and white paint being introduced on the production line in Germany, the colour charts looked quite different, with Arctic White, Black and Mars Red in non-metallic shades, and Diamond Silver, Iridium Silver, Pewter,

Left and below: The US catalogue for the 2007 season was again pretty much the same as the original version. This is the cover, and the section relating to the off-the-peg Designo versions of the SLK offered in the States.

A controversial set of adverts for the SLK 55 AMG. Some said the series mocked the poor, but that was certainly not the intention, or reality, for that matter. PC thoughts aside, like the toupee, they are actually quite humorous ...

Obsidian Black, Capri Blue, Caspian Blue and Storm Red in the metallics listing; there was a $700 premium for metallic paint, incidentally. The interior options stayed the same as the 2006 US offerings, which made life easy.

The 2007 V6 SLKs were offered at prices just $450 higher than those of the last season in the States, which was reasonable enough considering speed-sensitive PAS became a standard fitment, while the SLK 55 AMG was $1000 more, commanding $62,500 from October 2006 onwards. Most of the regular options were given a small price hike of between $10 and $25, although the AMG Sport Package went up by $50 (to cover the cost of the newly-added rear spoiler, new shift paddles and the manual mode switch on the gearbox), and the Designo packages by $100 apiece.

Meanwhile, the automatic air-conditioning became a stand-alone option at $710, while the windblocker (previously standard) and heated seats were now offered only as part of the $970 Heating Package. At the same time, the Trim Package was

An advert from a German company specializing in scissor door conversions for a number of popular vehicles.

British advertising from 2007 featuring the SLK.

replaced by the Appearance Package, which included the earlier interior trim components, but added a 17-inch version of the European Sport Package wheels with star and laurel centres, dark headlight surrounds, and a black headliner; this cost $1290 on the SLK280 and $990 on the SLK350. The Comfort Package was combined with the old Premium Package minus the air con and renamed the Premium 1 (or P1) Package, while the $3650 (or $1400 for the AMG model) P2 Package included the P1 items plus what used to be the basic Entertainment Package. The P3 Package was an additional $1200, but brought with it the P2 Package plus a DVD-based navigation system.

The last of the original R171s

The new C216-series CL, presented to the press in Stuttgart in June, made its public debut at the 2006 Paris Salon, where the S 63 AMG and CL 63 AMG models also made quite a splash. Soon after, in November, when the Maybach 62S was launched, the 25,000,000th postwar Mercedes car was built, but sports car fans were able to celebrate another landmark at the end of the month with the release of the 'Edition 10' SLK, which was produced to celebrate ten years of the popular two-seater.

The 'Edition 10' model was basically an option package (code P38), costing between €1200 and €1500 depending on whether it was fitted to the SLK200 Kompressor, SLK280 or SLK350. Limited to 350 units in Germany, the signature colour was 040 black, with 197 metallic black and 775 silver adding €575 to the invoice if the buyer went that route, while the fourth coachwork colour option was a dark grey Magno shade (044), which cost €2099. Special features included 17-inch ten-spoke wheels with unique centres and a dull chrome finish, darkened rear light units, black leather trim with perforated inserts and a silver underlay and contrast stitch, black Nappa leather on the centre console (like the SLK 55 AMG), leather gearshift, a red ring on the main instrument faces along with red pointers, Sport Package dash trim, a black headlining, and commemorative badges on the front wings, seatbacks and floormats.

The relentless stream of minor changes continued unabated, with the four-cylinder engine having gained a new sump in September 2006, and then revisions to the ECU, knock sensor, camshaft position sensor, cylinder head, inlet valves, ignition coils, sparkplugs, exhaust manifold and front downpipes two months later. The 7G-Tronic gearbox was given a new sump in January 2007, and all SLKs – including the AMG model – were fitted with a redesigned front shock absorber bump stop and a new lower steel link (or cross strut) for the front suspension at around the same time. The SLK350 also gained a revised propshaft and modified driveshafts. There were also changes

Continued page 155

Above, opposite and overleaf: The German version of the 'Edition 10' model, this example being finished in the special Magno paint. Note the dedicated gauge pack.

Ab Start
0 km
0:24 h
0 km/h
0.0 l/100km
PRND C
+28.5 °C

S FA 7194

made to the heater and air-conditioning assembly, along with the air con compressor, and the tyre pressure sensor unit that screwed into the tyre valve.

The German VAT rate increased from 16 to 19 per cent on the first day of 2007, which naturally necessitated a new price list. However, the base price (before VAT) remained the same on each of the four SLK grades and all the factory options – only the cost of accessories changed, with some going up and some going down a touch. The important thing is that the list content was left untouched, although it is worth noting that there was a dramatic reduction in the cost of the 'Sadachiba' and 'Alresha' alloys at this time.

January 2007 also saw the launch of the new 204-series C-Class. Variants followed quickly, with a string of four-wheel drive models arriving in the summer, and a line of estates at the Frankfurt Show later in the year. Meanwhile, soon after the New York Show, where a number of exclusive AMG products made their debut, plans were laid on the table to break the Chrysler partnership. A deal was ultimately concluded in early August, with the Chrysler contingent leaving the

The SLR McLaren Roadster looked like the SLK on steroids!

boardroom in Stuttgart with immediate effect. On 4 October, the shareholders agreed to the renaming of the company – it becoming known as Daimler AG. The final ties between the German and American firms were severed once and for all in the spring of 2009.

Before all that, though, a new SLK price list was issued in July 2007, just in time for the 2008 season. Each of the four models offered in Germany went up by €300, which took the price of entry in the SLK world to €30,200 plus taxes. All cars came with an updated 'Assyst Plus' service reminder system, and there were a few more AMG options added for the SLK 55 AMG model, including the Performance Package wheels on their own (SA 786) at €2000, the uprated chassis components from the same package (486) at €1000, the carbonfibre trim (H73) at €1500, and AMG velour floormats (U26) at €75 a set. Incidentally, regular velour floormats moved from the accessory list to the factory options list at this time; carrying the SA U12 code, they were also priced at €75. Other than the loss of the expensive Designo Chromaflair paint and 388 mobile phone options and the arrival of four-way lumbar adjustment (SA U22, priced at €380) and ready-to-roll wheel and winter tyre sets, though, there were no other changes compared to the list issued previously. Even the accessories were carried over, with one major exception – the €20 reduction on the cost of the ribbed floormats, which made sense given that the velour ones had become a lot cheaper since becoming a factory option.

Price list for the domestic SLK 'Sport Edition' model.

As it happens, the SLR McLaren Roadster had been launched in July 2007, taking the place of the coupé version in the showrooms and the Woking production facilities. Sales began that September, which is when another SLK special edition put in an appearance.

Costing between €2100 and €3000, depending on whether the base car was a four-cylinder or one of the V6 models, the 'Sport Edition' (order code P84) came with Sport Package wheels and brakes, a lowered suspension, a sports air filter for the V6s, darker headlight surrounds, an AMG rear spoiler, black leather trim, an 'Airscarf' heater, air-conditioning for the SLK200 Kompressor, seat heaters, an Audio 20 unit, red stitching on the leather steering wheel and gearshift, as well as the seats and door furniture, red seatbelts, a black headlining, red instrument pointers, Sport Package dash trim, and velour floormats with red edging.

A few more minor modifications could be spotted in the parts book by this time, with the SLK line getting a revised rear bulkhead in April 2007, along with a new fuel tank and first aid kit the following month. The ESP sensor cluster had been modified in April also, at least on the four-cylinder cars, with the V6 models getting the same change six months later, in October, by which time the manual transmission casing and clutch had received some attention, too. Meanwhile, the SLK280 got new injector nozzles in March 2007, and both V6 machines were given new exhaust manifolds in May, as well as new back boxes in September. At the end of 2007, the 7G-Tronic gearbox received a few tweaks to the B1 brake disc and K1 clutch plate carriers.

In the States, the 2008 range was basically a carry-over from the 2007 season, although a 700-off US version of the 'Edition 10' was launched. Based on the automatic SLK350, this came with the same wheels as its European counterpart, complete with a dull chrome finish, the same interior tweaks, and special edition badging.

Continued page 160

Above and overleaf: A selection of pictures showing the US version of the 'Edition 10,' based on the automatic SLK350.
Note the special finish on the alloy wheels.

SLK 350
Maryland
1A69166
Dealer

V6

Right and below: Cover from the US 2008 Model Year catalogue, and one of the pages showing an SLK280 with a brown leather interior.

The face-lifted R171 making its debut at the 2008 Detroit Show, which opened on 19 January and ran for just over a week.

The final batch of original R171s was sold at a price around £1000 higher than those posted in the 2007 MY in the UK, with the cost of entry now being £29,710. Meanwhile, Japanese prices were carried over, and the Australian 2008 Model Year cars were announced in August 2007. Modest price increases were witnessed across the board, with the SLK200 Kompressor starting at $86,374, and the SLK 55 AMG now commanding $164,474. A newcomer at this time was the $123,500 SLK350 Designo model, which came with special paint, leather and 'Tamo' wood trim, and every option imaginable. There was another subtle price increase as the season rolled on, adding about $2000 to the invoice, but this was a final fling as far as the 'Mark I' R171 was concerned, for the face-lifted 'Mark II' version was announced in January 2008.

It's worth noting for the record that, despite dramatic cuts in the workforce, car production increased to almost exactly 1.3 million units in 2007 – up from 1,230,951 in the previous year. As we will see from the next two chapters, though, the company was far from willing to rest on its laurels ...

5

The R171 Face-lift

"With its 2009 refresh, the SLK continues its march toward macho with styling and engineering changes that turn it into a far more sporting – and thus, likable – proposition." – *Car & Driver.*

Over 185,000 R171 SLKs had been sold already, with almost a third of them staying in Germany, but the sales pace was falling off quickly, and something needed to be done to maintain the status quo rather than let the figures continue in a downward spiral. A set of measures – including a fresh look, a new engine line-up to comply with the stricter EURO 5 (2009) emissions regulations about to kick in, and a few chassis mods to further enhance the car's sporting image – were duly put in place, involving the creation of no less than 650 new components.

The first couple of months of 2008 represented a busy period for the executives in charge of the Mercedes-Benz brand. At the tail-end of January, the face-lifted SLK made its debut at the Detroit Show, taking centre stage alongside a pair of GLK concept cars. A few days after the show was coming to an end, the CLC-Class was launched at the Mercedes-Benz Fashion Week in Berlin, the new line taking the place of the earlier C-Class coupé models.

The Mercedes-Benz stand at the 2008 Geneva Show, with the SLK closest to the camera, sitting next to a heavily-face-lifted SL. Despite what the bright lights say, it was not a new generation, as it retained the R230 chassis code.

In the following month, the Maybach Landaulet (first shown as a prototype in November 2007) was launched, and then, from 6-16 March, everyone was full of smiles at the Geneva Show – with face-lifted versions of the R230-series SL and C219-series CLS coming online, plus a European debut for the SLK, there was plenty to be cheerful about. The SL 63 AMG took a bow at the same time, and was duly named the FIA's official F1 Safety Car, while hybrids, four-wheel drive systems and the 'Blue Efficiency' direct-injection system also made a splash in Switzerland.

For all this sparkle, it is naturally the SLK that interests us, though. Home market deliveries of the face-lifted car began in April 2008, but what were the differences? These next few pages will guide you through the changes ...

The various refinements made at the front of the face-lifted R171 made it look far more sporty. Indeed, one is reminded of the way in which the original SLK was given a sportier nature in its mid-cycle revamp.

A new look

As one magazine succinctly put it, you would need to be a real Mercedes fan to spot the subtle styling changes. But they were there alright, and however small they were in number, they certainly made a difference.

Starting with the front mask, leaving the bonnet lines intact, the nose was made more masculine thanks to a new front bumper/air dam assembly. On the face-lifted cars, the shape of the pointed surround framing the three-pointed star was shorter, following the profile of the badge's outer ring, and appearing to sit within the grille instead of dropping down to merge with the bumper moulding. Following this move, if anything, the Formula One influence was even more obvious than before.

The grille surround, which was nothing more than a strong feature line in the bonnet and bumper moulding rather than a traditional frame (the old chrome shells were incredibly stylish, but were sadly out of place in the modern era), aped that of the face-lifted R230 SL in its latest guise, looking more pronounced due to a deeper lip at the bottom, while the latter also fell into line with the SLK by adopting a single slat on either side of the three-pointed star, instead of the three used previously. Incidentally, the aerofoil-style slats on the SLK were heavier than before, sitting ahead of a new black grille screen that followed contemporary SL practice.

The bumper's inserts were deleted and a crease was added down its centreline – again as per the SL – while the tow hook cover was made round instead of square. The headlight washer covers were still the old shape, though, when fitted, and, with the inserts gone, the sensors for the optional 'Parktronic' system now sat flush on the main bumper panel.

Moving below the bumper blade level, the intakes were reprofiled, with stronger shapes and dressed with the same netting as that employed for the radiator grille. The soft, organic outer edges and foglight housings were dropped in favour of something that looked like the old 772 AMG styling kit apron, with the two centre uprights moved closer together to a position underneath the star on the nose. The transverse fin between the two vertical bracing pieces was blacked out, which gave the new

This SLK350's colouring and position in relation to the camera highlight the front-end changes just a little better, although one would rarely see a car from this angle in real life. These are the standard wheels for this grade, by the way.

The sharper nose profile, with the bumper section flowing back off a central crease, becomes obvious when the face-lifted car is viewed from above.

design another F1 styling cue. The front-end makeover, which added 14mm (0.55in) to the length of the car, was completed by new foglights with chrome surrounds.

The new mirrors employed on the latest SL were called up for duty on the SLK, too. As far as the SLK is concerned, they were larger and squarer than before to give a greater glass area for improved vision, with stylish LED-based repeater indicators integrated into the design. Being bigger, the new mirrors added 43mm (1.7in) to the R171's overall width, even though most of the extra bulk was visible in the mirror housing's height.

Continuing down the sides, there were new wheels, which we'll come to in a moment, and a shorter aerial mast that didn't have to be removed if the owner went into an automatic car washing machine. For the record, it was still a fair bit longer than the aerial used on the SL, but the change was welcomed nonetheless.

The latest mirror design, which was shared with the contemporary SL.

This action shot of the SLK200 Kompressor shows the new rear bumper assembly up nicely, as well as the shorter aerial on the nearside wing. Note also the high-mount rear brakelight – red on the regular cars, but darkened on the AMG cars, while all face-lifted SLKs now shared the same darker rear combination lamps.

Where the stylists had previously tried to break up the panel that made up the rear bumper and valance with inserts and character lines, for the face-lifted car, the bulk was manipulated to give the vehicle a more substantial look. The bumper inserts were dropped again, in line with the changes made at the front of the car, while the dressing piece surrounding the exhaust pipes was reduced in height and given five ribs to lend it the impression of being a diffuser.

The new rear bumper added 7mm (0.27in) of extra overhang, and combined with the revised front bumper, took the car's overall length to 4103mm (161.5in). Oddly, though, in conjunction with darker taillight lenses (like those found on the AMG models) and beefier trapezoidal exhaust finishers, the various styling changes all came together to make the face-lifted machine look significantly more compact than its predecessor.

As for the AMG styling kit, which kept the SA 772 code, by the way, the side skirts and bootlid spoiler were the same as before, while the rear bumper was much the same, but with a modified section around the reprofiled exhaust pipes. The front air dam witnessed the only real change, copying that of the kosher AMG model but with the entire assembly in body colour. It doesn't sound like much, but the impression is quite different if one puts the two spoiler variants side-by-side.

As always at these times, the opportunity was taken to refresh the coachwork colour palette, with Tellurium Silver being replaced by Palladium Silver, and Prehnite Green taking the place of Benitoite Blue on the colour charts.

Refresher course

In conjunction with the exterior update, the interior was given a mild makeover at the same time. Again, this was a series of small revisions rather than a batch of revolutionary changes, but the differences were immediately obvious, giving the car an altogether more classy appearance.

The press release highlights the steering wheel as the biggest difference, and that's probably correct, for the new three-spoke

An American-spec SLK350 with standard trim. Note the new steering wheel, the toned-down switchgear, and the latest dressing piece above the glovebox, which was given a convex profile to allow light and shadow to play on it.

wheel was much sharper-looking than its predecessor. Perforated leather was used on the sections of the rim touching the upper pair of spokes, with plain leather above and below, and a silver clasp added at the base of the lower spoke. The centre pad was slimmer, too, playing host to a new multi-function button arrangement – the buttons did the same jobs, but were arranged in a circular array and blacked out to tone things down. A wood/leather steering wheel was still available, with plain leather to the sides and the wood sections at the top and bottom of the rim.

New gearlevers were adopted, too, with the silver tops giving way to black leather and matt chrome. The mode switch on the automatic transmission was also changed to black, while the selector guide was given a new insert with a flat black finish rather than a high-gloss one.

Continuing the theme of making the face-lifted car more driver-focused, the gauge pack was given fresh graphics and new silver pointers with red inserts. The heavy calibration rings and chrome bezels over the clock and fuel gauge looked a little

The optional wood/leather steering wheel. This is the Light Burr Walnut wood, although Black Ash was also available, along with Designo Natural Poplar.

heavy-handed compared to the simplicity of the original dials, but the designers obviously felt something was needed to bring back a bolder feature, given that in so many other areas the visual impact had been watered down.

Most of the silver buttons strewn across the centre console were changed for black ones, although a few remained, such as the roof and mirror switches aft of the gearshift. The thumbwheels

The new manual gearlever.

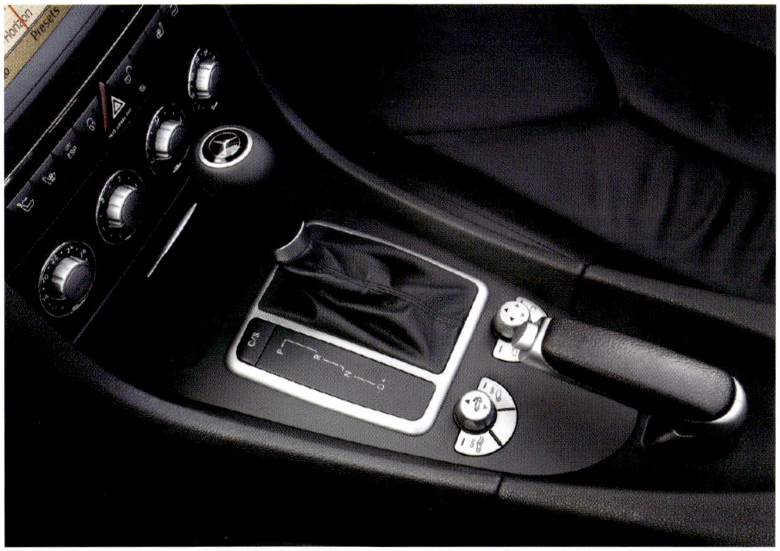

The redesigned automatic transmission selector. This is a UK car, by the way, so the roof and mirror controls are on opposite sides of the handbrake on left-hand drive models.

A gauge pack from a German-registered SLK350, readily identified by the exotic red-line (lesser models had a limit marked at 6500rpm). Certain countries, such as America and Britain, had the speedometers calibrated to 160mph, but the cluster was otherwise the same. AMG machines had their own set of gauges.

The centre console buttons were changed to black during the face-lift, giving the car's interior an altogether more serious aura.

on the HVAC controls continued in silver, too, with only the pushbuttons being changed to match those either side of the hazard warning switch. At the end of the day, there were still far too many buttons for traditional sports car guys like Jack Yamaguchi and myself, but at least they were more subtle-looking now, making the overall design look less fussy. Granted, the old silver buttons were probably a tad easier to locate, but with so many situated close together, one needed to look carefully at what was being pressed in any case.

The air vent thumbwheels and direction levers were also changed from silver to black with chrome inserts. At the same time, the silver flashes on the trays below the central air vents and HVAC controls were changed to brighter chrome highlight pieces, matching the new chrome insert added below the audio-visual unit housing.

While the finishing trim either side of the steering wheel was now black in regular guise, the insert above the glovebox was changed to a brighter silver and given a convex shape to add interest. The old optional Vavona wood trim was dropped in favour of a Light Burr Walnut veneer, with Black Ash also available for the new car, along with Designo Natural Poplar. When specified, the wood trim was extended to either side of the steering column, as well as the steering wheel, gearlever,

Above and top: A manual SLK200 Kompressor (chassis code 171.445 on the face-lifted cars) with Gullwing Red upholstery combined with Black Ash wood trim.

handbrake and door handles. The door furniture was carried over, incidentally, except for the power window switches, which looked a lot better in their updated guise.

The seats were the same as before, although the electrical switches were blacked out and new trim colours were listed – a Natural Beige Nappa hide to replace the old dark brown shade, and Gullwing Red was added to take the place of the existing red on the colour charts; the Orient Beige leather was given a new code number, too.

Rounding off the interior changes was an overhaul of the AV head units – the three restyled Audio 20, Audio 50 APS and Comand APS units now coming with a more user-friendly NTG 2.5 telematics setup. A hands-free Bluetooth connection was now standard, along with a socket for connecting portable audio devices, such as an iPod. There was also the option of a glovebox-mounted UCI media interface that allowed tracks from external music devices to be accessed more readily, replacing the Aux socket. The optional state-of-the-art Harman Kardon sound system was upgraded, with output going from 380W to 500W, while the Comand unit was given an SD-card slot and the 'Linguatronic' voice control system – something already available on top-end Benz models, but listed for the first time on the SLK.

An automatic SLK350 with the Natural Beige trim, along with the Light Burr Walnut wood option. The vents in the seat headrests point to this domestic car having the 'Airscarf' heating system installed, too. Incidentally, the new SLK350 tipped the scales at 1485kg (3267lb), which was 30kg (66lb) heavier than the other V6 grade, with the seven-speed automatic transmission adding a further 20kg (44lb).

The latest power window switches.

The Audio 20 and Audio 50 APS head units were basically the same, with only their capabilities being different – the APS version came with a DVD-based navigation system, whereas the basic Audio 20 model didn't.

The top-of-the-range Comand APS audio-visual unit, complete with HDD navigation and voice control. The larger screen was a useful identifying feature.

Under the skin

Forgetting the AMG engine for the time being, which we'll look at towards the end of this chapter, we can say that each of the four- and six-cylinder powerplants used in the SLK-series gained brownie points in the fuel economy stakes (and thus reducing CO2 emissions along the way), with two of them also gaining more power.

Thanks to a few tweaks to the ECU, new pistons that reduced the compression ratio to 8.5:1, fresh injectors, a revised supercharger and new back boxes for the exhaust system, the 1.8-litre four (Type 271.954) developed 21bhp more than the outgoing engine with the same bore and stroke. Maximum torque also increased, and although it was only by 7lbft, the spread of torque was far wider than that found in the old M271 unit. Notwithstanding, the four-cylinder lump was on average 11 per cent more frugal than before, and released 12 per cent less carbon dioxide into the atmosphere. Despite a new flywheel and propshaft, transmissions (both the standard 6MT and optional 5AT) were carried over, but a taller 3.27:1 final-drive was adopted (previously 3.46:1). Not only did this increase the top speed on the manual cars to 147mph (236kph), but, combined with the meaty torque curve, it also brought the 0-60 time down to 7.6 seconds.

The changes were less dramatic on the SLK280, although it did pick up the more suitable SLK300 moniker in many markets following the face-lift. This was probably to help differentiate the new and old cars, as both the chassis code (171.454) and engine number (272.942) were retained, the latter despite a fractionally higher compression ratio being employed. Ultimately, though, the power and torque outputs remained unchanged, the peaks were simply developed at a slightly different point in the rev-range. Not surprisingly, the 6MT and 7AT gearbox options

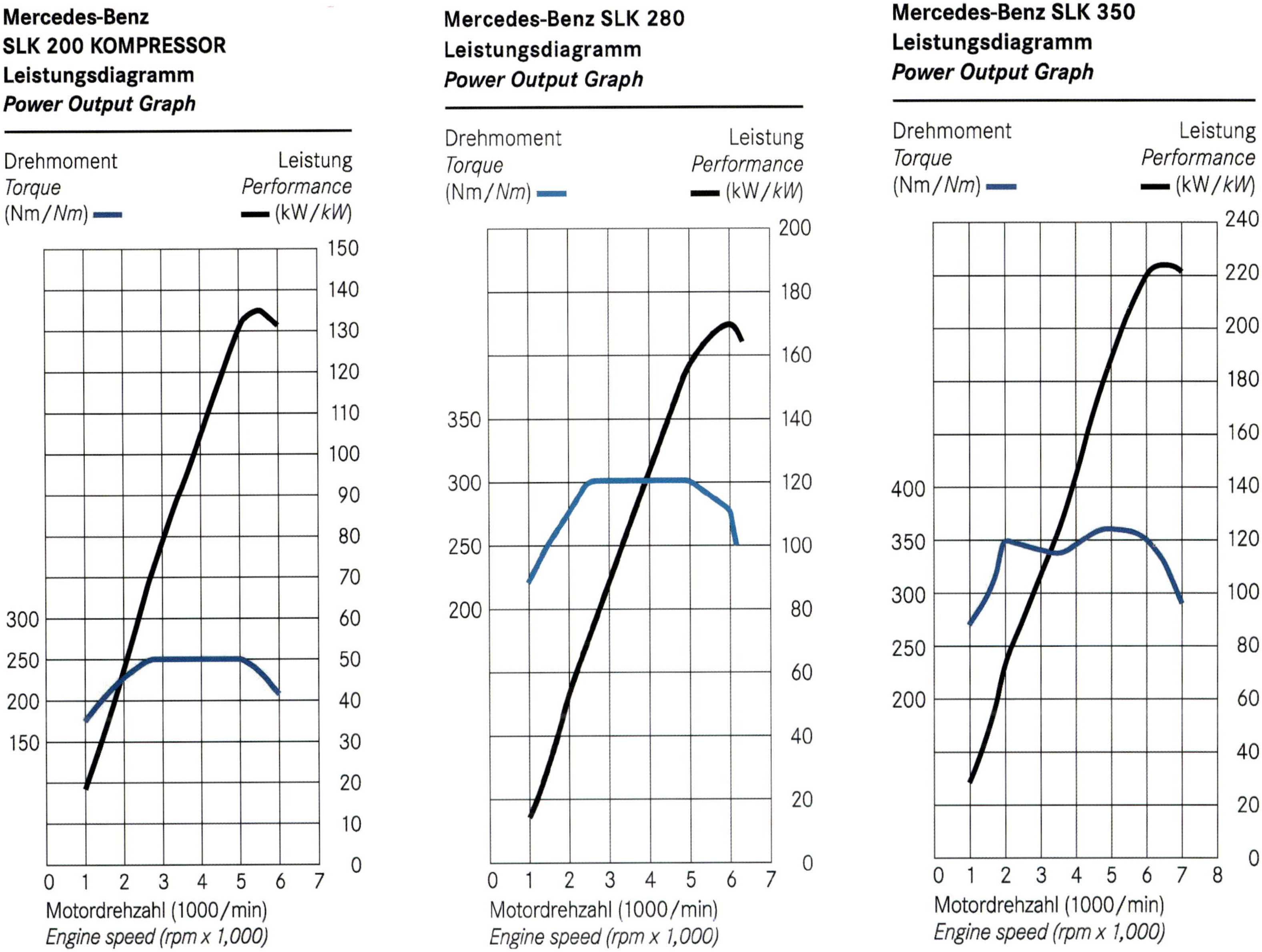

Power and torque curves for the revised four- and six-cylinder engine line-up.

were carried over, as was the 3.27:1 back axle ratio, so the only noticeable difference in performance was in terms of fuel consumption, with the latest unit being around four per cent more economical.

The big news was reserved for the SLK350, which gained a revised 171.458 chassis code thanks to its new, high-revving M272 E35 engine. In reality, the V6 looked much the same as before on paper, retaining the same bore and stroke and 3498cc displacement, but on opening the bonnet and catching a glimpse of the red vee on the engine cover, it was apparent that this particular unit was less conservative than its predecessor – on firing her up, the different character became all the more obvious, and one was left in no doubt that this was something a little special.

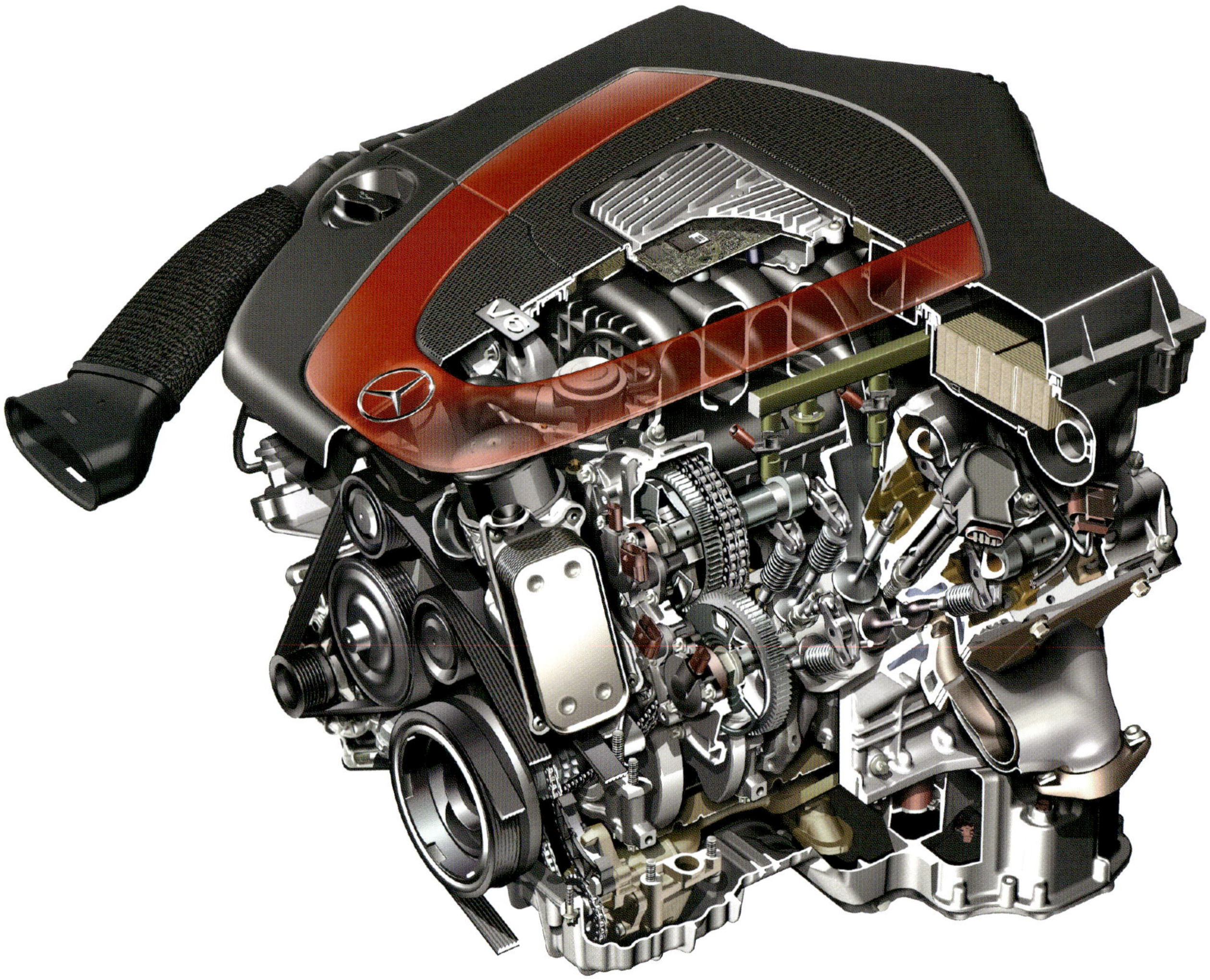

Cutaway drawing of the new 3.5-litre V6 Sportmotor, which was easy to distinguish thanks to its red vee in the engine cover. A similar unit was released in the R230 SL at the same time.

So, what made the new 3.5-litre engine (Type 272.969) into such a sporty unit? Well, the first rule in the creation of a high-performance engine is to lighten every component until its weight can be reduced no further without inducing reliability problems. This improves response, and for this particular engine, the pistons and sodium-cooled valves were made a lot lighter to help take the red-line into a loftier zone. At the same time, the higher 11.7:1 c/r – adopted to enhance economy, particularly on a light throttle – called for extra strengthening in the piston's gudgeon pin area, so it's a clever balancing act that engineers have to perform. Ultimately, the V6 Sportmotor had a documented acceptable limit of 7200rpm for brief bursts, which is quite remarkable.

This was not a temperamental unit, though, as the team that developed the engine knew that smooth power delivery was part of the V6 SLK's charm. It was realised that a reasonably good spread of torque was needed, too, for many of these cars would be linked to an automatic transmission, and in today's environment, one also needs to think carefully about fuel consumption and emissions.

Engine bay of the domestic market SLK350. In the face-lifted cars, 305bhp/266lbft was available, as opposed to 272bhp/258lbft on the earlier 350s.

In a bid to strike the necessary balance, the ME 9.7 ECU was reprogrammed and a new single-stage intake manifold was adopted to improve top-end performance. This was made from plastic to allow a greater amount of design flexibility, and came with the advantage of staying cooler than an equivalent die-cast part. This in turn kept the intake air cooler, which had a beneficial effect on the cylinder charge. However, to make the engine work well at idle and at engine speeds below 4000rpm, the valve timing needed to be advanced by five degrees to compensate. As it happens, the cylinder heads featured revised intake porting and the valves were given new cam followers and conical springs to cope with the higher revs involved, while modifications to the water jacket and valve seats dealt with any long-term reliability worries brought about by the higher compression ratio. And thanks to modern black boxes and knock sensors, the ability to run on 95-octane fuel was retained.

By the time the engineers had finished, there was a gain of 33bhp, along with an extra 8lbft of torque, although the latter was developed a lot further up the rev-range to fit in with the car's overtly sporting character. Peak power was now reached at a heady 6500rpm, while the 87bhp per litre output was close to racing engine standards not all that long ago. The unit sounded good, too, with the air cleaner assembly giving the latest 3.5-litre V6 its "emotion-charged soundtrack."

Amazingly, though, average fuel consumption improved by ten per cent, curbing CO2 emissions by a similar amount. A lot of this came courtesy of the longer 3.07:1 final-drive that was fitted on face-lifted cars (previously 3.27:1), duly connected to the familiar Type 716.664 gearbox – the same six-speed manual unit as used before, albeit with a new propshaft on its tail. The governed top speed was unchanged, but the 0-60 dash could now be completed in 5.4 seconds (0.2 quicker than before, as an extra gearchange was unnecessary thanks to the taller gearing).

The optional W7C700 automatic gearbox was modified slightly to handle the extra horses, coming with a fresh 722.904 code, although the internal ratios were the same as before. The automatic transmission was combined with a 3.27:1 back axle, incidentally, so the performance difference was negligible – the new car was only 0.1 seconds faster than before, although economy and emissions were about ten per cent better. A rich, sporting sound was emitted, too, courtesy of the automatic double-declutching feature during downshifts on the 7AT unit. It not only impressed onlookers, but also helped reduce wear on driveline components.

Chassis upgrades

With the appearance of the exterior and interior, as well as powertrain development, taking on a more sporting disposition, it would have been unthinkable to leave the chassis components alone. The shock absorbers were recalibrated slightly, but not to the extent that anyone would have noticed. However, with sports suspension tuning available as an option, there wasn't that much that could be done beyond fresh wheel designs if one was to retain a reasonable ride/handling compromise. Even though a revised brake servo was adopted and the SLK200 Kompressor and SLK350 got new front brake calipers, everyone was happy with the braking system, too. But the Mercedes engineers had one more trick up their sleeves – the 'Direct Steer' system.

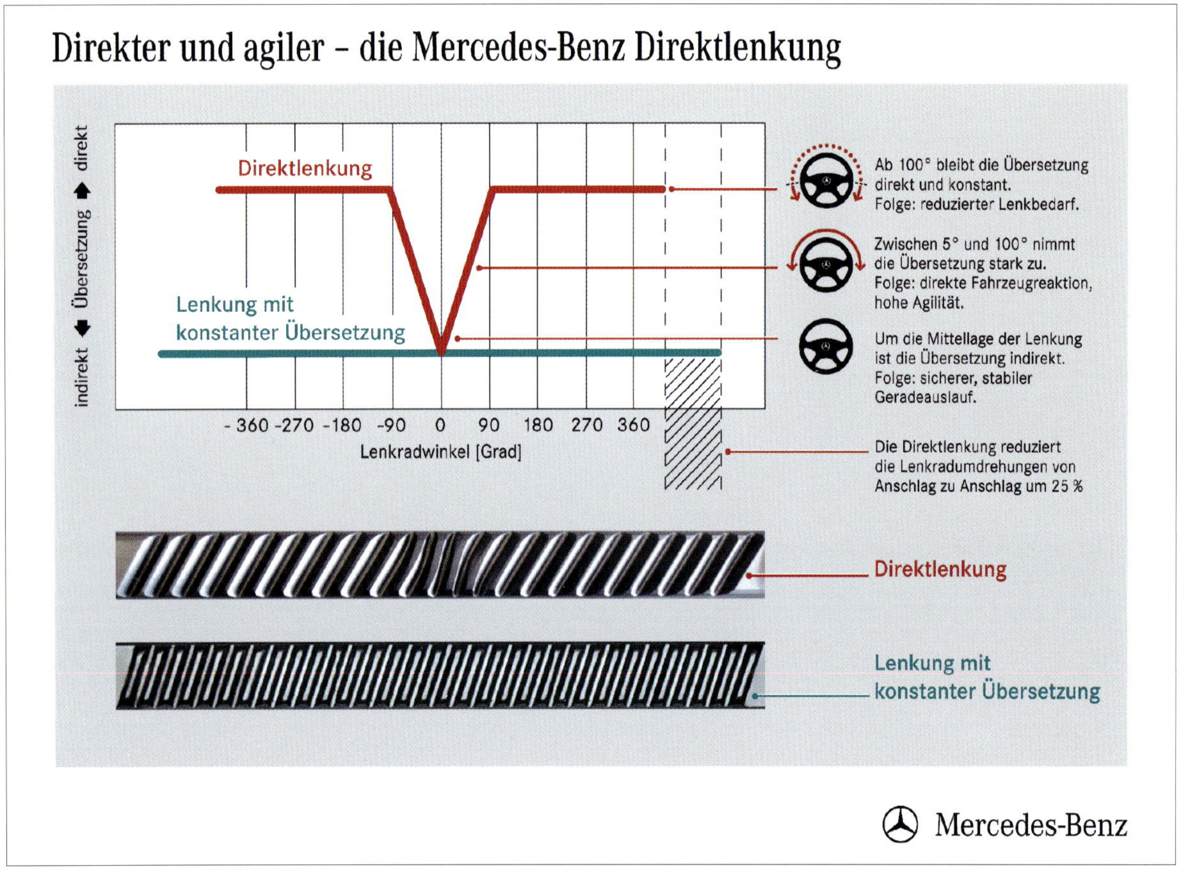

The 'Direct Steer' system explained, albeit in German.

Optional on the non-AMG machines, and based on the earlier speed-sensitive PAS system, which basically made parking light and easy and increased steering effort as vehicle speed rose, there were no sensors or actuators involved, so the new system saved a great deal of weight and also erased a potential reliability problem as the cars stacked up mileage.

In simple terms, the evenly-spaced gear teeth one finds on a regular rack were replaced by odd-shaped and unevenly-spaced teeth. As a result, the further the steering angle moved off-centre, the quicker the ratio became. It endowed the car with excellent straight-line stability, smaller steering movements, and greater precision and consistency in cornering. It also made the car more agile if evasive action was needed, with emergency lane changes being accomplished 22 per cent faster in terms of the required steering angle to execute a certain manoeuvre.

As *Motor Trend* noted: "[There's] a decided improvement in steering feel. Mercedes implemented its new Direct Steer system on the SLK and it's a throwback – a mechanical solution in the age of complicated electronics and algorithms. The problem Direct Steer attempts to address is the balance between freeway-cruising comfort and canyon-carving sharpness. The heart of this variable ratio system is a steering rack with specially shaped and spaced teeth. A standard pinion gear rides on top, but as it turns the steering ratio can change dramatically and instantly because it's all done mechanically (with hydraulic power assist, of course). Mercedes claims the number of turns from lock-to-lock has been reduced by 25 per cent, and on the road, the SLKs felt noticeably sharper, without that dead spot on-centre. More important is that the system is natural and progressive, free of that disconnected, artificial feel many of the steer-by-wire systems have. It's not perfect, but it is a definite improvement."

On the alloy wheel front, only the 16-inch wheels found on the SLK200 Kompressor were carried over as far as the domestic market was concerned, with 205/55 VRs on a 7J rim with all-round.

The three-litre car was given a new 16-inch, five-spoke wheel (SA R19), although the rim and tyre sizes were retained, with a 7J and 205/55 combination up front, and 8J alloy shod with 225/50 WR-rated rubber at the back. The SLK350 also had the sizes carried over, but the design was quite different, with the latest 17-inch alloys (SA R95) having five twin spokes. There were three new optional alloy wheels for Germany, too, but we will deal with those in the next chapter when we start to look at individual markets.

The R19 rim adopted on the face-lifted three-litre machine.

The familiar seven-spoke wheels that came as standard on the SLK200 Kompressor model.

The new R95 17-inch alloys adopted on the SLK350, featuring 7.5J rims with 225/45 tyres at the front, and 8.5Js with 245/40 WR-rated rubber at the rear. Note also the new brake calipers employed on the SLK350, complete with 'Mercedes-Benz' script.

Various views of the face-lifted SLK 55 AMG, which featured fewer styling changes than the regular cars. The front mask received the greatest level of attention. This German-registered vehicle has the standard 18-inch wheels, by the way.

The AMG variant

The styling changes for the SLK 55 AMG were less obvious, as the grille aerofoil arrangement was still blacked out, and one needed to look carefully to spot the heavier screen behind it – just like the one in the regular models, and repeated in the foglight housings. As it happens, there was a finer mesh in the area below the number plate on the AMG cars, although not as fine as that found behind the three-pointed star.

A close look, however, revealed the revised styling around the famous badge on the car's nose, as well as the sharp creaseline below it. The headlights gained dark surrounds, and the tow hook cover below the offside one was new, but interestingly, the bumper inserts were retained on the AMG model, providing a mounting point for 'Parktronic' sensors if the system had been specified. Lower down, the basic shape and foglight size and styling was pretty much carried over from the original SLK 55 AMG, but with sharper lines, while the lowermost transverse piece between the bracing uprights was finished in black to bring it in line with the revamp's concept. In addition, the vents on the outer edges of the air dam were kept, albeit with different styling for the new car.

The latest mirrors were naturally adopted, along with the shorter aerial, although the side skirts, the main rear bumper moulding and valance, and the bootlid spoiler were carried over without change. The exhaust pipe shapes were also retained, so the only other styling revision was on the 18-inch wheels – the familiar multi-spoke rims that were fitted as standard on the V8 car were now finished in Titanium Grey.

Inside, the changes applied to the run-of-the-mill models were adopted, including the 7H72 Avus Silver insert above the glovebox and the matt finish on the piece next to the gearlever, although the leather-wrapped steering wheel was subtly different, having a stronger ridge in the thumb area and a slightly flattened lower edge, as well as a set of aluminium shift paddles

Interior shot of the face-lifted AMG car, with the new three-spoke steering wheel being the main change. Note the slightly flattened edge at the bottom of the wheel, the aluminium shift paddles beyond it, and optional (SA H73) carbonfibre trim pieces. As with the regular SLK range, the treadplate designs were carried over.

The revised AMG gauge pack. This is the US-spec version, so has a 200mph speedo instead of a 320kph one.

The 360bhp V8 that powered the SLK 55 AMG was left untouched. It is seen here in one of the first face-lifted cars to make it to the USA.

The revised braking system employed at the front of the face-lifted AMG cars. The rear brakes were also modified, being smaller in diameter, ventilated only, and having two-pot calipers in place of the old four-pot ones.

on each side of the upper spokes. The instrument graphics were also revised in line with the regular cars, but the AMG variant continued to sport dedicated gauges nonetheless, with a 320kph speedometer and the 'AMG' logo on the tachometer face. Other than the new hide colours, the unique upholstery was retained without change.

The 5439cc M113 engine was left untouched, so its code number remained the same, as did that of the 7G-Tronic transmission and the 1575kg (3465lb) vehicle's chassis designation. Interestingly, while shift speed times were supposed to be faster and 'Direct Steer' was adopted as standard, there was a backward step on the braking system, for the stock car now came with one-piece drilled and ventilated 345mm (13.6in) diameter front discs being served by four-pot calipers, and ventilated 300mm (11.8in) rear discs being paired-up with two-pot calipers. Although fractionally bigger than the old standard front disc, the six-pot calipers and composite-style disc could only be brought back via the Performance Package, while the rear setup was inferior all-round. On saying that, of course, those who did a lot of track days had the chance to upgrade, and for normal road use, the latest system was more than enough.

Naturally, given that so few fundamental changes had been made to the basic AMG car, performance was the same as before, with the 3.06:1 final-drive allowing a 0-60 time of 4.9 seconds and a governed top speed of 156mph (250kph). With the basic changes brought about by the face-lift all covered, we can now take a look at how they affected the cars in the showrooms of each of the major markets ...

6

End of the Second Generation

"During our preview drive in southern France, we were reminded that, despite its position below the SL and SLR McLaren on the Mercedes totem pole, the SLK still gets plenty of looks – even in Monaco, where Bentleys are a common sight." – *Car & Driver*, February 2008.

Following the end of the Geneva Show, domestic deliveries of the SLK began in April 2008 – the same month as the A- and B-Class models were launched, and car number 5,000,000 left the Bremen plant. In reality, domestic SLK specifications and equipment levels were much the same as before, but it's worth recapping at this stage, if only to clarify option prices, and so on.

The latest version of the 1390kg (3058lb) SLK200 Kompressor model was €475 more than before the face-lift, listed at €30,675 plus taxes, with the SLK280 commanding €4500 more – its new price tag being €525 higher than the last of the small V6s with the same name (the 280 moniker was retained in Europe, at least). The SLK350 added another €4300 to the invoice, representing a €625 price hike on the pre-face-lift car, while the SLK 55 AMG was priced at a hefty €58,025 (€775 more than before). Apart from the AMG model, with its 7AT gearbox, each came with a six-speed manual gearbox as standard.

Even the base car came with the signature power metal folding roof with a heated rear window, 16-inch alloys, H7 projector headlamps with automatic headlight control, front and rear foglights, darkened taillights, chrome exhaust trim, power mirrors with heating elements, ABS with Brake Assist, ESP and ASR traction and stability programmes, PAS with a multi-function leather-wrapped steering wheel and adjustable

Above and opposite: A selection of publicity photographs showing the face-lifted SLK200 Kompressor for the home market. This manual car has the SA R52-type 17-inch alloy wheels and Gullwing Red trim.

S OU 9348

Above and opposite: This batch of stunning press photographs shows the updated version of the domestic SLK350. This vehicle has the correct (as in standard) wheels for the 3.5-litre model, along with Natural Beige upholstery and Light Burr Walnut trim.

column, a leather-trimmed gearshift, cruise control with 'Speedtronic,' sports pedals, and power windows with tinted glass and pinch protection. Other interior appointments included dual front and side airbags, seatbelt pretensioners and force limiters, sports seats with height adjustment and adjustable headrests, a childseat and passenger recognition system, stainless treadplates, an advanced automatic heating system with a 'Rest' facility, black cloth upholstery, full instrumentation including a tachometer, a trip computer, analogue clock, outside temperature gauge, brake pad wear indicator, an audible warning for the handbrake or lights being left on, the 'Assyst Plus' service reminder system, and a power socket in the passenger footwell and the box in the base of the centre stack (where the optional ashtray was fitted). There was also a centre console box that doubled as an armrest, a second storage box on the rear wall between the seats, a chrome SmartKey hooked up to the car's remote-control central locking and immobiliser, a remote trunk release, roof-mounted reading lights, door pockets, along with a map net in the passenger-side footwell and behind the driver's seat, and a first aid kit.

The three-litre car added a staggered wheel and tyre setup, and an uprated battery to cope with the manual air-conditioning. The SLK350 came with 17-inch alloy wheels and larger brakes, as well as the SLK300's goodies and an upgraded interior lighting package. As for the AMG model, this built on the SLK350's specification with a 'Speedshift' automatic transmission, 18-inch wheels, 'Direct Steer,' the AMG styling kit with a unique air dam and rear spoiler, darker headlight frames, bonnet vents, AMG brakes and suspension, AMG sports seats with Nappa leather trim and seat heaters, a sports steering wheel with aluminium paddle shifts, special gauges with a 'Racetimer' feature, and stainless treadplates carrying the AMG logo.

Moving onto options, the five-speed automatic gearbox (SA code 423) for the SLK200 Kompressor model added €1810 to the invoice, and 25kg (55lb) to the car's body weight. The seven-speed version for the V6 models (427) was €1900, while the €2130 '7G-Tronic Sport' variant (427+428) brought with it steering wheel shift paddles and reduced shifting times. As it happens, the shift paddles could be bought separately for the 5AT and 7AT transmissions, simply by specifying SA 428 and handing over €230. The 'Direct Steer' upgrade (213) was priced at €265, a lowered suspension (486) was €220, an uprated battery for the four-cylinder model (673) was €80, a fire extinguisher (682) was €110, and the tyre pressure loss warning system (477) €55.

On the alloy wheel front, the five-spoke 16-inch rims fitted to the SLK280 (SA R19) were available as a €280 option on the SLK200 Kompressor. Likewise, the standard 17-inch SLK350 wheels (R95) were listed at between €660 and €835, depending on whether they were destined for a four- or six-cylinder model, and came combined with a lowered suspension. There were three factory options listed for alternative rims, with the 17-inch R52 wheel being very similar to the R95 one, listed at €375 to €1105, while the 17-inch R93 design was basically a variation of the old R35 one. Painted in a Chrome Shadow hue, this ten-spoke wheel cost between €255 and €985, but, like the other rims, was only available on the non-AMG cars. The final option was the 18-inch AMG 795 alloy wheel, which was a no-cost option on the AMG machine. This rim had five split spokes and could be ordered for just €600 if the owner bought the Sport Package for regular cars, or between €1425 and €2155 if specified as a stand-alone option. Winter tyres (645) were €120 a set (unless they were bought as one of the three wheel and snow tyre combinations listed – 1R4, 1R6 or 1R7), run-flat tyres (R66) €250, while a spacesaver spare (669) could be ordered for €50 to replace the 'Tirefit' system.

The AMG styling kit (772) came in at €2980, Bi-Xenon headlights with washers (614) were listed at €835, washers for the regular lights (600) at €255, a heated windscreen washer system (875) at €165, rain-sensing wipers (345) at €100, remote control for the roof (880) at €110, fitted baggage for the boot (U23) at €170, and a luggage rack foundation kit (726) at €80, with an aluminium crossbar set (721) at €350 extra. The folding mirrors (500) and self-dimming interior and exterior mirrors (249) were put together as a €540 P49 package from now on, while the 'Parktronic' system (220) commanded €690, and a fabric windblocker (285) €70, or €255 for a clear acrylic version (283). An alarm could only be bought with the interior security upgrade after the face-lift (P54), priced at €425 as a set, and a garage door opener (231) was available for €225.

Above and opposite: The SLK 55 AMG in face-lifted guise. The multi-spoke alloy wheels are stock items, but this car has the optional AMG carbonfibre trim (H73).

S MA 5582

S MA 5582

A car fitted with the AMG styling kit and AMG alloys.

Air-conditioning for the four-cylinder car (580) was priced at €1200, while the top-of-the-range 'Thermotronic' system (581) was basically listed as an upgrade of the SA 580 option, costing an additional €540 for all cars. The Audio 20 CD audio-visual head unit and nine speakers (523) was €750, or €1000 if combined with a CD-changer (510). The Audio 50 APS unit (525) was €1560, with the CD-changer and voice control adding an extra € 400 (SA code 511), while the 'Comand' system (527) justified a €2860 price tag, or €3160 if bought with a CD-changer (512). To go with these stereos, there was the surround sound system upgrade (810) at €700, mobile phone installation (386) at €350, and a UCI media interface (518) at €160, although it was no longer possible to order speakers on their own.

The ambient lighting package (SA 876, although it was already standard on the SLK350 and AMG model) was €135, velour floormats (U12) €75, the 'Airscarf' heater (403) €395, including a cloth windblocker, a heated steering wheel (443) €250, an ashtray and cigarette lighter (301) €35, cupholder insert (309) €30, a suit bag for behind the seats (U07) €130, four-

The cupholder insert (SA 309).

A bag for suits or dresses which could be hung behind the seats (SA U07).

way lumbar adjustment (U22) €380, seat heaters (873) €310, and a power seat and memory package for the seats, mirrors and steering column position (P64) cost €1225. Leather trim was €1130, with Nappa grade hide commanding a €380 premium on top of that, and a full leather gearshift (280) was €35. For those looking for an extra touch of luxury, Light Burr Walnut trim pieces (H12) were priced at €750, as were the Black Ash (736) ones.

Metallic paint was a €580 extra. At the same time, Designo Metallic paint was priced at €1650, and Designo Mystic at €2375 – both quite a bit more expensive than before the face-lift. As for the three Designo leather options, at €2750, these were only €100 more, with trim in a single shade, a two-tone colour scheme, and black or grey leather/Alcantara upholstery being available. Only the two-tone trim was available on the AMG car, although at €1370, it cost a lot less.

Other Designo items included a black Alcantara headlining (Y83) at €1190, along with a grey version (Y85) at the same price, while a new option was a black vinyl headlining (Y90), like the one included in the Sport Package, and this was priced at €330. A leather/wood gearshift (Y94) was listed at €250, while the equivalent steering wheel (Y95, but not available on the AMG car) was €760; a two-tone leather wheel (Y96, and again only for the non-AMG line-up) was also listed, costing €510. Designo leather on the roll-over bars (Y98) was €610, which was the same cost as the regular or Nappa leather (the same SA code number was used, too). The last Designo option was a Natural Poplar wood trim package (W61) at €585, and €390 leather dash trim (Y97) – both being carried over from before, although the Black Ash option had gone.

The Sport Package (SA 952) was available for the non-AMG models, and, as long as they had a black leather upholstery option in place, depending on the grade, was priced at between €1065 and €1465 by the time April came around. It was basically the same package as that previously offered, so added the now-familiar 18-inch alloys with six double spokes, shod with 225/40 and 245/35 rubber, a lowered suspension (although it was possible to delete option this), the same uprated braking system up front (identical to the latest SLK350 spec), shift paddles on automatic machines, and a sports air filter for the three-litre V6 (the SLK350 engine came

An SLK with the optional Sport Package, ordered via the SA 952 code.

with one as standard). There was also a darker headlight surround and an AMG rear spoiler to finish off the exterior, while the interior featured its usual red contrast stitching on the steering wheel, gearshift, seats and door furniture, as well as a black headlining, red seatbelts (black could be specified if the owner preferred), a 7K79 'Carbon Optik' carbonfibre-style insert to replace the Avus Silver one above the glovebox, and velour floormats with red edging. For the record, the old package's red meter pointers were no longer used, as they were hardly needed, and all cars now came with the black trim to either side of the steering wheel, so that item was also unnecessary.

The boy-racer package available for the SLK 55 AMG model was the €4500 P30 Performance Package, which was the same as before, with the same 18-inch alloys, uprated braking and suspension systems, and carbonfibre trim and a different steering wheel for the interior. However, the bigger 360mm (14.2in) diameter composite discs and six-pot calipers that came with the P30 option up front, along with the old 330mm (13.0in) discs and four-pot calipers that used to be standard, were more important now, of course, seeing as a lesser braking system had been adopted on the face-lifted car's specification sheet. As it happens, AMG owners could individually specify the alloy wheels (786) for €2000, the stiffer suspension (486) for €1000, the 'Performance Steering Wheel' (281) for €400 (something never offered as a separate item before), and the carbonfibre trim (H73) for €1500, but if one wanted the uprated brakes, the P30 option was the only way to go. The only other option listed for the SLK by the AMG Performance Studio was a set of velour floormats (U26), priced at €75.

A final selection of press photography, with this batch showing the SLK 55 AMG with the Performance Package. It's useful because of the view of the correct alloy wheels and the interior updates. One should be aware, though, that the rear brakes are wrong on this car – despite what the German price list says, those that made it to the showrooms had larger discs at both ends, not just the front.

Colour & Trim Guide

These are the coachwork and trim colours introduced on the face-lifted cars in early 2008. There were very few changes to the colour palette thereafter, so, as before, it's easier to chart them in one block.

Standard Paintwork Options

Black (040), Fire Opal, aka Mars Red (590), and Calcite White, aka Arctic White (650).

Metallic Paintwork Options

Obsidian Black (197), Periclase Green, aka Jade Green (300), Jasper Blue, aka Orion Blue (345), Tanzanite Blue, aka Capri Blue (359), Prehnite Green, aka Hampton Sand (430), Thulite Red, aka Storm Red (541), Cubanite Silver, aka Pewter Silver (723), Iridium Silver (775), and Palladium Silver (792). From June 2009, Indigolite Blue (230) replaced Jasper Blue, and Tenorite Grey, aka Steel Grey (755) superceded Cubanite Silver.

Interior Trim Options

Black 'Sienna' cloth (081); regular leather in Black (801), Alpaca Grey, aka Ash (808), Orient Beige, aka Beige (815) and Gullwing Red (817); 'Nappa' leather in Black (851/861), Orient Beige, aka Beige (855), Alpaca Grey, aka Ash (858), Natural Beige (874) and Gullwing Red (887); 'Designo' leather in Black (X11) and Classic Red/Black two-tone (X83), and 'Designo' leather combined with Alcantara in Black (X20) and Alpaca Grey (X21). The optional wood trim came with a choice of Light Burr Walnut, Black Ash or 'Designo' Natural Poplar veneers.

NB. The 851 black, 855 beige, 887 red and 858 grey 'Nappa' leather shades were reserved for the SLK 55 AMG model; the red and grey hides came in two-tone colour schemes matched up with black on AMG cars.

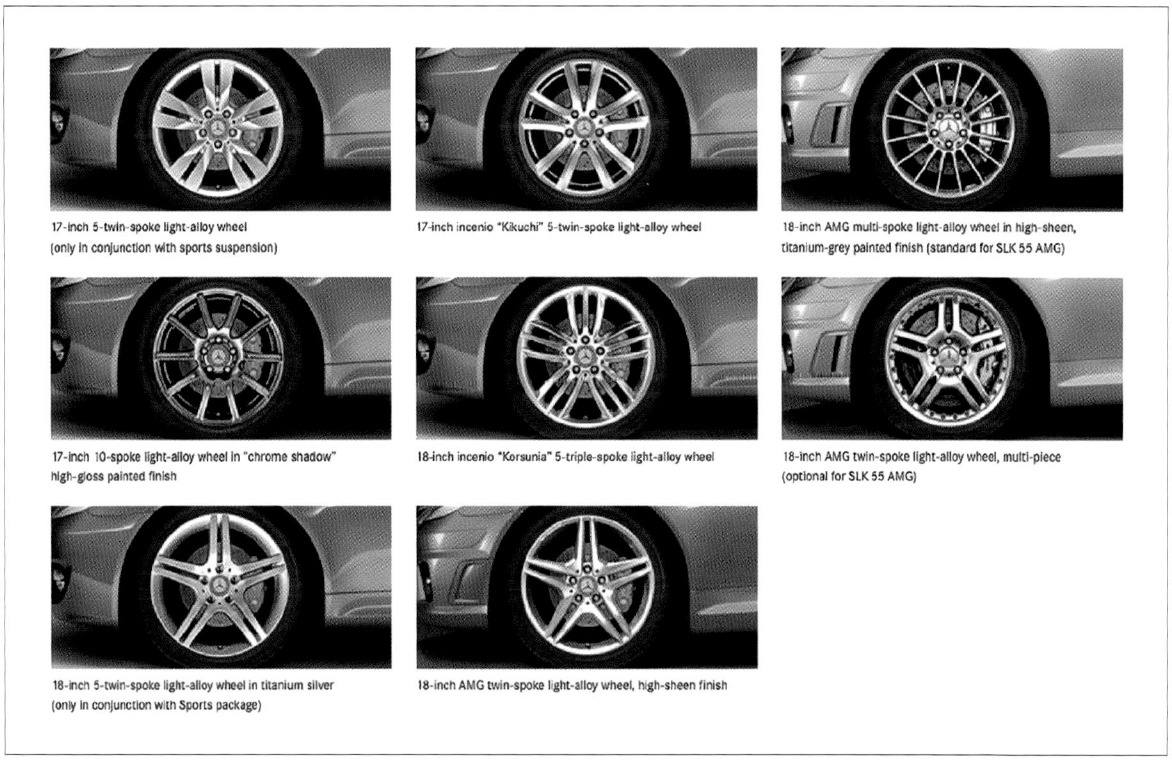

A useful page from the catalogue, showing a good cross-section of the contemporary alloy wheel line-up. The standard wheels are pictured in the previous chapter, while the earlier rims sold as accessories are illustrated in the fourth chapter.

One would have thought there was more than enough in the way of standard equipment and optional extras, but German dealers were armed with another catalogue containing accessories that could be fitted at the showroom's workshop. Most things were the same as before, but, again, a brief recap would be worthwhile.

Perhaps the most significant accessories were the additional alloy wheel designs offered by the dealerships. There were the Acubens, Elarneb, Sadachiba and Alresha patterns carried over from the previous season, albeit priced a touch higher, which were now augmented by the 17-inch Kikuchi rim with five double spokes and the 18-inch Korsunia rim with five triple spokes. The new 17-inch wheels cost around €1030 a set, while the 18-inch ones were €1160 a set. As a matter of interest, the Algedi alloy was basically the familiar R35/R93 option, and most of the earlier wheel designs were still available, including a replica of the Sport Package rim in 17- and 18-inch guise. Anyway, one could also order locking wheel bolts, and wheel centres with a plain three-pointed star or a more traditional star and laurel design.

Illuminated treadplates for the SLK, sold as an accessory.

Picture showing an SLK with a number of dealer accessories fitted, including roof-rack attachments, front spoiler corners, chrome grille inserts, chrome mirror housings and door handle cups, and Algedi alloy wheels finished in silver.

Contemporary advertising from the Belgian arm of Mercedes-Benz.

A typical mobile phone cradle, fitted in the central armrest box.

Other accessories included front lip spoiler corners (€349 including tax), a three-piece chrome trim set for the aerofoils in the radiator grille and bracing piece below the front number plate (€199), chrome door handle backing plates, chrome mirror housings, a flare section for the rear wheelarch whenever wider tyres were used, front mudflaps, illuminated treadplates (€641, and now featuring 'Mercedes-Benz' script rather than an 'SLK' logo, or an 'AMG' logo), a dedicated childseat (€246), various roof-rack attachments, black ribbed floormats (€75), a black cover for the driver's seat (€131), luggage nets for the boot (€26) or a slim oddments bag (€66), a trunk liner (€78), a non-slip mat for the boot (€35), a spare bulb set (€28), a car cover, cooler boxes, media interface kits for connecting gizmos, and mobile phone cradles and connections.

There was a change made to the 7G-Tronic's bell-housing and B2 clutch in June 2008, and a modification to the instrument cluster a couple of months later, although nothing was visible as far as the cars on the showroom floor were concerned.

The US market

The face-lifted car went on sale Stateside in May 2008. Prices were up a touch, with the freshly-named SLK300 commanding $44,950, the SLK350 $5000 more, and the SLK 55 AMG $64,300 plus delivery charges. Basic specifications were roughly the same as those of the home market machines, although there were a few significant changes.

The SAE and DIN measurements were paper differences only, with 228bhp, 300bhp and 355bhp being listed as the maximum power output on the three models in the States, even though the engines were the same. The transmissions were the same, too, although the manual gearbox option was dropped on the 3.5-litre car, and the standard wheel combinations were quite different. The US-spec SLK300 came with twin six-spoke 17-inch rims (of the type often seen in 18-inch guise in Europe), the SLK350 with a twin five-spoke pattern (the R52 alloys), and the AMG model with the 18-inch 795 AMG-designed wheels.

Above and opposite: The US-spec SLK300 for the 2009 season, with the standard wheels, an automatic gearbox, a grey leather interior, the regular air-conditioning, 'Airscarf' heater, power seats, and the Comand unit with its integral navigation system.

SLK 300

Right and below: A 2009 SLK350 for the US market, complete with the standard alloy wheels. At first glance, they looked similar to the domestic car's wheels, but the spokes were slightly different where they met the outer rim.

All US-bound cars came with 'Direct Steer,' a tyre pressure monitor, knee-level airbags, the 'TeleAid' service, an alarm system, leather trim, the Audio 20 unit with a CD-changer, velour carpets, an ashtray and cigarette lighter, and a cupholder insert. The AMG model added things like shift paddles on the steering wheel, ambient lighting, remote control for the top, a garage door opener, Nappa leather trim, heated and power-adjusted seats with the memory package, and auto-dimming mirrors.

Options were therefore rather limited, with an automatic gearbox for the SLK300 costing $1460, automatic air-conditioning $730, metallic paint $720 (coachwork colours were the same as those listed in Germany except for the lack of a Jade Green shade), Natural Beige leather at a $595 premium, and walnut trim for the non-AMG cars, $310. Several option packages were put together, including the $2950 Premium One (P01) Package (already standard on the AMG machine), which included rain-sensing wipers, remote control for the hardtop, auto-dimming mirrors, power steering column adjustment, power seats with lumbar support and memory facility, a media interface, garage door opener and interior lighting upgrade. The $2980 Multimedia Package included the Comand unit with CD-changer, navi and a surround sound system, while the $1030 Lighting Package contained Bi-Xenon lights and heated headlamp washers, and the $990 Heating Package boasted heated seats, the 'Airscarf' system and a fabric windblocker (the latter option was $480 cheaper on the SLK 55 AMG, as the heated seats were already a standard fitment). For the SLK300 and SLK350 only, there was the $2500 Sport Package, which came with an AMG styling kit, the familiar multi-spoke AMG alloys fitted to the home market SLK 55 AMG, an uprated suspension, and steering wheel-mounted shift paddles, plus a manual control mode on the gearbox. Lastly, there was the $6910 AMG Performance Package for the V8 car, coming with the 18-inch alloys used on European cars with the same upgrade, uprated brakes and suspension, a modified governor to allow a greater top speed, the Performance steering wheel, and carbonfibre trim components.

Above and overleaf: The SLK 55 AMG for the North American market, with the stock alloys for US buyers and very few interior upgrades, although the Comand head unit, 'Airscarf' heater and fully automatic air-conditioning were options.

So, what did the press think of the new model? *Car & Driver* wrote in its February 2008 issue: "Away from the crowded city streets and up into the mountain roads that provide the setting for the Monte Carlo Rally, the SLK is sure on its feet. The variable-assist power steering is a bit over-assisted, but the Direct Steer system does indeed feel direct even though, technically, it's not direct at all – it's progressive. No matter, because the system works, and the SLK350 moves through switchbacks without any frantic hand-over-hand spinning of the steering wheel.

"The power is a welcome addition, too. We'd say the grunt's just right, but we're not Goldilocks, and we'd never turn down the excess of the SLK 55. Still, Mercedes charges some $13,000 more for the extra horses in the AMG model, and the SLK350 does not want for power. Actually, the SLK350 is fast in a slightly sneaky way – a way that you wouldn't notice unless you were paying attention. Kind of like a mid-cycle face-lift."

A few months later, the same magazine was able to test the SLK350 on home turf. "Ride is pretty damn phenomenal for a car with such a short wheelbase. I guess that's what 17-inch wheels will do for you," said Erik Johnson. "Also, body roll is beautifully contained, and the 0.87-g skidpad rating is more than respectable."

Johnson concluded: "Ultimately, we appreciate the cleverly packaged, reasonably attractive, and arguably more masculine roadster that is the 2009 SLK350. Brandishing many luxury features, a retractable hardtop, 300 horses, and a three-pointed star, the SLK350 occupies its rightful spot in the prestige brand's line-up."

The UK

With the SLK280 moniker retained on the three-litre machines, it would have been easy for those who take no more than a passing interest in sporting machinery to miss the face-lift if one only looked at the price lists. However, the new models were, according to *Autocar*, "hugely improved," commanding between £29,710 and £51,975 initially, although prices were reduced a fraction at the end of 2008 due to a temporary reduction in the VAT rate (back down to 15 per cent).

Not all testers were as impressed as *Autocar* with the changes, though. When *Auto Express* brought together a three-litre SLK, a BMW Z4 and Porsche Boxster, it noted: "Get out on the road, and it's immediately apparent that the SLK can't match the sharp driving dynamics of its rivals. However, the SLK's more laid back nature and comfortable ride mean it's a great long-distance cruiser, and it can easily match the refinement offered by the new BMW Z4 ... The Mercedes isn't the most expensive

Interior of the UK-spec SLK200 Kompressor. This car has an automatic transmission, the Audio 20 or 50 unit, and black leather trim.

Above and overleaf: A selection of shots showing various aspects of the SLK280 for the British market. This particular car has the R93 alloys.

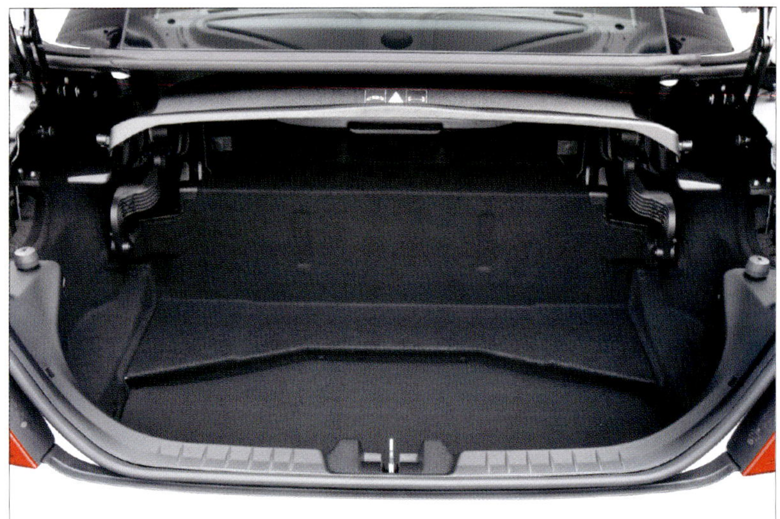

car here – that honour goes to the Boxster – but it costs £3500 more than the equally fast and well-equipped BMW. The SLK is the original folding hardtop roadster, yet on this evidence, it's going to struggle to hold on to its claim to be the best."

When this test was conducted, in the spring of 2009, SLK prices stood at £29,445 for the SLK200 Kompressor, £32,290 for the SLK280, £36,580 for the SLK350, and £51,585 for the flagship AMG model – still less than the base SL, but twice the price of a Morgan 4/4. In the summer, there was a four-cylinder '2LOOK Edition' added, priced at £31,235, but more on that in a moment.

Japan

Japanese pricing had been revised in the spring of 2008, with SLK prices now ranging from 5,620,000 yen to 10,380,000 yen. At this time, the A170 was the cheapest Mercedes offered, listed at 2,570,000 yen, but there were several AMG models approaching the 30,000,000 yen mark, and even these were positively reasonable compared to the 70,000,000 yen being asked for the SLR McLaren Roadster.

By the end of the year, the SLK280 had fallen by the wayside, and the cost of entry went up to 5,700,000 yen for the

Interior of a UK-registered SLK350 with black ash trim components to contrast with the grey leather.

face-lifted SLK200 Kompressor (AT and rhd only). The revised SLK350 and SLK 55 AMG variants were also given slight price increases, commanding 7,540,000 yen and 10,560,000 yen respectively from the autumn onwards; although both came with an automatic gearbox only, there was a choice between lhd and rhd on these two grades, as for some reason, left-hand drive still held a certain kudos for owners of imported machines in the Land of the Rising Sun. Incidentally, the cheapest SL at this time was the 12,000,000 yen SL350, while Porsche Boxster prices ranged from 5,820,000 to 7,510,000 yen. It should be noted, however, that around half-a-million yen had been added to Boxster prices by the end of 2009, while those of the three SLKs remained unchanged, even as the 2011 season drew to a close and the R172 models took their place in the showrooms from July that year. The BMW Z4 was also creeping up in price, with the top model listed at 8,150,000 yen in October 2010.

Australia

The face-lifted range was launched in June 2008 in Australia. The SLK200 Kompressor provided the entry-level model, priced at $88,520 in manual guise, or $91,825 with an automatic gearbox. With the 280 gone, the SLK350 was next in line at $115,637 (or $119,365 for those who preferred two-pedal driving), while the new version of the SLK 55 AMG cost a hefty $171,270.

For 2009, the old prices were rounded off a little, making the SLK models range from $90,100 to $175,000. At this time, the Mazda MX-5 (NC-series) started at $42,460 and went up to just under $50,000, while the Porsche Boxster ranged from $113,000 to $140,000 for a manual S. As one can see, the SLK was hardly a cheap alternative for open car lovers – sales were achieved on merit. SLK prices increased by about 1.5 per cent for the 2010 Model Year, with the existing three machines joined by a $100,050 SLK300 grade in April 2010. Everything then remained the same until July 2011, when the R172 was released, with prices starting at just $82,900.

Other 2009 season news

Although diesel power was taking a leading position in Daimler AG marketing at the time, July 2008 witnessed the debut of the SL 65 AMG Black Series at Hockenheim. Powered by a 670bhp twin-turbo V12 from the M275 series, it was every bit as wild as the new 650bhp SLR McLaren Roadster 722S launched at the Paris Salon that year. The timing was good for this type of vehicle, as McLaren-Mercedes pilot Lewis Hamilton was crowned world champion soon after following a nail-biting finale to the 2008 F1 season. The New Year saw the release of the last of the 199-series SLR models – the 75-off 'SLR Stirling Moss' roadster. In reality, though, it was the more conventional GLK, and the launch of the new 212-series E-Class at the 2009 Detroit Show that mattered more to most people, with electric cars looking good for the future.

Lewis Hamilton in action in the 2008 Canadian Grand Prix. (Courtesy Wikipedia Creative Commons, Mark McArdle)

The tuners were as active as ever. This is a 2009 car modified by the German Piecha concern. (Courtesy Piecha)

Just looking

The 2009 Geneva Show saw the C207 E-Class Coupé take a bow, along with the Maybach Zeppelin, and a new line of 'smart' microcar variants. In addition, to coincide with the announcement of the forthcoming adoption of a SLK300 moniker for the three-litre SLK (a move that was ultimately carried through at the end of June, in time for the 2010 season), Mercedes released a new limited run SLK at Geneva, and christened it the '2LOOK Edition' model.

Marketed as an upgrade package (option code P25) on the non-AMG cars, it was painted in 040 Black or 650 Calcite White, although it was also available in 197 Obsidian Black or 048 Designo Mystic White if one was willing to pay a premium – €590 in the case of the metallic black paintwork, and €1990 for the white hue. Regardless of the exterior colour, there was a dark

Exterior and interior shots of the '2LOOK Edition' of 2009 vintage, as well as a close-up of the special badging that graced the front wings.

surround on the headlights, 18-inch alloy wheels that looked like the optional five-spoke AMG rim (code 22R in silver, as used on the contemporary SL, or R70 in Chrome Silver), an acrylic windblocker, a two-tone interior trimmed in black and white Designo Nappa leather with contrast stitching (with the same theme carried over to the door inlays and centre armrest), seat heaters, contrast stitching on the steering wheel, white trim above the glovebox and to either side of the steering column, the Audio 20 CD setup, a black headlining, model-specific floormats, and special badging. Before options and tax, the '2LOOK Edition' SLK200 Kompressor was priced at €34,825 (with air-conditioning as an additional bonus), the three-litre version €38,375, and the SLK350 one €42,275. It was limited to just 300 units in Germany, but was sold as a special edition in most parts of the world.

As it happens, dealers were issued with a new price list at the time of the Swiss event, although it didn't take effect until 30 June 2009. Compared to the prices of a year earlier, the cost of the non-AMG cars had increased by €600, while the SLK 55 AMG was hit with a rise of €650, taking it to €58,675 plus tax.

As for options, there wasn't that much to report. The standard wheel in the 952 Sport Package became an open five-spoke design – basically an 18-inch version of the 19-inch R17 rim supplied in the SL's Sport Package. The 'Thermotronic' air-conditioning and AMG styling kit went up by €50, the media interface kit by €40, leather trim, the 7AT and run-flat tyres by €30, the 'Airscarf' and memory package by €25, the 5AT and basic air con by €20, the Bi-Xenon lights, a spacesaver spare and alloy wheel options by €15, metallic paint, winter tyres, the rain-sensing wipers, alarm, remote control for the roof, wood dash trim, ashtray and cupholder inserts, heated steering wheel rim, uprated battery and luggage rack by €10, and the headlight washers, heated screen washer system, 'Direct Steer' option, seat heaters, both windblockers, interior lighting upgrade and tyre pressure loss warning system by €5 apiece.

The SLS AMG model, evoking memories of the 'Gullwing' 300SL.

At the same time, the cost of Designo Metallic paint went up by €150, and the Mystic range by €175. Designo leather trim prices, meanwhile, increased by €50 across the board, while the two-tone steering wheel and gearshift option increased by €40, the W61 wood dash trim by €15, and Designo headliners and leather fascia trim went up by €10. Other Designo options also suffered a price hike, with the leather roll-over bar trim going up by €90, and the leather/wood steering wheel and gearshift by €140 and €100, respectively. In addition, it's safe to say that the price of accessories increased by a tiny amount, virtually across the board.

On the mechanical front, in March 2009, the four-cylinder engine gained a new cylinder head cover, a new air mass sensor, modified rocker arms and the hydraulic adjusters that sat underneath them, and a revised ancillary belt tensioner; it also had a new subframe placed beneath it. A little while later, the same unit was given a new crankcase, along with fresh breather hoses and check valves to match. By May that year, different horns were being fitted to the SLK range, and the non-AMG machines gained new rear shock absorbers.

Meanwhile, the E63 AMG, plus face-lifted versions of the GL-Class and ML450 Hybrid, were launched at the New York Show in April 2009, while the face-lifted S-Class (W221) was displayed at the Shanghai event in the same month.

The 2010 Model Year

The sporting image craved by the Mercedes-Benz marketing men was further enhanced in September 2009 when the new 197-series SLS AMG model made its debut alongside the E-Class estate, a plug-in hybrid version of the S-Class and a fuel cell version of the B-Class at the Frankfurt Show. The stunning SLS had an all-alloy gullwing body, and was powered by a 571bhp, 6.2-litre V8.

Above and overleaf: The domestic 2010 MY catalogue was virtually the same as the one issued in the spring of 2008 – only the cover, colour listing, accessory pages and a few minor details were different. This is the cover and a few selected pages from the 2010 edition, printed in December 2009.

As it happens, Mercedes power had been chosen by no less than three F1 teams for the 2009 season. Jenson Button was duly crowned world champion in his Brawn-Mercedes BGP001, with Brawn also taking the constructors' title. This prompted Daimler AG to take a 75 per cent stake in Brawn to secure the team for a new works F1 effort starting in 2010. At the same time, AMG-Mercedes was classed as DTM champions, keeping the Stuttgart brand firmly in the motorsport spotlight.

For 2010, the SLK200 Kompressor engine received a new balance shaft housing and valve seals, while the six-speed manual transmission gained a fresh clutch bearing release assembly and new fifth-sixth synchro rings. The front and rear bumper support bars were replaced by stronger items, and the array of electrical relays in the boot was changed. In early spring, the rear axle carrier subframe was modified, with the underbody panelling at the front end receiving attention soon after. And by April, the central sun gear in the 7G-Tronic transmission had been overhauled, too.

Meanwhile, as the E-Class convertible (207-series) was being presented in Detroit in January 2010, the home market dealerships received two new SLK price lists – one for the run-of-the-mill models, and a second one for the 'Grand Edition' model. There was also a single sheet informing them of a 'Sport Edition' released at the same time.

Starting with the regular SLK line-up, prices increased by a small amount, taking the SLK200 Kompressor to €32,025 plus taxes, the SLK300 to €36,525, the SLK350 to €40,825, and the SLK 55 AMG to €59,450 – a price that broke the €70,000 barrier as soon as Germany's 19 per cent VAT was added on. In reality, though, the price hike was easy to justify, as the Audio 20 stereo (complete with nine speakers) was now a standard fitment on all cars, and the increase hardly covered its cost. Otherwise, the standard specifications and equipment levels were all carried over.

As for factory options, the AMG Driver's Package (SA 250) was an interesting newcomer, allowing owners to have the AMG car's governor adjusted upward to 175mph (280kph) after attending a driving academy run by the tuning company. At €2000, though, this was only for the most dedicated of enthusiasts.

With the Audio 20 unit becoming standard, the cost of the CD-changer for that particular stereo (510) was now €300, while the cost of the Audio 50 and Comand units was reduced by €300, with or without the changer. The 952 Sport Package was carried over, albeit €10 more expensive. The seven-speed automatic gearbox was also €10 more than before, as was the 'Parktronic' system, leather trim, and the interior lighting package; the cost of seat heaters went up by just €5.

The SLK 'Grand Edition' (right), sitting next to the SL 'Night Edition' launched at the same time.

A view of the SLK 'Grand Edition' model's special interior, and the special badging applied to the vehicle. Note also the additional trim pieces on the bonnet.

Like the standard metallic paint, the price of Designo paint also increased by €20, and the Magno range was added to the catalogue at €3320 – almost double the cost of regular Designo metallic paintwork. The cost of Designo leather trim went up by €10, while a dashboard insert in the same material was now €420 – €20 more than before. There were no other changes on the options front, however, and no significant changes on the accessory listing, either.

The SLK 'Grand Edition' (P61) was offered in all the standard coachwork colours except Indigolite Blue, Prehnite Green and Periclase Green, although the signature hue for this limited edition was 041 Designo Graphite Metallic, which commanded an €1800 premium over and above the €35,525 being asked for the SLK200 Kompressor version, the €39,375 base price on the SLK300 version, and the €43,125 asked for the SLK350 version.

The 'Grand Edition' featured the 18-inch Korsunia alloys from the accessories brochure (although the AMG 795 rims could be specified for just €835 extra), the silver bonnet fins, dark headlight surrounds and dark third brakelight found on the AMG cars, and a tasteful interior upgrade. The Designo Basalt Grey Pearl leatherwork featured embossed accent lines in the seat inlays and door trim inserts, and also graced the dashboard inserts, carrying a discreet logo, while black Nappa hide was used on the central armrest and gearshift. The 'Airscarf' system was combined with seat heaters and an acrylic windblocker to provide comfort during the winter months, with the four-cylinder car also inheriting the air-conditioning that was already standard on the V6 models. The package was completed by grey seatbelts, black velour floormats with a 'Grand Edition' logo and grey edging, and special badging on the front wings.

The 'Sport Edition' was basically for those who wanted a sporty looking machine but couldn't be bothered going through option catalogues! Costing a €2875 premium on the four-cylinder model due to the addition of air-conditioning, and around €1950 on the V6s, the 36P package included Sport Package five-spoke alloys covering the 3.5-litre car's braking system, an uprated suspension (if required), a sports air filter for the SLK300, a rear spoiler, darker headlight surrounds, black or grey leather trim, red contrast stitching, carbon-style trim above the glovebox, the 'Airscarf' system and seat heaters, red seatbelts (black was an option), a cloth windblocker, black headliner, and velour floormats with red edging; automatic cars also came with steering wheel-mounted shift paddles. By choosing an off-the-shelf package, home market buyers saved between €1000 and €1700, with the smaller-engined models offering the best value.

Soon after the newcomers were announced, the new 571bhp AMG M157 twin-turbo 5.5-litre V8 was presented to the press at the AMG head office, in March 2010. A few days later, in Geneva, the F800 research vehicle took a bow, along with the SLS AMG in its F1 Safety Car livery. At the same time, the 'MercedesSport' brand was launched to allow buyers greater scope for individuality.

There was no let up in the pace, as the Mercedes range continued to expand. The new R-Class made its debut at the New York Show, along with the SLS AMG GT3 for race enthusiasts. The face-lifted Maybach and a lwb version of the E-Class followed, and in May, the M276 (V6) and M278 (V8) power-units were presented to the press in Stuttgart. Featuring advanced direct-injection and ignition control, as well as a stop-start facility to enhance fuel consumption, they delivered more power and more torque, yet could boast an average of 23 per cent better fuel efficiency. Their debut came in the new CL-Class (216-series), released in July in conjunction with the seven-speed 7G-Tronic Plus gearbox, and the C218 CLS, launched at the Paris Salon later in the year. There was also a great deal of activity on zero-emissions vehicles, with the E-Cell concept being another area of green technology to augment the F-Cell, LPG and advanced diesel systems being fielded by the company.

Contemporary American advertising for a dedicated insurance service designed for Mercedes-Benz owners.

Front, rear and interior views of the US market's 'Diamond White Edition,' released for the 2010 season.

America's last cars

The SLK 55 AMG found itself in a precarious position in the States for 2010 – it was still available, but it was hardly promoted. Indeed, it didn't even appear in the catalogue produced for the 2010 season. As such, the SLK brochure was far smaller, albeit similar in content with regard to the SLK300 and SLK350.

For 2010, the SLK300 inherited the same wheels as its bigger brother, and the US colour palette was revised, with only Arctic White, Palladium Silver, Iridium Silver, Steel Grey, Black, Obsidian Black, Capri Blue, Mars Red and Storm Red being listed. While prices started at $46,900 plus $875 delivery charges, options, apart from those relating to the AMG car, were basically the same, with only illuminated door sill trim and the Harmon Kardon sound system being added to the individual options list.

The Americans were treated to a limited edition for 2010, though – the US equivalent of the '2LOOK Edition'. Finished in 048 Designo Mystic White paint, the SLK300-based 'Diamond White Edition' was restricted to no more than 100 cars, so it's something of a rarity. There was only really one major difference compared to the European version, and that was the choice of alloy wheels, the US car coming with AMG multi-spoke rims.

For 2011, there was absolutely no doubt that the AMG variant had gone. This left only the 1458kg (3208lb) SLK300 and 1508kg (3318lb) SLK350 in the SLK line-up, with prices starting at $47,650 – less than half the cost of the cheapest model in the contemporary SL range.

Interestingly, both cars were fitted with an AMG styling kit and given dark headlight surrounds for the 2011 season, with the SLK300 now sporting the R95 17-inch rim off the home market SLK350, while the US SLK350 was given the 18-inch wheel found in the European Sport Package. Quartz Blue was added to the US colour charts, although it was actually the 230 Indigolite Blue shade that had been used on the German range

Right and overleaf: Cover and a couple of pages from the American 2011 Model Year brochure. The car on the cover in an SLK350 in standard guise, at least as far as the Stateside 2011 season was concerned.

during the previous season. As for options, following the change in standard specifications, the Sport Package came minus the bodykit from now on, of course, but two Sport Packages were listed for 2011 – one with the multi-spoke AMG alloys, the other with the 795 five-spoke version. Otherwise, apart from the illuminated treadplates going back to the accessories list, there were no other changes.

UK update

The UK fell into line with other EU countries by rebadging the SLK280 as the SLK300 in September 2009, in time for the 2010 Model Year. Soon after, on the first day of January 2010, the VAT rate went back to 17.5 per cent, and a 0.8 per cent inflationary hike was added to the SLK line at the same time. During 2010, SLK prices stood at £30,755 for the SLK200 Kompressor, £33,870 for the SLK280, £38,260 for the SLK350, and £53,790 for the SLK

The arrival of the R172 SLK range, with a diesel variant included in the line-up soon after the launch, signalled the end of the R171's run. The outgoing car had been very successful, however, with almost a quarter-of-a-million units sold.

Tailpiece.

55 AMG model, and then on the first day of January 2011, the VAT rate increased to 20 per cent, taking prices up still further. By June 2011, the last of the R171 models were being listed, with the AMG gone, and the other grades ranging from £31,410 to £39,065. Later that month, the R172 came online.

Swansong

Having fallen to just over a million cars built in 2009, along with 425,000 trucks, Mercedes production picked up in again 2010, increasing to 1,312,456 units, as well as more than 625,000 commercials. As it happens, the last of the R171 SLKs were built in 2010, the final batch having a new tyre pressure sensor attached to the tyre valve. However, a few were sold beyond this year, with most of them staying at home – in fact, 612 were sold in 2011, and the last 12 in 2012. By the end of the run, no fewer than 78,928 R171s had been sold in Germany.

On 29 January 2011, Mercedes' boss Dieter Zetsche was on hand to present the R172 SLK, with its launch lined up for March 2011. Lining up alongside the new C-Class Coupé at Geneva, the R172 featured such novel ideas as the 'Magic Sky Control' glass roof, and there was even a diesel version released in time for the 2012 season. Things would never be the same ...

Appendix I
Year-By-Year Range Details

This appendix brings together the brief specifications for all R171-series models, arranged in chronological/engine size order. Column one shows the vehicle type, the second column shows the basic engine details (to be used in conjunction with Appendix II), whilst the third contains any useful notes, including the main market (if nothing is listed, one can assume worldwide sales, while the cars with 'European market' against them are not always restricted to EU countries – please refer to the main text for definitive details). Only production road cars are listed for each model year (MY), with the Black Series not included, as it did not appear in regular price lists.

2004

SLK200 Kompressor (171.442)	M271.944	Pilot build from January 2003. Full-scale production starts December 2003. European market.
SLK350 (171.456)	M272.963	Pilot build from February 2003. Full-scale production starts May 2004. Officially classed as a 2005 model.

2005

SLK200 Kompressor (171.442)	M271.944	European market.
SLK280 (171.454)	M272.942	Pilot build from June 2004. Full-scale production starts May 2005. Classed as a 2006 model in the US.
SLK350 (171.456)	M272.963	
SLK 55 AMG (171.473)	M113.989	Pilot build from November 2003. Full-scale production starts September 2004.

2006

SLK200 Kompressor (171.442)	M271.944	European market.
SLK280 (171.454)	M272.942	
SLK350 (171.456)	M272.963	
SLK 55 AMG (171.473)	M113.989	

2007

SLK200 Kompressor (171.442)	M271.944	European market.
SLK280 (171.454)	M272.942	
SLK350 (171.456)	M272.963	
SLK 55 AMG (171.473)	M113.989	

2008

SLK200 Kompressor (171.442)	M271.944	European market. To February 2008.
SLK280 (171.454)	M272.942	To February 2008.
SLK350 (171.456)	M272.963	To February 2008.
SLK 55 AMG (171.473)	M113.989	To February 2008.
SLK200 Kompressor (171.445)	M271.954	Face-lift model. Pilot build from June 2007. Full-scale production starts February 2008. European market.
SLK280/300 (171.454)	M272.942	Face-lift model. Production starts February 2008. Classed as a 2009 model in the US, and badged as the 300; retained the 280 badge in mainland Europe and the UK.
SLK350 (171.458)	M272.969	Face-lift model. Pilot build from June 2007. Full-scale production starts February 2008. Classed as a 2009 model in the US.
SLK 55 AMG (171.473)	M113.989	Face-lift model. Production starts February 2008. Classed as a 2009 model in the US.

2009

SLK200 Kompressor (171.445)	M271.954	European market.
SLK280/300 (171.454)	M272.942	Badged as the 300 in the US, and 280 in Europe and the UK.
SLK350 (171.458)	M272.969	
SLK 55 AMG (171.473)	M113.989	

2010

SLK200 Kompressor (171.445)	M271.954	European market.
SLK300 (171.454)	M272.942	
SLK350 (171.458)	M272.969	
SLK 55 AMG (171.473)	M113.989	To September 2010.

2011

SLK200 Kompressor (171.445)	M271.954	European market. To November 2010.
SLK300 (171.454)	M272.942	To November 2010.
SLK350 (171.458)	M272.969	To November 2010.

Appendix II
Engine Specifications

The following is a survey of all the mainstream production engines employed in the R171-series models featured in this book, complete with the leading specifications and any other notes of interest. One should bear in mind that engines with 'Europe' listed as the main market are not always restricted to EU countries, and are occasionally restricted to certain areas – please refer to the main text for definitive details.

Type 113.989 (M113 E55 AMG)

Production (MY)	2005-2011
Cylinders	90-degree V8, water-cooled
Main bearings	Five, in alloy block
Valve operation	Sohc, 24v, in alloy head
Bore & stroke	97.0 x 92.0mm
Cubic capacity	5439cc
Compression ratio	11.0:1
Fuel delivery system	Fuel-injection
Engine management	Bosch ME 2.8
Power @ rpm	360bhp (265kW) DIN @ 5750
Torque @ rpm	376lbft (510Nm) DIN @ 4000
Main market	Worldwide
Notes	Used in the SLK 55 AMG model from September 2004 to September 2010. Tuned to give 400bhp/384lbft in the Black Series model.

Type 271.944 (M271 E18 ML)

Production (MY)	2004-2008
Cylinders	Straight-four, water-cooled
Main bearings	Five, in alloy block
Valve operation	Dohc, 16v, in alloy head
Bore & stroke	82.0 x 85.0mm
Cubic capacity	1796cc
Compression ratio	9.5:1

Fuel delivery system	Fuel-injection, plus supercharger
Engine management	Siemens SIM 4 LKE
Power @ rpm	163bhp (120kW) DIN @ 5500
Torque @ rpm	177lbft (240Nm) DIN @ 3000-4000
Main market	Europe
Notes	Used in the SLK200 Kompressor model from December 2003 to February 2008.

Type 271.954 (M271 E18 ML)

Production (MY)	2008-2011
Cylinders	Straight-four, water-cooled
Main bearings	Five, in alloy block
Valve operation	Dohc, 16v, in alloy head
Bore & stroke	82.0 x 85.0mm
Cubic capacity	1796cc
Compression ratio	8.5:1
Fuel delivery system	Fuel-injection, plus supercharger
Engine management	Siemens SIM 4 LKE
Power @ rpm	184bhp (135kW) DIN @ 5000
Torque @ rpm	184lbft (250Nm) DIN @ 2800-5000
Main market	Europe
Notes	Used in the SLK200 Kompressor model from February 2008 to November 2010.

Type 272.942 (M272 E30)

Production (MY)	2005-2011
Cylinders	90-degree V6, water-cooled
Main bearings	Four, in alloy block
Valve operation	Dohc per bank, 24v, in alloy head
Bore & stroke	88.0 x 82.1mm
Cubic capacity	2996cc
Compression ratio	11.1:1
Fuel delivery system	Fuel-injection
Engine management	Bosch ME 9.7
Power @ rpm	231bhp (170kW) DIN @ 6100
Torque @ rpm	221lbft (300Nm) DIN @ 3500
Main market	Worldwide
Notes	Used in the SLK280 model from May 2005 to February 2008, and the SLK280/300 model from February 2008 to November 2010. The compression ratio was increased to 11.3:1 for the face-lifted car, and although outputs remained unchanged, maximum power was developed at 6000rpm, while maximum torque was available between 2500-5000rpm.

Type 272.963 (M272 E35)

Production (MY)	2005-2008
Cylinders	90-degree V6, water-cooled
Main bearings	Four, in alloy block
Valve operation	Dohc per bank, 24v, in alloy head
Bore & stroke	92.9 x 86.0mm
Cubic capacity	3498cc
Compression ratio	10.7:1
Fuel delivery system	Fuel-injection
Engine management	Bosch ME 9.7
Power @ rpm	272bhp (200kW) DIN @ 6000
Torque @ rpm	258lbft (350Nm) DIN @ 2400-5000
Main market	Worldwide
Notes	Used in the SLK350 model from May 2004 to February 2008.

Type 272.969 (M272 E35)

Production (MY)	2008-2011
Cylinders	90-degree V6, water-cooled
Main bearings	Four, in alloy block
Valve operation	Dohc per bank, 24v, in alloy head
Bore & stroke	92.9 x 86.0mm
Cubic capacity	3498cc
Compression ratio	11.7:1
Fuel delivery system	Fuel-injection
Engine management	Bosch ME 9.7
Power @ rpm	305bhp (224kW) DIN @ 6500
Torque @ rpm	266lbft (360Nm) DIN @ 4900
Main market	Worldwide
Notes	Used in the SLK350 model from February 2008 to November 2010.

Appendix III

Chassis Numbers and Production Figures

Chassis numbers

The body codes and chassis start numbers for each model type:

Type	*Model Year*	*Body code*	*Chassis no.*
SLK200 Komp.	2004-2008	R171.E18	WDB171442**
SLK200 Komp.	2008-2011	R171.E18	WDB171445**
SLK280	2005-2008	R171.E30	WDB171454**
SLK280/300	2008-2011	R171.E30	WDB171454**
SLK350	2005-2008	R171.E35	WDB171456**
SLK350	2008-2011	R171.E35	WDB171458**
SLK 55 AMG	2005-2011	R171.E55	WDB171473**

Note: The first asterisk in the above chassis numbers is to be replaced by a '1' for left-hand drive, or a '2' for right-hand drive. The second asterisk is to be replaced by a letter ('F' through 'H') to show the car was built in the Bremen plant, followed by a sequential six-digit production serial number, starting on 000001.

For America and certain other countries, the 17-digit VIN number starts with 'WDB' to identify Daimler-Benz (later Daimler AG) as the maker. The next four digits describe the model (with 'W' for 171-series, followed by 'K' for a drophead body, then a model key, such as '56' which is a shortened version of 171.456). The eighth digit shows restraint systems, and the ninth is simply a check digit, which is a number ('0' to '9') or an 'X' in place of the number ten. The tenth gives the year of manufacture, which is defined by numbers and letters (3 = 2003, 4 = 2004, 5 = 2005, 6 = 2006, 7 = 2007, 8 = 2008, 9 = 2009, and A = 2010). Next is a letter for the Bremen plant ('F' through 'H'), followed by a six-digit sequential serial number.

Build numbers

Production quantities for each model type, arranged by engine size and basic type:

Type	*Model Year*	*Number built*
SLK200 Kompressor	2004-2011	140,094
SLK280/SLK300	2005-2011	40,415
SLK350	2005-2011	52,134
SLK 55 AMG	2005-2011	9541

A different breakdown of the build numbers, this time showing how many of each model type was produced within a given calendar year (CY), including the pre-production prototypes. Unfortunately, the early SLK280 and the later version badged as either the SLK280 or SLK300 were batched together in the original annual data provided to the German government, hence the lack of a more accurate number for each type:

Year	*SLK200K*	*SLK280/300*	*SLK350*	*SLK 55 AMG*
2003 CY	391	-	80	1
2004 CY	34,378	18	17,038	1036
2005 CY	31,349	9408	15,892	3904
2006 CY	22,273	11,070	7397	1931
2007 CY	16,635	8638	4304	1282
2008 CY	17,961	6237	4679	976
2009 CY	8822	1830	1211	227
2010 CY	8285	3214	1533	184

Overall production figures

A table showing a summary of the annual production (by CY) for all R171 SLK models combined (including prototypes), followed by a cumulative figure, valid at the end of each calendar year:

Year	*Number built*	*Cumulative production*
2003 CY	472	472
2004 CY	52,470	52,942
2005 CY	60,553	113,495
2006 CY	42,671	156,166
2007 CY	30,859	187,025
2008 CY	29,853	216,878
2009 CY	12,090	228,968
2010 CY	13,216	242,184
Total R171-series models built		**242,184**

Also from Veloce Publishing –

The 300 SL's 1952 debut was the culmination of a long, difficult road back to racing for Mercedes-Benz after a 13 year break. This book vividly depicts the 300 SL's performance in the five races in which it competed in that year, and tells the story of how it became the most successful competition sports car that season. Through dramatic photographs and stirring text, one of the greatest years of sports car racing is brought to life, filled with automobiles prepared by great factory teams, driven by men who were national sporting idols, and raced under gruelling conditions unique to the age.

ISBN: 978-1-845846-17-6
Hardback • 25x25cm • £75* UK/$120* USA • 144 pages • 126 colour and b&w pictures

For more info on Veloce titles, visit our website at www.veloce.co.uk • email: info@veloce.co.uk • Tel: +44(0)1305 260068
* prices subject to change, p&p extra

Index

Mercedes-Benz, as well as Daimler-Benz and Daimler AG, along with their subsidiaries and products, are mentioned throughout the book.